# The Business and Economy Internet Resource Handbook

# The Business and Economy Internet Resource Handbook

*edited by*
Phil Bradley

LIBRARY ASSOCIATION PUBLISHING

LONDON

Published by
Library Association Publishing
7 Ridgmount Street
London WC1E 7AE

Library Association Publishing is wholly owned by The Library Association.

First published 2000

British Library Cataloguing in Publication Data

A catalogue record for this book is available from the British Library.

ISBN 1-85604-351-7

Typeset from editor's disks by Library Association Publishing.
Printed and made in Great Britain by MPG Books Ltd, Bodmin, Cornwall.

# Contents

# List of contributors

**Stephen Adams** is Managing Director of Magister Ltd, an information and training consultancy specializing in patents documentation. He holds a BSc in Chemistry from Bristol University and an MSc in Information Science from City University, London. He has worked in the information industry since 1981, in central government, research associations and the commercial sector, including nine years with Zeneca Agrochemicals as Principal Patent Searcher. Magister Ltd provides consultancy services to patent database producers, online hosts and users.

**Karen Blakeman** has worked in the information profession for over 20 years and has been a freelance consultant for 11 years. Her company (RBA Information Services) provides training and consultancy on the use of the Internet, and on how to access and manage information resources. Prior to setting up RBA she spent ten years in the pharmaceutical and health care industry before moving to the international management consultancy group Strategic Planning Associates. Karen is currently Chair of the UK Online User Group and writes the Internet column for *Business Information Searcher*. She also produces a monthly, electronic newsletter entitled *Tales from the Terminal Room*. Her publications include *Search strategies for the Internet*, the UKOLUG *Quick guide to effective use of the Internet* and *Business information on the Internet*.

**Jill Bradley** started her career in public libraries before moving into the industrial sector at Esso Engineering and BOC Cryogenics as Librarian. She established a library at BIS Group, working in Corporate MA and marketing. Jill then moved to Harris Research to set up one of the first optical archiving projects in the UK. She is now the

Information Manager at Taylor Nelson Sofres and is responsible for their archiving system as well as running an information service and sampling department.

**Phil Bradley** has worked in the field of electronic publications for 20 years and is an independent Internet consultant. Phil runs numerous training courses in the field for Government departments, library authorities and blue chip companies. He also designs and maintains websites for a number of clients and speaks on Internet-related issues at conferences at home and abroad. He is the author of a number of books, such as *The advanced Internet searcher's handbook* (Library Association Publishing), and writes a monthly column in the *Library Association Record*.

**John Coll** is Head of the Scotish Science Library at the National Library of Scotland. He is also responsible for SCOTBIS (Scottish Business Information Service) based within the Scottish Science Library which provides a national business information service to the Scottish community. He has been involved in library work for 16 years and has spent the last 11 at the National Library. Professional interests include business information, web development and the role of IT in information services.

**Julia Dagg** is Academic Liaison Librarian at St George's Library, University of Sheffield, which serves the Faculty of Engineering, including Computer Science, Sheffield University Management School and the Departments of Economics and Computer Science. She is also a subject consultant for EEVL, the pioneering guide to quality engineering information on the Internet, now integrated into the Resource Discovery Network. She has a particular interest in the way in which world wide web resources offering useful free information can be integrated with libraries' traditional resources.

**Diana Grimwood-Jones** is an independent information and management consultant with particular interests in organizational effectiveness, content management and training and development. Her career includes 12 years in academic libraries as a Middle Eastern specialist, and nine years at The British Library in a variety of managerial roles. She was Senior Consultant at Aslib from 1992–7, where she began to develop an interest in the small business sector. One major recent project has been the establishment of the London Reference Database of business support services for London-based SMEs for the Business Link London network. She has also worked extensively within Europe, notably for the Community's Research and Development Information Service (CORDIS).

**Ben Heald** is Director of Communities at Sift, a company which he co-founded in 1996. He spent six years with KPMG, before establishing his own consulting business. Sift owns a portfolio of professional online communities, including AccountingWEB, LawZone and TrainingZone.

**Jane Heath** BA DipLib MIInfSci has been Business Information Manager since 1993 at Aon Risk Services, a UK subsidiary of leading insurance broker Aon Corporation. Current projects include setting up an online library of technical insurance information. She began her professional career in public reference libraries (Wimbledon and Kingston-upon-Thames) and was subsequently Information Analyst at Eagle Star (1991–3) and Information Officer at Bacon and Woodrow (1988–91).

**Keith Rose** gained an MSc in Information Science at City University in 1989, before taking his first post in the Library at Oftel. After this he worked in the Department of Trade and Industry's Information and Library Service for several years, answering a wide range of enquiries from sections supporting a wide range of industries, and building up a knowledge of official websites on the way. He is currently working as an Information Analyst with the Department's Business Analysis Team.

**Dr Iain Swadling** is the Food Information Officer at the International Food Information Service (IFIS Publishing). IFIS Publishing is best known as the producer of the databases *FSTA (Food Science and Technology Abstracts)*, the world's premier source of food related information, and *FNII (Food and Nutrition Internet Index)*, a searchable website describing and indexing food and nutrition resources available on the Internet. Dr Swadling has a background in food microbiology; he is a regular contributor to the scientific literature relevant to the food sector worldwide, and has specialist knowledge of information available via the Internet.

**Ian Tilsed** is a Computing Development Officer for the University of Exeter Library and Information Service, where his responsibilities include CD-ROM networking, the departmental website, and some popular pages on library and information science resources. He is a member of the Editorial Advisory Board for *Online Information Review* (formerly *Online & CD-ROM Review*), the *Internet News* column editor for the *UKOLUG Newsletter* and a regular reviewer for a number of publications. He is a corporate member of the Institute of Information Scientists.

**Sheila Webber** is a lecturer in the Department of Information Studies at the University of Sheffield. Her particular areas of interest are the marketing of information services, information literacy, and business information. She has maintained a list of Business Information Sources on the Internet since 1994, and has given numerous talks and seminars on the topic, including a series for the British Library. She is a Fellow of the Institute of Information Scientists, and has also been actively involved in the UK Online User Group, the European Bureau of Library Information and Documentation Associations, and the American Society for Information Science. Previous posts include Headship of the British Library's Business Information Service, responsible for free and priced services.

**Martin White** BSc FIInfSc FRSA is Managing Director of Intranet Focus Ltd, which he established in 1999. He has 30 years' experience in the information business, in information management, publishing and consulting roles. Much of his work has been in the areas of electronic publishing and high-technology market strategy development. His current areas of interest include the design and management of trans-national intranets (based on his experience of working for clients in 26 different countries), the development of enterprise information portals, and business development strategies for companies providing electronic information services to both the business and scientific sectors. In addition he tracks developments in electronic intellectual property, and advises on compliance with data protection, electronic copyright and database copyright legislation. Martin is a Past President and Honorary Fellow of the Institute of Information Scientists, a member of the Editorial Board of the *International Journal of Information Management* and is on the Executive Board of Online Information 2000.

# Introduction

Welcome to *The business and economy Internet resource handbook*. This guide is designed to appeal to a wide range of people – from those with little or no knowledge of the subject at all who wish to obtain a good overall understanding of how the subject is covered on the Internet, to those who are experts in one particular subject, and who wish to see how their subject fits into a larger overall scheme. Finally, each chapter, and indeed each guide, can be read either as part of the whole or by itself as a quick reference to point you towards key Internet resources.

*The business and economy Internet resource handbook* has been compiled from the work of practitioners who use the Internet every single day to locate and obtain information to assist them in their day-to-day work. As a result, the guide is based on their practical experience and is an invaluable 'starter pack' for people who are similarly going to be using the Internet for practical reasons.

The guide opens with three chapters that are designed to help set the scene, and put the chapters that follow into perspective. The first is an overview of the whole subject area, which identifies common issues, draws out similar threads and tries, as much as is possible, to summarize the strengths and weaknesses of the Internet as a whole when it comes to the coverage of business and the economy. The second chapter looks at how to make the best use of the different types of search engines that can be found on the Internet, as well as highlighting several particularly useful ones in this subject area. The third chapter covers resources that are designed to keep the researcher or practitioner up to date in the field and discusses various ways of turning this from a 24-hour-a-day job to a simple task that lasts for 24 hours a day.

The second section of *The business and economy Internet resource handbook* looks at the subject in more detail. Each chapter introduces the subject matter at hand, then looks at the resources that are available, and describes and summarizes them, as well as highlighting any particular strengths and weaknesses.

The handbook has not been compiled in an attempt to cover every single aspect of business and economy; that would need a book many times the size of this one! Rather, the intention is to highlight specific areas of interest and to provide various access points to the Internet and particular websites which can then be used by readers to further their own explorations of the Internet.

Also included is a chapter on e-commerce, which is slightly different in that it is about e-commerce on the Internet in general, rather than about the way in which business subjects are covered on the Internet, as with the other chapters. However, it is included because e-commerce is an important new area, which is expanding at a tremendous rate, and in a book on the Internet, business and economy would not be complete without some discussion of it.

This handbook should appeal to anyone who has an interest in business or financial information, be they researchers or information professionals. If you've just begun working in this area, or even if you've been doing so for many years, you should find useful information here – from overviews of the subjects to in-depth discussions on how well the Internet covers them, and detailed descriptions of individual websites. The handbook is intended to be a constantly useful resource, offering both an in-depth understanding of different aspects of business and financial information, and a quick-reference tool where you can find excellent websites to enable you to further your own research, or answer queries for others.

I should like to thank all the contributors for their hard work and unfailing patience and courtesy in the compilation of this work.

Phil Bradley

# 1
# Overview

*Karen Blakeman*

## Introduction

If, five years ago, you had merely hinted that you were using the Internet for locating business information, you would have been greeted with either total incredulity or hysterical laughter. There was very little available and what you did find had to be treated with extreme caution. In 1994, *The Daily Telegraph* was the first traditional information provider to give wholehearted attention to the job of providing access to its product via the Net. Today, the *Electronic Telegraph* at **http://www.telegraph.co.uk/** remains a key business resource. The BBC (British Broadcasting Corporation) also entered the fray and it was clear from a report in *The Guardian* (Schofield,1994) that, like most of us at the time, they were not sure what to do with the web:

> The BBC is building a public access server on the Web at **http://www.bbc.co.uk/**. It admits that 'there is not much here yet, but we're working on it'.

And work on it they did. The BBC site is now one of the most popular European portals for business and general information.

As for USA-based sources, SEC filings have long been available, but in the beginning one had to go through a tortuous process of downloading an index of filings, search it and then use FTP (file transfer protocol) to retrieve the document – hardly point and click.

Training courses tended to concentrate on discussion lists and Usenet newsgroups where one could request help from colleagues and experts on a specific subject. Discussion lists are still a useful aid to research – joining BUSLIB-L at **http://www.willamette.edu/~gklein/buslib.htm** is a must for any serious business researcher. As far as the web was concerned, one was hard-pushed to fill an A4 page with business sources.

Quality of information was, and still is, a major problem. The information was free, but unless it came from an established and trusted source, one had to subject it to rigorous scrutiny. Anyone can establish an Internet presence at very little or even no expense. Free Internet service providers abound and, with free web space and cheap domain name registration, it is possible for totally unqualified, inexperienced individuals to proffer advice and information.

Today, the Internet is mainstream. All serious information providers and publishers have web-based interfaces. Charging for quality is becoming more common but the 'free' sources still far outweigh priced services; it is tempting for information managers to cancel online subscriptions and rely on free or cheap, pay-as-you-go options for the bulk of their information needs. For some, this may be an appropriate strategy – for example, if you are only interested in current news stories, in checking name and contact details for a company, or in pulling off a facsimile of a company's annual report.

If, on the other hand, you need to be able to search several years of archival news stories, or pull together a mailing list of, say, Belgian, Swiss and Austrian organic chocolate manufacturers with more than 50 employees, then in the majority of cases you will have to revert to subscription services. As for annual reports and company accounts, company websites may satisfy your requirements with a PDF facsimile of the documents, but as soon as you want to start comparing and analysing a range of companies, the data has to be in a format that can be imported into your applications software – for example, .CSV, .RTF or Excel formats. You could struggle to convert HTML and PDF documents, or rekey the data into your system, but subscription services offer a more cost-effective and efficient solution.

# Identifying appropriate resources

There is a lot of good, free or low-priced business information out there – and I really do mean a lot! Every area of business is covered: news, share prices, interest rates, company information, taxation, official government documents, statistics, telephone directories, doing business, export markets. However, each site has its own *raison d'être*, strengths and weaknesses, and one can waste a considerable amount of time not just locating a site but also assessing the coverage, options and quality of the service that it provides. This is where a guide such as this is so useful. People who work with business and economic information, and use resources regularly, are able to provide expert advice on what is available and the limitations.

# Keeping addresses of key sites

Once you have found a site that you are going to use on a regular basis, add the site to your browser's bookmarks or favorites. It is all too easy to forget to do this when you are under pressure and the MD is screaming from his taxi that he needs that company interim report *now*, but you can bookmark after the event. If you are a Netscape user, pull up the history screen by pressing the Ctrl and H keys simultaneously, highlight the page you want, right-click on it with your mouse, and from the pop-up menu select 'add to bookmarks'. If you use Internet Explorer, click on the history button, right-click with your mouse on the page that you want, and select 'add to favorites'. Do not leave it too long, though, because your Internet connection may have been set up to 'expire' or clear the history on a daily basis.

A final comment on bookmarks and favorites: do make regular back-ups of them. They can disappear without trace, usually after a browser upgrade. Maybe you have already experienced that horrible feeling in the pit of your stomach when you have discovered that the bookmarks you have painstakingly and lovingly collected and organized have vanished into thin air.

# Search tools

Extensive as this publication is, it is no longer possible to list and comment on every single site that could be of use in a business environment. Sooner or later you will have to resort to Internet search tools. Chapter 2 goes into this subject in more detail and gives excellent advice on how to select and use the key search tools, as well as pointing out why and where search engines go wrong. It is worth repeating here that search tools miss and exclude pages and sites for a variety of reasons:

- web page design flaws such as home pages with graphics and no text
- dynamic pages that are created 'on the fly' – for example, a page that pulls together news and share price information from underlying databases in response to a visitor's request
- password protection – a large number of free business sites are overlooked by search engines because of this.

So, as well as learning how to use search engines effectively, it is vital that you build up a collection of addresses to key resources in your sector. In addition, identifying relevant, evaluated subject listings or portals in your subject area will save you a considerable amount of time. Here are some suggested starting points:

➠ *Yahoo!* at **http://www.yahoo.co.uk/**, as well as being an excellent directory of websites, carries a significant amount of content in the form of news, share price and financial information.

➠ *Corporate Information* at **http://www.corporateinformation.com/** is an excellent starting point for news sources, company financials, stock exchanges, business directories etc from across the world.

➠ *Exportall* at **http://www.exportall.com/** concentrates on European sources, with sections on directories for each country and country-specific search tools.

➠ *RBA Business Sources on the Internet* at **http://www.rba.co.uk/sources/** is a blatant plug for the author's own listing.

➠ *Sheila Webber's Business Sources* at **http://www.dis.strath.ac.uk/business/index.html** is an excellent list of business sources on the Internet compiled by Sheila Webber at Strathclyde University.

➠ The *BBC* **http://www.bbc.co.uk/** is one of the more popular European portals.

➠ *Online Newspapers* at **http://www.onlinenewspapers.com/** is a good starting point for locating web versions of newspapers.

➠ *Governments on the Web* at **http://www.gksoft.com/govt/** is *the* listing of government websites across the world. Nothing else comes anywhere near it in terms of coverage or currency.

➠ *Delia Venables Legal Links* at **http://www.venables.co.uk/** is a well respected and authoritative listing of legal sites.

➠ *Official Statistics on the Web* at **http://www.auckland.ac.nz/lbr/stats/offstats/OFFSTATSmain.htm**.

➠ *IRN Research* at **http://www.irn-research.com/** includes an excellent listing of trade and research associations, with descriptions and comments on the availability of statistics.

➠ *Telephone Directories on the Web* at **http://www.teldir.com/** is an excellent evaluated list of telephone and fax directories by country.

➠ *Google* at **http://www.google.com/** is not a portal or evaluated subject listing but it is a simple, fast and accurate search engine.

# Quality and information management issues

## Quality

Quality has always been an issue when it comes to business information and, to be honest, it is not just the Internet that presents a problem. We have all found errors in the so-called traditional subscription online services and we all have our personal hate list of databases that we would not touch with a bargepole. It has to be admitted, though, that the nature of the Internet provides ample opportunity for individuals, companies and organizations to present biased, misleading and incorrect information.

Questions that you need to ask and points to bear in mind include:

### Who is providing the information?

Are they well known in the industry or sector? Are they qualified to offer advice or to write on the subject? What is their background?

### The source of the information

Is there an indication of how it has been gathered? Is it from a journal or newspaper article, personal research or another website? Has it been copyright cleared?

## Why is the information being provided (especially if it is free)?

What is the motivation of the information provider? Does the person or organization have an axe to grind over political or economic issues? Or are they trying to discredit others? Is the information free as a means of tempting you into the site to use other, priced services? If it is a Government-funded site, it may be a cost-saving exercise (for example, the provision of free statutory instruments and acts of parliament). If it is offering advice on doing business in a specific country or region, it may be to encourage inward investment. The latter is often true of sites providing extensive information on emerging markets.

## Coverage

Are you being offered access to the full collection of data or to a limited selection? If the latter, what are the selection criteria? News sources in particular may offer you only today's main headlines and restricted or no archives.

## Search options

Are there options for keyword searching? Do you have to browse lists of headings or drill down through menus?

## Display options

Can you, for example, view the results of a company directory search as a continuous list, or are you forced to look at each company one at a time? Can you specify which fields or types of information are displayed? Is the information in HTML, PDF or another format such as Word, Excel?

## Printability

When printed, does the information fit onto a sheet of paper or do you have to fiddle around with your browser and printer settings? Does it print out at all? Can you print off documents in one go or do you have to print them as separate sections? The latter is a common problem with UK Acts of Parliament, and so frustrating when you subsequently realize that you have missed a section.

## Directories

What do they mean by a directory? Many are lists of hypertext links to company websites, while others are searchable databases. If they are the latter you must check coverage, selection criteria for inclusion, search, display and print options, mail-merge and mailing label options (usually only available as a priced service).

## Company financials

Is the information being provided directly by the company itself? If the site is not the primary source, is it the official repository for official filings (for example, the SEC in the USA), a site providing links to company websites (for example, *CAROL* at **http://www.carol.co.uk/**), or a secondary content aggregator (for example, *Hemmington Scott* at **http://www.hemscott.co.uk/** or *FT Company Briefings* at **http://www.ft.com/**)? Free company financials are often just key figures such as turnover, number of employees, or profit before or after tax. Furthermore, the figures may not be as they appear in the original accounts: they may have been harmonized or processed so that companies from different countries can be directly compared – for example, on *FT Company Briefings*.

## *How up to date is the information?*

All too often this is impossible to ascertain. In the early days of the web, seeing a 'page last updated on . . .' or 'links checked on . . .' was an indication of its currency. Unfortunately, the technology that is now used to create so-called sophisticated sites enables today's date to be displayed on a page without any expenditure of effort on the part of the person responsible for the content. Therefore, one has to assume that dates on web pages are meaningless.

Netscape does have an option (view, page info) which sometimes tells you when the page was loaded onto the web server. But again, this is unreliable as some web publishing packages automatically reload the whole site or update the page information every time one page is amended. Also, the date is sometimes given as unknown.

# Accessibility and availability

## *Accessibility*

For the users of information 'content is king'. The whole purpose of visiting a website is to look for information, not to admire the technical wizardry that has gone into the design. Nevertheless, far too many web designers still concentrate on the gadgetry with the result that sites are slow to load, do not display correctly or are not displayed at all. In order to make the most of the Internet as a business resource, you will have to use both Netscape and Internet Explorer as some pages will display correctly in one but not the other. An extra complication with Internet Explorer is that the security settings can affect whether or not a page is displayed. Even low to medium security will block some scripting and Active-X functions, so that the browser defaults to an error message page. This is not your IT department being paranoid or awkward – these are sensible precautions. The recent spate of script viruses – for example, the 'I Love You' and 'Life Style' viruses – are proof of that. These are not only transmitted via e-mail but also within web pages.

## Availability

The web is a medium that facilitates rapid publication. Information and entire websites can be loaded and updated in a matter of minutes. Unfortunately, the converse is also true. A page can literally be there one second and gone the next. If you know that the information you are looking at really is essential, do not just bookmark it but save it to disk or print it out. Future availability of archives is another potential problem to be aware of. Sites rarely spell out their policy on this, so cancelling a paper subscription may not be a sensible thing to do if you rely heavily on archival material.

# Copyright, terms and conditions

Finding out what you can and cannot do with the information, especially from free websites, can be a nightmare. The copyright symbol is usually present on the page, but even well-known publishers do not always elaborate on what is permissible. Terms and conditions vary considerably from one publisher to another:

- no stated policy whatsoever, in which case try and contact the web page owner to clarify the situation (though you may have difficulties finding an appropriate e-mail address or telephone number on the website)
- yes, you can pass the information on to other parties provided you do not charge for it and you include the source of the information
- you can only use the information for your own personal use
- you can only use the information for your own personal use and

under no circumstances are you to use it for any business purposes or application

- several screens of legalese that, in essence, threaten you with dire consequences if you use or store the information in any form and that if taken to their logical conclusion forbid you to even look at the data.

# Conclusion

Even those of you who have had limited experience of using the Internet will know that 'everything' is not on the Internet. In fact, everything is not in electronic form and neither is it in hard copy. The best business information is inside people's heads! This guide to business information concentrates heavily on locating data and information directly, but when you are out there, remember that the Internet can also be used to identify individuals and companies who can pull together the information you need and place it in context.

The above does seem to include a preponderance of negative points, but despite these the Internet is an incredible source of information. Its development over the last five years has been astounding and few of us dreamt that so much would be made so freely available. Tasks that once took a few hours or days – finding the latest news on a company, looking up currency exchange rates or checking up on VAT and tax regulations – can be done in a matter of minutes if you know where to look. And if you do not know where to look, read on . . .

# References

Schofield, J (1994) Netwatch, *Guardian Online*, (17 November), 5.

## URLs mentioned in this chapter

*British Broadcasting Corporation* http://www.bbc.co.uk/

*BUSLIB-L* http://www.willamette.edu/~gklein/buslib.htm

*CAROL* http://www.carol.co.uk/

*Corporate Information* http://www.corporateinformation.com/

*Deila Venables Legal Links* http://www.venables.co.uk/

*Exportall* http://www.exportall.com/

*FT Company Briefings* http://www.ft.com/

*Google* http://www.google.com/

*Governments on the Web* http://www.gksoft.com/govt/

*Hemmington Scott* http://www.hemScott.co.uk/

*IRN Research* http://www.irn-research.com/

*Official Statistics on the Web* http://www.auckland.ac.nz/lbr/stats/
    offstats/OFFSTATSmain.htm

*Online Newspapers* http://www.onlinenewspapers.com/

*RBA Business Sources on the Internet* http://www.rba.co.uk/sources/

*Sheila Webber's Business Sources*
    http://www.dis.strath.ac.uk/business/index.html

*Telephone Directories on the Web* http://www.teldir.com/

*The Electronic Telegraph* http://www.telegraph.co.uk/

*Yahoo!* http://www.yahoo.co.uk/

# 2

# Using search engines to find business and economics information

*Sheila Webber*

## Introduction

This chapter contains an overview of search engine characteristics, some searching tips, a list of search engines, and some sources for further information.

The definition of a search engine adopted in this guide is 'a searchable catalogue, database or directory of websites, of a reasonably large size'. A search engine normally consists of:

- a database, with each database record relating to a specific web page
- information retrieval software used to search the database.

The amount of information stored about each web page, the frequency with which each record is updated, the way in which the records are searched and output, and the total size and scope of the database, will all vary depending on the search engine. There is a trend towards search engines using more than one database, typically providing access to both a large computer-compiled database and a smaller human-compiled database, which can be browsed by category as well as searched. Examples are *Yahoo!* at **http://www.yahoo.com/** (with its own smaller, classified directory, and the very large Inktomi database) and *AltaVista* at **http://www.altavista.com/** (with its own very large computer-compiled database, and the smaller human-compiled Open Directory).

This chapter does not contain detailed search instructions for particular search engines. This is because the layout and search features of the more popular engines change constantly, and a printed book is not really the best place to go for this information. You are recommended to bookmark the *Infopeople* search tools chart and the *Searchenginewatch* site at **http://www.searchenginewatch.com/**, in particular, to keep abreast of changes. Both these sites have been stable for some time and are very frequently updated (see the end of this chapter for more details).

# What are search engines useful for?

They can obviously be useful to identify a company's own website. They are not so useful for identifying all the current news about a company, since search engines will not index all news stories immediately. Older news stories may turn out to be broken links, as they have been moved to an archive or removed completely from the original news site. However, you may well turn up a few news stories relevant to your company. You will not find the entries from most company directories (see the section below on What search engines do not cover), but some directories consist entirely of web pages, and those will be found.

You might retrieve commentary about the company from other companies' sites (eg on a client list or on an academic site). You may also find references to the company and its products in discussion list postings. If the company has disgruntled customers or is being attacked by a pressure group, then there may be 'alternative' information about the company.

Market information can be more difficult to track down, as it is harder to express the concepts fully and unambiguously. There is also a limit to the amount of full-text market information available free of charge on the publicly accessible web. Government sites can provide useful information on some specific markets, as well as general background information about a country. Both *Google* at **http://www.google.com/** and *Northern Light* at **http://www.northernlight.com/** have options to limit searches to US Government sites.

More theoretical business and economic topics can be difficult to research, as some words which you might want to use (such as 'marketing') occur frequently in sites for commercial marketing companies. You may have to try several engines, and reformulate your strategy, or limit by type of site (eg specifying educational sites). The browsable search engines can help, since you can drill down the categories to identify relevant sites.

Finally, search engines can be useful because of external information which is incorporated into the search or which is linked from the engine's home page. Examples are *Yahoo!*'s finance page (with stock quotes, news stories and so forth), and the data on US quoted companies which is found by *Excite* at **http://www.excite.com/**.

# How search engines compile their databases

This will vary. The main difference is between databases compiled by humans and those compiled automatically by computers. The human-compiled directories will tend to be smaller, more selective and have one record per website. The computer-compiled ones will be larger, and will tend to have multiple pages from each website. In the case of human-compiled search engines, editors will also search for relevant sites and will decide which sites to include and exclude. In the case of computer-compiled search engines, programs will be set up to check through the records on the search engine's database and find out whether the pages are still there, and to follow up any links on these pages in order to discover new pages. The terms 'spidering' and 'crawling' are used for this process, because of this process of following links to discover new resources.

In both cases, website creators will notify search engine providers of new or changed websites. Third parties may also recommend sites for inclusion.

The information that is indexed from each web page will vary. Human-compiled engines are likely only to record the title, and provide a site description of one or two sentences. Computer-compiled search engines are likely to index the whole text, although some of them are programmed just to create sets of keywords and phrases which are meant to express the content of the page more meaningfully.

The frequency with which the search engine's database is updated will also vary, and you will rarely see any open statement about this aspect, or statements about the size of the database. The aim will be to revisit all the pages stored in the database periodically, but search engines will tend to revisit popular websites more frequently and index them more thoroughly.

Search engine providers do not all create their own search engines: many of them buy in a search engine. For example, Inktomi sell their search engine to a number of sites (eg *UKMax*, *Yahoo!*, *HotBot* at **http://www.hotbot.com/**): this means that there is a large degree of overlap between the services using Inktomi, but they are not all the same, as each is likely to have a certain amount of customization (including a slightly different range of sites and search options).

A few databases include material that is not based on the web. The most obvious example is *Northern Light*, which allows you to search both the web and a range of well-established business sources.

# What search engines do not cover

No search engine covers all web pages in all publicly accessible websites. Lawrence and Giles (1999) estimated that no engine indexed more than about 16% of the estimated publicly indexable web. This study was carried out scientifically, and although there is debate about the results, you only have to compare the rates at which search engines and the web have increased in size (the web has increased a lot faster) to realize that search engines cannot be keeping pace.

Search engines will tend not to cover very new websites. The search engine has no way of knowing about a new site, either until a human has notified the search engine provider of a site's existence, or until an already indexed site links to the new site. Non-text files are not well indexed in search engines. There are specialist engines which focus on them (for example, *Lycos* has separate engines for graphics etc), but they are still not well covered.

Importantly for business searches, material held in separate searchable databases will not be listed on search engines. Since most company directories (eg yellow pages directories) are held as separate databases, this means that it is vitally important that you identify relevant company directories and then search the directories individually – a two-stage search.

When you search, for example, a yellow pages directory, although the output will be in the form of a web page, this is just a transient page created 'on the fly'. A program will have first translated your input into a query for the separate database, and then coded up the reply into a web page. This means that although the page you see appears as a web page, it only exists on your own computer as created by the program – it isn't available as a separate web page.

Much material in password-protected sites will also be excluded from search engines (even if the registration for the sites is free). Webmasters can put coding into their sites to encourage users to follow links into the site and visit it frequently, as well as adding relevant keywords to enhance retrieval. Unfortunately, though, useful sites may sometimes not be very skilfully coded from this point of view. A lot of very useful business information is contained in password-protected sites or in separate directories. Altogether, then, search engines can only give you access to a portion of the business information on the Internet.

# How do search engines carry out searches?

In order to search effectively, it is useful to have an idea of how the search engines work. Most search engines default to *relevance-ranked* searching. If nothing is said about how the engine works, it is probably relevance-ranked. A number of them also have *Boolean search* options. Additionally, on some engines, site owners can *pay* in order to rank more highly on the hit lists.

## Relevance ranking

This means that the engine has been programmed to give higher weighting to particular types of search term. The rules for this will vary, and you will not usually find a statement of what the rules are.

There are two key reasons for this. Firstly, if someone has come up with an effective set of weightings, they will want to keep the exact rules to themselves so as to retain competitive advantage over the other search engines.

Secondly, some website owners (particularly commercial website owners) are constantly tweaking their websites to try to come as high as possible in hit lists: to be in the number-one spot when someone searches on particular keywords. The search engine providers are keen to stop website owners from manipulating the results in this way.

The end result is that it is difficult for searchers to work out how best to refine search strategies. Not only will there be little information on the rules for ranking results, but the search engine provider will change the rules periodically, both to improve performance and to outwit the website owners.

The most common factors in relevance ranking are:

1   Higher weighting given to words in the title and main headings of a web page. The title is the set of words which appear at the very top of the browser (with the Hypertext Markup Language (HTML) coding <title>).

2   Higher weighting given to words taken from web pages' meta tags. These are keywords and phrases added by the creator of the web page to describe the page's content (the HTML code used is <meta>, hence 'meta tags'). These words are not displayed when you view the web page normally, but are listed in the invisible header portion of the page.

3   Higher weighting given to pages which mention the search terms several times.

4   Higher weighting given to pages in which your search terms are adjacent.

5   Higher weighting given to words which appear infrequently on the search engine's whole database. For example, if you searched on the words *ptarmigan information*, then it is likely that *ptarmigan* would be given a higher weighting than *information*, since many more web pages contain the word *information*.

You will almost always be able to use the plus and minus signs to increase or decrease the weighting of a particular search term (see the section below on search strategies), or specify that a set of words are to be searched as an exact phrase.

Weighting factors relating to other people's evaluation of a website are being used more and more. These include:

1   Higher weighting given to web pages which have a lot of external links to them, the idea being that if many people link to a website, then they are probably recommending it as a useful site. *Google* is an example of a site that gives this factor priority.
2   Higher weighting given to sites which have been frequently selected from hit lists by other searchers. *Direct Hit* is an example of a service which uses this method.
3   Higher weighting given to sites which have been voted for by users, eg by searchers sending in e-mails recommending a site.
4   Human compilers of the search engine giving the websites rankings – for example, allocating stars to a website, with four-star sites ranking higher in results than one-star sites.

# Boolean logic

Some search engines allow you to use Boolean logic: normally Boolean AND, OR and NOT. You may also be able to use brackets in order to group search statements, and some engines have more features for word adjacency (eg NEAR on *AltaVista* to specify words appearing within ten words of each other).

It is worth remembering that, when you are doing a Boolean search, you are defining what the retrieved search set is going to be. You are not necessarily determining what the output order is going to be. If you are a library and information professional, accustomed to searching systems like DIALOG, you are probably used to the default order being by date, usually with the most recent items displayed first. On a search engine this is far less likely to be the default. It is more likely to be relevance ranking or a random order. This makes it even more important to consider scanning several pages of search results, and not just the first page.

On *AltaVista* advanced search you have two search boxes: one in which you input your Boolean search, and one in which you type the words which will determine which results are displayed first. In a few systems you can specify how the output should rank (eg on *Northern Light* power search, you can select output ranked by relevance or by date).

## Paying for higher rankings

This usually involves website owners paying to have their site highly ranked when a particular search term is used. Some search engines have been started with the stated aim of persuading advertisers to pay in order to make their sites rank higher: examples are *GoTo* and *FindWhat*. In fact, since a comparatively small proportion of search terms and sites have been paid for, results may not be significantly different from, or worse than, other engines.

This is a controversial area, and some of the major engines have flirted with this approach, introducing and then withdrawing it. One option has been to highlight paid-for links separately. The more usual approach for the major engines is to link keywords to banner advertising rather than to higher website rankings. For example, if you used the search term *travel* you might get an advertisement for holidays; if you searched on *printers* you might get an advertisement for computer peripherals.

## Meta search engines: why not use them all the time?

Meta search engines are sites which take your search query and run it against several search engines. They usually just present the top hits from each engine. Some of them combine the results, but more of them present the results engine by engine. They may make it easy for you to go directly to the engine of your choice, having perused the hit list and identified which engine gave particularly good results.

There is a case for always starting with a meta search engine, particularly if you do not use search engines very often. It is likely that at least one of the engines will have found something at least mildly relevant to your interests. It helps to avoid the problem of accidentally using an inappropriate strategy (eg using Boolean logic on an engine that does not accept Boolean input) since the chances are that the strategy will be appropriate for one of the engines being searched. If you are using an unusual search term, which occurs in a web page that only one or two engines have indexed, then there are obvious advantages to searching across many engines.

However, if you want to get the best out of an individual search engine, then you need to optimize your search to use the unique features of that engine. It is also possible that the most relevant pages (to you) will not occur within the top 10 or 15 hits. Therefore, you will probably want to get to know a few individual search engines really well (including at least one search engine focused on your own country), and also use meta search engines.

Which you prefer to use first will depend on the type of search and your own personal style of information-seeking. Meta search engines are certainly useful for difficult searches, eg when you have tried your favourite engine with no result and want an overview of what other engines might produce. They can be useful for company website searches, since it is possible that at least one of the engines will rank the company's own website top. *Debriefing* is a good meta search engine to produce a few 'serious' hits. The meta search feature of *Ask Jeeves* at **http://www.askjeeves.com/** has a nice compact format.

# Search strategies

Strategies that work on just about every engine are:

- using a plus sign to indicate a word must be present, eg *+Nescafe*
- using a minus sign to indicate that a word must not be present, eg *– blend*
- using double quotes to indicate a phrase eg *"Gold Blend"*
- words without pluses or minuses to be searched for, but ranked lower.

Thus you might type into the search box: *+Nescafe –"Gold Blend"* to find pages that did contain the word 'Nescafe' but did not contain the phrase 'Gold Blend'. Synonyms or alternatives should be added with no plus signs, eg *+Nescafe "market share" "market size"*.

It is a good idea to look at the help pages or examine all the search menus and forms before trying other searches (eg Boolean).

There are yet more ways of increasing search precision (retrieving fewer items):

# Include or exclude search terms

1   Restrict to *<title>*. This is possible, for example, on *AltaVista, HotBot, Northern Light* (format on these systems is *title:searchterm* eg *title:glaxo*), and Yahoo! (*t:searchterm* eg *t:glaxo*). On a number of other engines you can opt to search for a term in the title by using the pull-down bars.

2   Use *and*. With some search engines there is an 'all the words [must be present]' option and/or a Boolean search option – a button or pull-down menu bar.

3   Use *not* (or *and not* on *AltaVista* advanced).

4   Specify upper case: on *AltaVista* and *HotBot* if you type in upper

case, that is all that will be retrieved, eg *Next* will find fewer pages than *next* (lower case retrieves both upper and lower case).

# Refine and limit your search

1   Search within your existing search set (eg *HotBot* and *Infoseek* at **http://www.infoseek.com/** allow this).
2   Restrict the search by language.
3   Restrict by date. It is not always made clear what the 'date' refers to: it may be either the date on which the page was added to the search engine's index, or the date when the page itself was created/updated.
4   Restrict to specific top-level domains, eg *.uk*.
5   Use very specific terms.

# Change search engines

1   Use smaller directories (that might just index a home page and/or a brief description of the site) rather than a massive search engine (that will have many pages from the same site, and irrelevant hits from all the full text).
2   Specialist engines will provide better precision.
3   National/local engines may give better precision.
4   Use a meta search engine to see which individual engine gives the most relevant results.

# Ways to increase recall (find more items)

1   Provide more synonyms to describe the search concepts.
2   Use *or* (or change to searching 'any of the words').
3   Try more than one engine.

4   Use meta search engines.

5   Specialist and national/local engines may give better recall as well as better precision.

6   Use 'related search' or 'more like this' features.

7   Try a different strategy (eg natural language if you were using Boolean search).

# Using search engines as company directories

1   Search on the full company name as a phrase, plus variations on the name. There are all the usual problems of company name searching (eg both W H Smith and WH Smith appear on web pages).

2   Categorized sites like *Yahoo!* can provide a directory of company websites, sometimes with whole categories devoted to parts of one company. If you search on a company name, you may be offered a company profile, with a tailored page with basic details, and links to the company website, news headlines and other relevant information.

3   Any search engine that just puts in one entry per site is easier to search if you want the home page of a website (rather than a more specific page within it).

4   *HotBot, Mirago, Infoseek* and the .COM version of *AltaVista* group pages from the same site together and just put the home page (or the page closest to the home page in what is retrieved) in the hits list. *Excite* also has an option to 'list by website'.

5   For names which appear commonly in other contexts, try linking the name with a word connected with its line of business or key product, eg *Next and clothes, Apple and Macintosh.*

6   *AltaVista* and *UK Directory* give you the option of finding the

*RealNames* entry. *RealNames* have a directory of company websites, but it is not comprehensive.

7    *Debriefing* seems to return useful results on company name searches.

8    *Excite* will offer you the page for the company in its company directory if you search for the name of a large (mostly US) public company on its own.

9    Local or national versions of search engines may well have links to the local yellow pages directory or some other business directory.

# What is in the search results page?

Some search results pages are confusing. The actual list of hits may not start until half way down the page. If you are using an engine for the first time, it is worth scrolling up and down the page carefully to try and work out what it is presenting. There may be information about the search output and whether you can change the defaults on the search engine's help pages.

The search engine's idea of relevance may not coincide with your own. It may well be worth scanning several pages of hits, rather than just the first one.

The engine will usually give a count of the number of web pages found. If the number is large, bear in mind that this may include pages which only contain part of one of the words you entered as a search term. Additionally, on a number of engines there is a limit to the number of hits you can display.

The page may start with advertisements (including links to carry out your search on affiliated sites like *Amazon.Com* at **http://www.amazon.com/**). If the search engine emphasizes its directory, then it may start by giving links to sections in its directory before listing individual websites (*Yahoo!* is one example of this).

Some computer-compiled search engines list just one entry per website, with an option to display further pages on that website. This is a very useful feature for business searches, as it makes it easier to identify the range of websites you have retrieved. In the tables below, the engines which have this feature are indicated. The human-compiled search engines tend to have just one hit per site anyway.

Some engines use different databases depending on what you have typed in. *HotBot* is the most obvious example (see entry in the listing below). Some of these features are designed to help people searching on the names of large companies (prioritizing the link to the company's website, or giving data about the company), and again these features are noted in the tables below. Where search engines are using someone else's database, there will often be a 'powered by . . .' (eg 'powered by Inktomi') statement at the end of the page of hits.

Some engines give a count of how many times each term was found, and which terms were ignored.

On some engines you can alter the number of hits displayed per page, and how much detail is displayed with each hit.

Some engines have a 'more like this' or 'related search' option. A few allow you to search within your existing search set, or add extra search terms.

*Northern Light* categorizes the search results into folders. Sometimes it groups by type of site, and sometimes by subject. You can either browse through the list of results page by page, as for any other search engine, or click on a particular folder, to browse just the results in that folder.

# Some key search engines

Notes to tables:

'**Boolean search**' means that you can at least use and, or and not (**NB** Relevance ranking is the default unless otherwise stated).

'**.COM version**' means the version of the search engine which has an address ending .com.

'**Groups by site**' means that the search engine groups together the pages from one site, and puts just one listing per site in the hit list.

'**Title search**' means that you can specify that a word must appear in the title of a web page.

'**Very large**' means over 100 million web pages; '**large**' means 50–100 million; '**medium**' means 2–50 million; '**small**' means 1–2 million; '**very small**' means less than a million.

**Table 2.1** *General search engines*

| Name, URL and origin | Notes | Features relevant to business searches |
|---|---|---|
| *AltaVista*<br>**http://www.altavista.com/**<br>(UK) **http://www.altavista.co.uk/**<br>Versions include Swedish, German and UK.<br>Owned by CMGI Inc and Compaq, USA. | Very large engine: over 200 million web pages (17 million in UK version), 25 million multimedia objects, plus Usenet messages (also has e-shopping, news). Smaller browsable directory is open directory. Boolean and title search in advanced search option. Translation feature. All versions have advanced search and text only options (look for links near bottom of home pages). .COM version groups by site. | Local versions have local news headlines and links to local yellow pages directories, eg Scoot yellow pages and Reuters news for the UK. Uses *RealNames* database. **http://money.altavista.com/** has news and stock quotes, with options to set up your own portfolio. |
| *Ask Jeeves*<br>**http://www.ask.com/**<br>(UK) **http://www.askjeeves.co.uk/** (planned)<br>Owned by Ask Jeeves Inc, USA. | Two services: a very small database containing answers compiled by humans (it gives you a list of questions it calculates may be like yours, and you choose the nearest); and a meta search engine (it searches several engines and presents the top hits in a handy format). | Some of the ready-compiled answers relate to business questions, but have a USA focus at present. |
| *Direct Hit*<br>**http://www.directhit.com/**<br>Direct Hit Technologies Inc, USA. | Ranks according to how many people have clicked on that link in the past. Used as part of some other search engine sites, either obviously (eg in *HotBot*) or behind the scenes. | Results can be good for broad topics and better-known companies. |
| *Dow Jones Business Directory*<br>**http://businessdirectory.dowjones.com/**<br>Owned by Dow Jones Inc, USA. | Human-compiled searchable directory. Very small but well-focused, with careful site reviews. Includes some non-USA sites. | Whole directory is business-focused. Includes entries for Dow-listed companies. For subscribers to the *Wall Street Journal*, there is extra hyperlinked data. |

| Name, URL and origin | Notes | Features relevant to business searches |
|---|---|---|
| *EuroSeek* **http://euroseek.net/** Interface in several European languages. Owned by Euroseek AB, Sweden. | European focus. Medium-sized. Boolean search. Uses open directory as browsable directory. | Good 'media guide': links to news sites worldwide. Strong on European news sites. Also European news headlines. |
| *Excite* **http://www.excite.com/** (UK) **http://www.excite.co.uk/** Versions for Australia, France, Germany, Italy, Japan, Netherlands, Sweden, UK and Chinese-speakers. Owned by At Home Corporation, USA. | Very large search engine. Boolean search: use in normal search box; 'advanced' search page doesn't really add to the search options. Option to display top 40 results grouped by website. Personalization options. Results page rather 'busy': includes categories, news stories, websites. Optimized for relevance-ranked searching. If your usual strategies fail, it is worth typing in ordinary sentences that describe your search. | If you type in the name of a major company (using .COM version), it will create links to company data (eg from Media General Financial Services and Standard & Poor's). Local news headlines, stock quotes on national versions. On 'business' page of .COM version, company search is of US companies, data from Dun & Bradstreet. UK *Excite* has link to BT yellow pages. |
| *FAST* (aka *AlltheWeb*) **http://alltheweb.com/** Owned by FAST and Dell, USA. | Very large search engine. Advanced search allows title search and some other options, eg filter by domain. The buttons for MP3 files, ftp files, graphic files are links to the relevant *Lycos* sites. | No features relevant to business searches, but it does seem to be large and fast. |
| *Google* **http://www.google.com/** Owned by Google Inc, USA. | Ranks sites mainly according to how many other sites link to them. If you click the 'I feel lucky' button, you are automatically taken to the site that *Google* has selected as number one. Google Scout feature identifies related pages. | Good for broad searches and for finding a few relevant sites. USA Government pages search (click on 'about Google'). |

| Name, URL and origin | Notes | Features relevant to business searches |
|---|---|---|
| *GoTo*<br>**http://www.goto.com/**<br>Owned by GoTo.Com Inc, USA. | Very large engine (uses Inktomi). Advertisers pay to feature higher up the search rankings. Boolean search. Lists one site per domain (but no feature to see the other pages on that site that have hit). | The yellow pages search option is for a USA directory, stocks are from Stockpoint. |
| *HotBot*<br>**http://www.hotbot.com/**<br>Owned by Lycos, USA. | Very large search engine (Inktomi); browsable directory is open directory. Boolean search. Title search. Groups by site. If you do a fairly simple search, the top hits returned will be from the *Direct Hit* database, not Inktomi (look at the bottom of the page to see which one has been used). Text-only option. You can search within a results set. | |
| *Infoseek*<br>**http://infoseek.go.com/**<br>(UK) **http://www.infoseek.co.uk/**<br>Local versions include Denmark, France, Italy, Japan, Netherlands, Spain, Sweden, UK.<br>Owned by Go.Com, and ultimately Disney, USA. | Medium-sized. Boolean and title search. Groups by site. You can search within a results set. For advanced search click 'search options' (under the search box). | On .COM version company profiles are from Hoover's (click 'search options' and select 'companies') and you can search recent newswires. |
| *LookSmart*<br>**http://www.looksmart.com/**<br>(UK) **http://www.looksmart.co.uk/**<br>Australian and Dutch versions.<br>Owned by LookSmart, USA. | Small, manually compiled, browsable by subject. There is a *LookSmart* Live service: if you type in a query, one of *LookSmart*'s editors will give you an answer. | Has a good business section, and the UK guide really does have a UK focus. |

| Name, URL and origin | Notes | Features relevant to business searches |
|---|---|---|
| *Lycos*<br>http://www.lycos.com/<br>(UK) http://www.lycos.co.uk/<br>Versions include Germany, France, UK, Belgium, Sweden etc.<br>Owned by Lycos, USA. | Large search engine. Browsable directory is open directory for .COM version; UK *Lycos* has a UK-specific but small and out-of-date browsable directory. Title search and Boolean search (including 'near', 'far'). Use normal search box; advanced search is not very advanced. There is also a search engine for pictures, sound. .COM version retrieves 'popular sites' (direct hit), then websites, then newswires. UK version groups by site. | On *Lycos UK* the yellow pages are Thomson. Some of the European versions have a link to the *Wer liefert was* (who supplies what) directory. Local news headlines on national versions, plus other local links. |
| *Microsoft Network*<br>http://search.msn.com/<br>Owned by Microsoft, USA. | Very large engine (Inktomi database). Boolean and title search options in advanced search option (click 'more options'). Can also group by site in advanced. The saved search feature is only available if you are using Internet Explorer 5. | |
| *Northern Light*<br>http://www.northernlight.com/<br>Also http://www.NLResearch.com/<br>(corporate searchers' site with extra options for searching market research reports and Wharton Econometric reports).<br>Owned by Northern Light, USA. | Very large search engine. As well as the usual searchable database of websites, there is also a 'special collection' of journals, magazines, newswire etc databases, which you search for free, but you pay to see the full text. Boolean and title search. As you search, the system creates a series of 'folders' grouping together sites by type or topic. Free alerting service (listing new websites and articles matching your keywords). | The special collection has a strong business focus. There are separate search screens for Investext, stock quotes, and news (last two weeks, searching 30 newswires).<br>In 'business search' you can limit search by broad industry, date, information types. Company name option only retrieves special collection items with a company name field. They operate *govsearch* (US Government sites, priced service) and the free database is also good for these sites. |

| Name, URL and origin | Notes | Features relevant to business searches |
|---|---|---|
| *Oingo*<br>**http://www.oingo.com/**<br>Owned by Oingo Inc, USA. | Experimental search engine that matches your search terms against thesauri and asks you to specify which meaning you want if a word has more than one. There is only a limited database (ie the open directory). | Thesaurus approach aids precision searching, but open directory is not very useful for non-USA business searches. |
| *Open Directory*<br>**http://dmoz.org/**<br>Owned by Netscape and thus AOL, USA. | *Yahoo!*-type human-compiled directory of websites. Used on a number of sites: the fact that it is free may be the reason for its popularity. | At time of writing, *Yahoo!* and *LookSmart* are preferred for European business searches. |
| *RealNames*<br>**http://web.realnames.com/**<br>Owned by RealNames Corp, USA. | Directory of companies, products and homepages. Used by other search engines. Companies normally pay to participate. | Business focus, but bias towards USA companies, and includes personal home pages. |
| *Thunderstone*<br>**http://dwarf.thunderstone.com/texis/websearch/**<br>Owned by Thunderstone, USA. | Concentrates on .com, .org and USA-only sites. Does not index all the text in the pages: their software automatically analyses and categorizes the sites with keywords. | |
| *Voila*<br>**http://www.voila.fr/**<br>(UK) **http://www.voila.co.uk/**<br>Versions include UK.<br>Owned by France Telecom. | Very large search engine. Boolean search. Groups pages by site. *Voila UK* has the Systran translator; French *Voila* has a French-to-English or German translator. | French and UK versions have Agence France Presse news and thematic search option (you can limit search to pages on finance theme: worth trying). On French version the *économie* section has links to stock exchange etc. |
| *WebSearch*<br>**http://www.WebSearch.com.au/**<br>(UK) **http://www.WebSearch.co.uk/**<br>Australia.<br>Versions include New Zealand, Hong Kong, UK. | Good coverage of Southern hemisphere, as one might expect. UK version does not have terribly good UK coverage. Chatty free e-mail newsletter. | |

| Name, URL and origin | Notes | Features relevant to business searches |
|---|---|---|
| *Yahoo!*<br>**http://www.yahoo.com/**<br>(UK) **http://www.yahoo.co.uk/**<br>Versions include UK and Ireland, Germany, Australia and New Zealand, Norway, Spain, Denmark, Sweden, France. | Small, human-compiled search engine. Local people are involved in compiling the local versions. Title search and an advanced search allow you to specify *and* or *or*. Personalization options. Searches on very large Inktomi database if your search terms do not hit on *Yahoo!*. | Structure means it can be used as a company directory, including companies with branches/sites worldwide. UK *Yahoo!* has a financial section with financial information: the state of the FTSE, Dax etc; latest business headlines from Reuters and the Press Association; a feature to search for share prices; and a link to search the Hemmington Scott UK company profiles. Similar sections on some other national versions. |

**Table 2.2** *UK search engines*
  See also *AltaVista, Ask Jeeves, Excite, Infoseek, LookSmart, Lycos, Voila and WebSearch* in Table 2.1.

| Name, URL and origin | Notes |
|---|---|
| *Financial Times business directory*<br>**http://www.globalarchive.ft.com/directory/topLevelNavigation.htm**<br>(or if they have moved it, go to **http://www.ft.com/**) | Very small *Yahoo!*-type directory focusing on business websites. |
| *Mirago*<br>**http://www.mirago.co.uk/** | You can specify how the pages should be ranked (eg most recent, image-rich, word density). Boolean search. You can group hits by site. There is a query parser which augments the search with US/UK spellings etc. As well as the main database there is a small browsable directory. |

| Name, URL and origin | Notes |
|---|---|
| *Scotland.Org*<br>**http://www.scotland.org/** | About 5,000 Scottish websites. |
| *SearchUK*<br>**http://www.searchuk.com/** | Small to medium-sized. Address search feature that supplies addresses (though it won't give results unless it can find a precise match). Data is from Capscan, residential and business addresses. 'Business' search is the Scoot directory. |
| *UK Directory*<br>**http://www.ukdirectory.com/** | Lists UK sites, grouped by sector, with business focus. *RealNames* search option for organization searches. |
| *UK Index*<br>**http://www.ukindex.co.uk/index.html** | Directory of UK (or UK-related) websites. They assign category headings, and the database is searchable. Alerting service available. |
| *UKMax*<br>**http://www.ukmax.com/**<br>Owned by Hollinger Digital and thus a stablemate of the *Daily Telegraph*. | Very large UK-based search engine using the Inktomi engine. Has UK news, weather, stock quotes etc. |
| *UKPlus*<br>**http://www.ukplus.co.uk/**<br>Owned by the *Daily Mail*. | Annotated, searchable directory of UK websites. |
| *WebScot business directory*<br>**http://www.webscot.co.uk/** | Directory of about 900 Scottish business sites. |

**Table 2.3** *Meta search engines*

| Name, URL and origin | Notes |
| --- | --- |
| *Copernic*<br>**http://www.copernic.com/**<br>*AltaVista, Deja.com, Excite, HotBot, Infoseek, Google, Lycos, SNAP, MSN* and *Yahoo!* (free version). | You need to download the *Copernic* software (available for PC or Mac). When you enter your search it will go online and pull down results. Priced version includes extra categories (news etc) and engines. |
| *Debriefing*<br>**http://www.debriefing.com/** | Australian meta search engine that is particularly good for business searches, as it tends to ignore personal pages etc. Unfortunately it does not group by site so you may find that all the selected hits come from the company's own site, but it is well worth trying, eg for company name searches. |
| *Dogpile*<br>**http://www.dogpile.com/**<br>Defaults to search *LookSmart, GoTo.com, Dogpile Web Catalog, Dogpile Open Directory, Direct Hit, About.com, Infoseek, RealNames, AltaVista, Lycos* and *Yahoo!*<br>Owned by Go2Net. | You can customize it to search up to 18 engines, in the order that you specify. Assumes 'and' if a phrase is entered. You can also search a selection of business news (mostly USA, some world). |
| *Metacrawler*<br>**http://www.metacrawler.com/**<br>*About.com, AltaVista, Excite, GoTo.com, Infoseek, LookSmart, Lycos, Thunderstone, WebCrawler* and *Google* are specified on powersearch page.<br>Owned by Go2Net. | Includes a powersearch page, on which you can select exactly which engines you search. |

| Name, URL and origin | Notes |
| --- | --- |
| *Inference* **http://www.infind.com/** *WebCrawler, Yahoo!, Lycos, AltaVista, Infoseek and Excite.* | Clusters results by type of site. *Inference Find 2* can search up to 51 engines and has a typo detector. There are French and German versions (though recall is not immediately impressive). |
| *Mamma* **http://www.mamma.com/** Searches 'ten of the major search engines': on the powersearch page it names *About.com, Yahoo!, Excite, Infoseek, Lycos, Webcrawler, Alltheweb, AltaVista.* | The powersearch option allows you to decide which engines to search. |
| *Multimeta* **http://www.multimeta.com/** *Aladin, Altavista, Eule, Excite, HotBot, Infoseek, Intersearch, Lycos, Yahoo! (Germany), Yahoo! (USA).* | Searches some major international and German search engines. |
| *Profusion* **http://www.profusion.com/** *AltaVista, Excite, Infoseek, GoTo, LookSmart, Magellan, WebCrawler, Yahoo!, Alltheweb.* | You can pick the ones you want, or choose 'best three' ('ProFusion will analyse your query and try to determine which subject or subjects your query is in') or 'fastest three'. |
| *Savvysearch* **http://www.savvysearch.com/** | There are a number of categories in which you can perform a metasearch, eg large search engines, 'guides' (directories like *Yahoo!*); search engines in particular languages (eg German, French, Spanish). |

**Table 2.4** *List of search engines*

| Name, URL and origin | Notes |
|---|---|
| *All-in-one*<br>**http://www.allonesearch.com/** | Lists 500 search engines and directories, grouped by type. Includes 'people search' engines listed and some other specialist database types. |
| *AlphaSearch*<br>**http://www.calvin.edu/library/as/** | Database of gateway sites, with academic emphasis. |
| *Beaucoup*<br>**http://www.beaucoup.com/** | Lists 2500 search engines and directory-type sites (including a reasonable range of non-USA engines). |
| *Invisible Web*<br>**http://www.invisibleweb.com/** | Indexes websites which contain databases that search engines cannot spider. You first have to identify the resource you want and then go to that specific site to search it. |
| *Searchability*<br>**http://www.searchability.com/** | The useful feature of this site is the description of the various search engines, grouped by category. |
| *Virtual search engines*<br>**http://www.dreamscape.com/**<br>**frankvad/search.html** | Links to 1000 search engines and directories, arranged by category. |

**Table 2.5** *Lists for identifying non-English-language engines*

| Name, URL and origin | Notes |
|---|---|
| *Searchengine Colossus*<br>**http://www.searchenginecolossus.com/** | Covers about 100 countries |
| *Search Engines Worldwide*<br>**http://www.twics.com/~takakuwa/search/** | Covers about 900 engines, arranged by country. |
| *7Alpha* (French)<br>**http://www.7alpha.com/** | Specifically indexes search engines and directories by country and by theme. There is a category for business directories/engines (enterprises). |
| *LookSmart*<br>**http://www.looksmart.com/** | Has a search tools category that includes a good list of country directories. |
| *LANIC search engines page* (Latin America)<br>**http://lanic.utexas.edu/world/search/** | Links to Latin American search engines (in Brazil, Chile, Mexico etc): scroll down the page to find these links. |

# Guides to searching search engines

The magazines *Online* and *Econtent* (with partial contents at **http://www.onlineinc.com/**) and *Searcher* (with partial contents at **http://www.infotoday.com/**) often have good articles about search engines, and some of the articles are available in full text and free on their websites. *Freepint* (**http://www.freepint.co.uk/**) is good for practical tips.

Blakeman, K (1998) *Search strategies for the Internet,* RBA Information Services (see details at **http://www.rba.co.uk/**). This includes search sheets for individual engines.

Richard Eskins' *Search Tools: a guide* is a packed but quick loading page, with links and brief tips concerning various web search tools (available at **http://www.mmu.ac.uk/h-ss/dic/main/search.htm**).

Hock, R (1999) *Extreme searcher's guide to web search engines: a handbook for the serious searcher*, Information Today. A practical guide, with sections on major engines.

Carole Leita's *InfoPeople search tools chart,* produced for the InfoPeople Project, based at the University of California at Berkeley, is a search chart with features of major search engines, very frequently updated. It can also can be downloaded in Adobe's PDF format. (Available at **http://www.infopeople.org/**).

Greg R Notess' *Search engine showdown* summarizes, reviews, and compares the search features and database scope of Internet search engines (available at **http://www.notess.com/search/**).

*SearchIQ* has reviews and news about search engines (available at **http://www.searchiq.com/**).

Danny Sullivan's *Searchenginewatch* is an excellent resource, with comparisons, facts, news (including a newsletter) and links (available at **http://searchenginewatch.com/**).

At **http://www.searchenginewatch.com/facts/index.html** there are links to useful pages with advice on searching search engines: this section would be a helpful starting point for a novice search engine searcher.

Ian R. Winship's *Comparative chart* is a handy one-page chart showing some of the features for *AltaVista, Excite, Google, Infoseek, HotBot, Lycos* and *Northern Light* (available at **http://www.unn.ac.uk/features.htm**).

The author's own site, *Business information sources on the Internet*, includes an annotated list of search engines and a list of search engine reviews and guides (available at **http://www.dis.strath.ac.uk/business/**).

## Reference

Lawrence, S and Giles, C L (1999) Accessibility of information on the web, *Nature*, **400**, (July), 107–9.

## URLs mentioned in this chapter

*7Alpha* **http://www.7alpha.com/**

*All-in-one* **http://www.allonesearch.com/**

*AlphaSearch* **http://www.calvin.edu/library/as/**

*AltaVista* **http://www.altavista.co.uk/**

*AltaVista* **http://www.altavista.com/**

*Ask Jeeves* **http://www.ask.com/**

*Ask Jeeves* **http://www.askjeeves.co.uk/**

*Beaucoup* **http://www.beaucoup.com/**

*Business information sources on the Internet*
       **http://www.dis.strath.ac.uk/business/**

*Comparative chart* **http://www.unn.ac.uk/features.htm**

*Copernic* **http://www.copernic.com/**

*Debriefing* **http://www.debriefing.com/**

*Direct Hit* http://www.directhit.com/

*Dogpile* http://www.dogpile.com/

*Dow Jones Business Directory* http://businessdirectory.dowjones.com/

*EuroSeek* http://euroseek.net/

*Excite* http://www.excite.co.uk/

*Excite* http://www.excite.com/

*FAST (AlltheWeb)* http://alltheweb.com/

*Financial Times business directory*
    http://www.globalarchive.ft.com/directory/topLevelNavigation.
    htm

*Free Pint* http://www.freepint.co.uk/

*Google* http://www.google.com/

*GoTo* http://www.goto.com/

*HotBot* http://www.hotbot.com/

*Inference* http://www.infind.com/

*infoPeople search tools chart* http://www.infopeople.org/

*Infoseek* http://infoseek.go.com/

*Infoseek* http://www.infoseek.co.uk/

*Invisible Web* http://www.invisibleweb.com/

*LANIC* search engines page http://lanic.utexas.edu/world/search/

*LookSmart* http://www.looksmart.co.uk/

*LookSmart* http://www.looksmart.com/

*Lycos* http://www.lycos.co.uk/

*Mamma* http://www.mamma.com/

*Metacrawler* http://www.metacrawler.com/

*Microsoft* Network http://search.msn.com/

*Mirago* http://www.mirago.co.uk/

*Multimeta* http://www.multimeta.com/

*Northern Light* http://www.NLResearch.com

*Northern Light* http://www.northernlight.com/

*Oingo* http://www.oingo.com/

*Online* and *Econtent* http://www.onlineinc.com/
*Profusion* http://www.profusion.com/
*RBA Information Services* http://www.rba.co.uk/
*RealNames* http://web.realnames.com/
*Savvysearch* http://www.savvysearch.com/
*Scotland.Org* http://www.scotland.org/
*Search Engines Worldwide* http://www.twics.com/~takakuwa/search/
*Search tools: a guide* http://www.mmu.ac.uk/h-ss/dic/main/search.htm
*Searchability* http://www.searchability.com/
*Searchengine Colossus* http://www.searchenginecolossus.com/
*Searchenginewatch* http://searchenginewatch.com/
*Searchenginewatch*
        http://www.searchenginewatch.com/facts/index.html
*Searcher* http://www.infotoday.com/
*SearchIQ* http://www.searchiq.com/)
*SearchUK* http://www.searchuk.com/
*Thunderstone* http://dwarf.thunderstone.com/texis/websearch/
*UK Directory* http://www.ukdirectory.com/
*UK index* http://www.ukindex.co.uk/index.html
*UKMax* http://www.ukmax.com/
*UKPlus* http://www.ukplus.co.uk/
*Virtual search engines*
        http://www.dreamscape.com/frankvad/search.html
*Voila* http://www.voila.co.uk
*WebScot business directory* http://www.webscot.co.uk/
*WebSearch* http://www.WebSearch.co.uk/
*Yahoo!* http://www.yahoo.co.uk/
*Yahoo!* http://www.yahoo.com/

# 3

# Keeping up to date

*Phil Bradley*

## Introduction

As we all know, the Internet is constantly changing, growing and adapting to different circumstances. New web pages are added at the rate of over a million a day, and it is still increasing at an almost unbelievable rate; use in the UK alone is doubling every six months.

Consequently, you would be forgiven for thinking that, because of this huge growth, there would be something in place to make it easy to keep up to date with new developments and advances – but unfortunately, quite the opposite is true. Keeping up to date with advances, both in Internet technologies and in the new materials that are added to the Internet, is one of the most difficult things to do easily.

This chapter will consider some of the ways in which you may be able to ensure that you keep as up to date as possible, not only in the fields of business and economics, but also generally. We shall consider some of the different ways in which you can do this, and the advantages and disadvantages of various techniques, and we shall look at some resources in detail.

# Search engines

If you want really current information, search engines (see also the previous chapter) will generally not provide you with it. They generally obtain their information in one of two ways. Those search engines that are free text, such as *AltaVista* (**http://www.altavista.com/**)*, Lycos* (**http://www.lycos.com/**)*, HotBot* (**http://www.hotbot.com/**) and *Northern Light* (**http://www.northernlight.com/**), use utilities called robots or spiders to crawl the web, looking for new or updated pages. Once they find a new page, or a page that has been updated since they last looked at it, they will copy the new data back to base, and will periodically update their indexes. Authors of web pages can of course go to the various search engines and inform them of new pages, which will put them onto a fast track for indexing, but it's still not a fast process. There are two elements to consider here: the first is the time it takes for the robot or spider programs to navigate the web (which is akin to painting the Forth Bridge), and this process can literally take months; the second is the interval between updates of their indexes. As a result, a web page may have been published for three months or even longer before search engines find and index it.

Other search engines such as *Yahoo!*, which are based on a directory or hierarchical approach, rely on web authors visiting their sites and registering pages directly into the appropriate categories. These pages can then be viewed by people employed by the search engines, and if they are appropriate can be included in the index. This obviously requires authors to remember to do this; if they don't, the search engine will not know about the existence of the web page, so you won't find it. Consequently, you are at the mercy of not only the authors, who need to register their pages in a timely manner, but also the search engine itself, which needs to ensure that it updates its index regularly.

Some search engines will allow you to run a search on date – the advanced search features in *AltaVista* and *Northern Light* are examples of this – and you can run a search, then ask the engine just to display the new web pages that it has found between two different points in time. This can prove useful in allowing you to see how fresh their index is, and of course a search of this nature will eliminate web pages that you have found previously. It is also possible to bookmark a search that you have run: when you go back to that bookmark in the future, the search will be re-run from scratch for you, and if the engine also provides a search-by-date feature this is an easy and effective way to provide yourself with a current awareness service. However, you should still keep in mind that you may well be searching on an index that is days (if not weeks) old, so it's not a perfect solution by any means.

# Personalized services

Since all the search engines are trying to get as much share of the market as possible, many of them have begun to offer personalized services in order to make themselves more attractive to potential users.

There are two aspects of this that may be of interest to the business and economics researcher. The first is that many of these personalized services will give access to stocks and shares quotes. Since this is a free service, you cannot expect to get up-to-the-minute quotes, but most of them are only delayed by about 15 to 20 minutes, so unless you're considering actively buying or selling stock, this information is as current as most people will need. The second factor that may prove useful is in providing news stories, which are updated throughout the day. It is possible to personalize the system to keep you updated on new and breaking stories in any number of different fields: simply log on to the system at various times during the day and your personalized page will be automatically updated to provide you with the latest headlines, allowing you to read the story in detail. The major disadvantage here is that it is generally not possible to focus these updating services tightly;

the most that you can hope for is something like 'Business information in the UK', for example. So although you may well get stories, news and information that closely match your particular interests, more often than not much of the material will be of little if any interest to you. However, on the plus side, it is quick to check – simply visit the personalized page with a click of your browser, or if you are lucky enough to have constant access, simply refresh the page every now and then to see if there are any appropriate stories.

Most of the larger search engines offer services of this nature, and they are often called 'My <name of search engine>'. Take a look at your favourite search engine to see if there is an appropriate link, and follow the on-screen instructions on how to set the system up – it should take no more than 30 minutes or an hour to do this, and other than changing any defaults from then on, the job is done for once and for all. A few examples are *My Yahoo!* (**http://www.yahoo.com/**), *My Excite* (**http://www.excite.com/**) and *Personalized Ask Jeeves* (**http://www.aj.com/**).

One service in particular that is worth mentioning is that of *CRAYON*, or 'Create your own newspaper', at **http://www.crayon.net/**. This is one of the better services, since it has a very wide range of subject categories, such as Politics, Biz, Tech, Science, Health, and allows you to gather content from a very wide variety of news sources. You are not limited to just those resources that a particular search engine has an existing relationship with. Instead, you can choose from American newspapers, television sources, many UK-based news information services and indeed news services from as far afield as India and Japan.

# News sites

Another useful resource is that of newspapers and other news sources.

Virtually all of the major newspapers now have web versions, and some of these are updated during the course of the day, rather than just once in the morning. These can of course be useful, but are only as useful as the printed version, naturally enough! You will generally find that they are not an exact duplicate of the printed version, and emphasis is usually given to technological news items, for obvious reasons. However, they can prove valuable, particularly since it's not possible to obtain copies of all of the newspapers available throughout the world.

There are too many news sources to list – that would take a book, not a chapter – but an excellent source for information of this nature is to be found at *Media UK* (**http://www.mediauk.com/directory/search.html**), which provides links to newspapers, journals, magazines, television and radio sources on the Internet.

There are, of course, some specialist news services, such as *Reuters* at **http://www.reuters.com/** and the *Press Association* at **http://www.pa.press.net/**. Both of these are excellent sources of current information, and the Press Association in particular provides news stories and links to a variety of different news sources, allowing you to read about a story from a variety of different viewpoints.

# Keeping up to date with particular pages

Once you've found a page that interests you, and provides valuable information, you'll obviously bookmark it, or add it to your favourites list. However, that means that you have to go back and revisit the page regularly, just to see if it's changed or any new information has been added to it – which can be a waste of time, particularly if nothing has changed! There are various ways that you can ensure that you keep this time down to the bare minimum, quickly and easily. One particularly useful utility is the *Netmind* service (formerly called URL-minder) at http://www.netmind.com/. This allows you to create a list of sites that interest you, list them with *Netmind* and then forget all about them. It's simple to use, effective and entirely free. *Netmind* visits each page you've listed every 24 hours, and if it finds any of those pages have changed it will send you an e-mail to this effect. You can then go back and visit the page, safe in the knowledge that something new has been added.

Recent versions of both major browsers also offer the opportunity of keeping up to date with specific pages by utilizing options in the bookmark (for Netscape) or favorites (in Microsoft Explorer). The methods of keeping up to date differ for each of them (and change according to the version of the browser that you're using), so the best advice is to use their help facility and choose bookmark or favorites as appropriate.

# Using bots to keep up to date

Bots – also known as robots, or most commonly intelligent agents – are becoming increasingly more common. Intelligent agents come in many varieties – free, commercial, based on a web page or downloaded onto your hard disk – and cover many different aspects – shopping, careers, searching, updating and so on. Perhaps the best single resource for information on these utilities is **http://botspot.com/**, which describes and lists many hundreds of them.

If you need to know what's happening in the world, news bots can be of assistance. A good bot will search through a wide variety of publications and also offer proper search facilities, not just pasting information into a template (which is a valid criticism of personalized newspapers). Some examples of news bots are: *Excite NewsTracker* at **http://nt.excite.com/**, which searches through over 300 news sites, utilizing a thesaurus, but doesn't allow the use of Boolean operators;

*NewsHub* at **http://www.newshub.com/** allows much greater precision in terms of search functionality, and updates every 15 minutes; *NewsTrawler* at **http://www.newstrawler.com/** has a very strong international bias, with a particular emphasis on business and financial information, but the interface is quite poor and quickly becomes irritating. *StockVue 2000* from Alpha Microsystems is a bot that is specifically designed for business and economics researchers. While much of the system is dedicated to keeping you up to date with various stocks and shares prices, an integrated module called BusinessVue also ensures that you can quickly obtain news, announcements, and other information within business sectors. The product is free of charge and can be downloaded at **http://www.stockvue2000.com/**.

Of course, there are times when you want to know what other people and organizations are saying about your own company, and *CyberAlert* at **http://www.cyberalert.com/** is an Internet monitoring and alerting service for market intelligence. It tracks information on your company (or indeed any other company that interests you) by checking websites, mailing lists, newsgroups and other resources relating to the company, products, services, brands or trademarks. It is, however, a commercial product and is quite expensive: at the time of writing the price is $395 per month per search string.

One of the author's personal favourites is *The Informant* at **http://informant.dartmouth.edu/**, which is another free service. *The Informant* allows you to create favourite searches using your preferred search engines (from, admittedly a limited list of three) to list useful web pages. At periodic intervals (3, 7, 14, 30 or 60 days) it runs the search on your behalf and sends you an e-mail once it finds new web pages that match your search criteria, or when it identifies web pages that you're interested in which have been updated since the last time *The Informant* visited the site. You then simply need to return to *The Informant* website and check out the new information that has been located. Another favourite is *Karnak* at **http://www.karnak.com/**, which works on a similar principle, although, since it is a commercial product, you are only able to store one free profile at a time. However, limited though that is, the utility is fast, effective and accurate.

Intelligent agents can save you a tremendous amount of time when it comes to keeping yourself up to date with what is happening in your particular subject area. While agent technology is still in its infancy, it is quite clear that this is an area which can only expand in the future.

# Mailing lists and newsgroups

Another useful and easy way to keep up to date in your areas of interest is to let other people do this for you. Careful use of mailing lists can ensure that you find out the majority of things that are happening, from conferences to exhibitions, to new websites, to news and events.

Mailing lists (or as they are often also called, discussion lists or even listservs) are simply glorified cc: lists. However, a mailing list has a lot of advantages over a cc: list that you would use with your own e-mail package. To begin with, you don't need to keep a note of everyone that belongs to the list – that job is taken care of by a central computer called a mailserver. The mailserver provides the administrative function of sending e-mails (or posts) out to all the people who subscribe to a particular list – almost like a postbox in fact. Rather than having to know all the hundreds, if not thousands, of e-mail addresses for people who subscribe to a particular list, it is only necessary to know one address: that of the mailserver. Once you post to it, your message will automatically be sent on to everyone who subscribes to that particular mailing list.

Mailing lists have many advantages: they allow you to 'talk' to other people who are interested in the same subject area, who may be able to offer assistance, thoughts or opinions if you have a particular problem; they are fast – queries posted to a mailing list usually have answers within a couple of hours; people use them for posting information about new resources that you might otherwise not come across. They are certainly one of the best ways of keeping up to date with what is happening in a particular subject area.

A good place to start a search for useful mailing lists is *Mailbase* at **http://www.mailbase.ac.uk/**, which has thousands of different lists covering a wide variety of subjects; a quick search for 'business' found a total of 45 different mailing lists, including discussions on ethics, research, teaching, trends, small business issues and so on. *Mailbase* lists tend towards the academic (indeed, all the lists are biased towards the UK academic field), so if you don't find the list that you want there, you might want to try *Liszt* at **http://www.liszt.com/**, which has over 90,000 lists available.

Newsgroups are perhaps less useful, but may still be worth researching. They work on a similar basis to mailing lists, but instead of having a mailserver they utilize a news server, and every ISP (Internet service provider) has one. When you subscribe to a newsgroup, usually by using newsreading software such as *Forte Free Agent* at **http://www.forteinc.com/**, the software connects to the newserver and downloads either all the messages in the group, or just the headers (or titles) of the posts for you to decide which ones you wish to read.

When you post to a newsgroup, the posting is sent to your ISP's news server, which then copies it onto other news servers around the world (commonly referred to as 'propagation'), thus allowing other people to download your posting. There are several hundred different business-related newsgroups available, but your ISP may not carry them all; if you are in any doubt you should contact their technical support department for assistance.

Another way of identifying or using newsgroups is to use a web-based service such as *Deja*, formerly known as *DejaNews*, at **http://www.deja.com/**. This is a (free) service that archives newsgroup postings and allows you either to search specific newsgroups or to do a general search for a subject that interests you. This can be a very effective way of finding out what people are discussing at the moment, and can be a valuable way of 'taking the pulse' of people. Consequently, if you wanted to find out what people's attitudes are towards, for example, a British Telecommunications announcement, reading newsgroup postings would provide you with exactly that sort of information. However, you do need to be aware that both newsgroups and mailing lists are generally people's opinions on subjects, rather than factual information that you can rely on without checking further. Nonetheless, they can be a very useful first resource.

# Virtual libraries

Virtual Libraries (VLs) are essential libraries on the Internet – hence their name. A virtual library is the creation of a number of experts, researchers and information professionals who work in a particular subject area and who dedicate a portion of their time to scouring the Internet looking for useful resources in their subject areas. These resources are examined, and if it is felt that they are of a high enough quality, will be included in an index or directory for people to use.

VLs are therefore a valuable resource, since they provide up-to-date, authoritative data on a very wide variety of different subject areas. Not only are they kept up to date (most VLs will check that their links are correct and working every 24 hours), but they can be a useful place to visit just to ensure that you are aware of all the websites that might prove useful in your work, and to check out what new material has been added to the VL. Consequently they are a superb starting point, not only for researching a particular topic, but for keeping up to date.

There are a great many VLs available on the web, and the following, while not being a complete list, is certainly a good starting point.

➠ The *WWW Virtual Library* at **http://www.vlib.org/** provides access to a great many VLs, covering serious subject areas and a few light-hearted ones as well.

➠ *ADAM* at **http://www.adam.ac.uk/** covers art and design issues.

➠ *ALEX* at **http://sunsite.berkeley.edu/~emorgan/alex/** is a catalogue of electronic texts.

➠ *Biz/ed* at **http://www.bized.ac.uk/** is probably the single most appropriate VL for readers of this handbook, and is an excellent starting point for anything to do with business and economics.

➠ *BUBL* at **http://www.bubl.ac.uk/** is a superb resource that covers over 11,000 subjects, and *BUBL Link 5:15* attempts to provide a minimum of five and a maximum of 15 top-quality resources.

➠ *Countryside Recreation Network* at **http://www.ilrt.bris.ac.uk/crn/** covers, unsurprisingly, data on countryside recreations.

➠ *EELS* at **http://www.ub2.lu.se/eel/eelhome.html** is a VL covering electronic engineering.

➠ *HISTORY* at **http://ihr.sas.ac.uk/** is self-explanatory.

➠ *HUMBUL* at **http://users.ox.ac.uk/~humbul** covers the humanities.

➠ *OMNI* at **http://www.omni.ac.uk/** is the abbreviation for Organizing Medical Networked Information, and is a good first step for anything medical.

➠ *SOSIG* at **http://www.sosig.ac.uk/** covers the social sciences.

➠ Finally, *AlphaSearch* at **http://www.calvin.edu/library/as/** is a small and effective search engine that finds VLs for you, and is an excellent place to start searching.

# Conclusion

There are many ways of keeping up to date with business and economics information on the Internet, or indeed, virtually any aspect of any subject! This is an area that is expanding at a rapid rate at the moment as more and more companies are recognizing that providing various mechanisms for keeping people up to date can be a profitable area to work in. Individuals are also realizing that it's becoming easier to keep up to date without having to put in hours and hours of work to do so.

# URLs mentioned in this chapter

*ADAM* http://www.adam.ac.uk/

*ALEX* http://sunsite.berkeley.edu/~emorgan/alex

*AlphaSearch* http://www.calvin.edu/library/as/

*AltaVista* http://www.altavista.com/

*Ask Jeeves* http://www.aj.com/

*Biz/ed* http://www.bized.ac.uk/

*BotSpot* http://botspot.com/

*BUBL* http://www.bubl.ac.uk/

*Countryside Recreation Network* http://www.ilrt.bris.ac.uk/crn/

*CRAYON* http://www.crayon.net/

*CyberAlert* http://www.cyberalert.com/

*DejaNews* http://www.deja.com/

*EELS* http://www.ub2.lu.se/eel/eelhome.html

*Excite* http://www.excite.com/

*Forte Free Agent* http://www.forteinc.com/

*HISTORY* http://ihr.sas.ac.uk/

*HotBot* http://www.hotbot.com/

*HUMBUL* http://users.ox.ac.uk/~humbul

*The Informant* http://informant.dartmouth.edu/

*Karnak* http://www.karnak.com/

*Liszt* http://www.liszt.com/

*Lycos* http://www.lycos.com/

*Mailbase* http://www.mailbase.ac.uk/

*Media UK* http://www.mediauk.com/directory/search.html

*Netmind* http://www.netmind.com/

*NewsHub* http://www.newshub.com/

*NewsTracker* http://nt.excite.com/

*NewsTrawler* http://www.newstrawler.com/

*Northern Light* http://www.northernlight.com/

*OMNI* http://www.omni.ac.uk/

*Press Association* http://www.pa.press.net/

*Reuters* http://www.reuters.com/

*SOSIG* http://www.sosig.ac.uk/

*StockVue 2000* http://www.stockvue2000.com/

*WWW Virtual Library* http://www.vlib.org/

*Yahoo!* http://www.yahoo.com/

# 4

# Company sources on the web

*John Coll*

## Introduction

For many business librarians, the impact of the web has had far-reaching effects on the provision of information. Nowhere has this been more evident than in the growth of websites that now allow one to carry out research on companies. This chapter attempts to summarize the key resources that currently exist on the web for such data. The emphasis here will be on UK sources, although some major international sites will also be covered. Given the larger number of websites that now provide such information, it is inevitable that this chapter can only provide an introduction. It will, however, attempt to feature what are, in the author's view, sites of particular importance, although it is recognized that any such selection must, by its very nature, be subjective.

## Types of company information

For the purposes of this chapter, company information is defined under three categories. These are as follows:

1   **Directories**
    This includes telephone directories, web directories (which are

primarily links to company websites) and other sites that provide company information in a basic directory style.

2   **Financial information**
This includes sites providing everything from profiles on companies through to detailed financial data and in some cases, the electronic equivalent of accounts or annual reports. It will also cover sites providing equity data, stockbroker research etc.

3   **News**
This will focus predominantly on news sites providing company information but news sites of a more general business nature will also be included.

In all cases the emphasis will be on sites providing some or all information free of charge. Sites providing information on a chargeable basis will be covered only if they are of key importance and provide either some free information or operate on a pay-and-display basis. A brief description and URL is given for each site although the transitory nature of the web may have made some of these out of date by the time this appears in print.

# Directories

Directories, along with news sites, have been one of the major areas of growth in terms of business information on the web. There are a variety of reasons for this. Directories on a national level are often based on existing electronic databases, which makes their migration to a web-based medium relatively easy. In addition, web directories can often be quicker or more flexible to search than the traditional printed medium through the use of a variety of search parameters such as keyword, post/zip code, fuzzy logic etc. Finally, the interactive nature of sites (ie the fact that you can submit your own details) allows for the creation of a multitude of regional or industry-specific sites at a minimal cost in comparison to their printed equivalent.

In this sense, directories on the web offer a valuable (and indeed at the local level often unique) resource tool for the researcher looking for company information. For the business librarian, they also present something of a double-edged sword in terms of their usefulness. On the one hand, they provide a new and often invaluable source for researching companies. On the other hand, the web by its very nature allows individuals to by-pass the librarian as the traditional gatekeeper of such information and obtain the information directly from their PC.

However, while in one sense such resources do create the beginnings of a 'virtual library' for the business researcher, they also present problems of their own. A 1998 study of UK companies by Coll and Murray (1999), suggested that many directories on the web performed poorly in terms of retrieval, compared with printed sources. In addition, unlike commercially produced printed sources, which by their very nature must demonstrate quality to survive, web sources are often difficult to establish in terms of purpose, ownership or depth of coverage. Thus the strength of the web becomes its own weakness. In other words, an ability to liberate organizations from the constraints of commercial publishing by transferring data directly onto the web has also allowed the creation of much 'information' that is in turn highly questionable in terms of value.

In spite of these concerns, it is evident that the exponential growth of the web will create a real demand for such resources. What is less clear is the future of many commercial publishers who have seen a decline in subscriptions to their printed sources but have not yet discovered a viable income stream from the electronic equivalent.

# Directories by region

## United Kingdom

There are a surprisingly large number of UK sites on the web providing directory-type information. This chapter concentrates on national sources. Useful sources for regional and industry-specific information are covered in the section entitled 'Other useful sources' at the end of this chapter. National sources tend to provide basic address and telephone details. The directories range in size from approximately 100,000 to over 2 million companies. However, there is often a trade-off between size and content, and directories with smaller coverage can sometimes provide considerably more detail than the 'telephone directory' sites. Some of the key resources include:

### *ASKALEX* http://www.askalex.co.uk/

A very fast site which allows you to search by names, products or services. A location can also be added to narrow the search. Coverage is in the region of 1.8 million companies, although the top names appearing in a search may be as a result of advertising. Searchable by name, product service or location.

### *BT PhoneNet* http://www:bt.com/phonenetuk

The BT site was a late addition to the web but was particularly welcomed given that it is perceived as the official site for telephone numbers. Unlike some other sites *BT PhoneNet* also includes personal numbers, although ex-directory numbers are excluded. A useful addition to telephone directories on the web, this resource is weakened by occasional difficulties in accessing the site as well as an inability to carry out national searches.

## Electronic Yellow Pages **http://www.eyp.co.uk/**

As the name suggests, this is an electronic version of the yellow pages directories and covers 1.6 million companies, searchable by business type, name or location. When searching by business type, EYP will prompt you with a list of categories if there is no exact match.

## Kellys **http://www.kellys.co.uk/**

An electronic version of the well-known Kellys business directory, this provides data on 135,000 companies, as well as (in some cases) a link to their website. You will need to register to use this site.

## Scoot **http://www.scoot.co.uk/**

A large site with 2 million companies covered. From the main search screen you can select business type and location. There is also a separate company search screen. When searching by business type you must specify location.

## The Biz **http://www.thebiz.co.uk/**

Provides web links and/or contact details for an unspecified number of UK companies. Searchable by keyword or browsable by sector.

## ThomWeb **http://infospace.com/uk.thomw/**

An electronic version of the Thomson directories, covering 2.2 million companies. Searchable by name, business type or location. As with *EYP* and *Scoot*, you are prompted with alternative categories if there is no match on the business type. As with *Scoot* you must also specify location when searching by industry.

## Trade UK http://www.tradeuk.com/index.html

Hosted by Dialog.com, this site is the official British Trade International source for exporters. The international buyers category allows you to select British exporters by product and destination.

## UK Business Finder http://www.infospace.com/uk/

Provided by TDL InfoSpace, this site provides similar search capabilities to *ThomWeb* (which seems to be powered by the same software). Use the 'business finder' option to search by name or category. Once again, you need to specify a location when searching by industry.

## UK Index http://www.ukindex.co.uk/

A site providing links to company websites. Searchable by name or category.

## UK Web Directory http://www.ukdirectory.com/

Another site that provides links to specific websites. Searchable by name, and browsable by category or via an A–Z listing.

## Webscot http://www.webscot.co.uk/

A listing of Scottish companies (approximately 1000). Links to company websites as well as containing basic contact information and description. Searchable by keyword, region and/or category.

## *Yell: UK Yellow Web* **http://www.yell.co.uk/ukweb/**

The web directory version of yellow pages. Searchable by name or browse by specific category.

# International

There are a range of other directories for the web covering specific countries or regions. For the purpose of this article we have divided them into broad geographical regions and concentrated on the main sources. For specific country and industry sources we would recommend the section on other useful sources published at the end of this chapter.

# Global sites

## *Global Source* **http://www.globalsources.com/**

Allows you to search on just under 80,000 products and over 75,000 suppliers in 120 companies.

## *Global Yellow Pages* **http://www.yellowpages.webguest.com/**

A somewhat selective listing of white, yellow and business directories on the web.

## *Infobel* **http://www.infobel.com/**

Provides links to white and/or yellow pages for 188 countries.

## *Kompass* **http://www.kompass.com/**

Provides details on over 1.5 million companies. You can search by name or product. Registration required for detailed data or for using the advance search.

### *Telephone Directories on the Web* **http://www.teldir.com/**

Links to white, yellow and selective business directories for 150 countries worldwide.

# Africa

### *Mbendi* **http://www.mbendi.co.za/**

Unspecified number of African sites with a particular emphasis on oil and gas companies. Browsable by name or industry.

# Asia

### *Asian Sources* **http://www.asiansources.com/**

Gives details on just under 76,000 suppliers and 80,000 products. A small number of non-Asian companies are also provided.

### *Orient Business Express* **http://www.accessasia.com/obehome.htm**

Provides basic information on almost a million Asian companies. Searchable by name or product. You need to pay to view records on this site.

# Europe

### *Europages* **http://www.europages.com/**

One of the few pan-European sources available, covering over 500,000

European companies. However, only very brief information is given and UK coverage seems poor, with some major companies not appearing in a recent test. Searchable by name or product/service.

### WLW Online http://www.wlw.de/

The web version of *Wer liefert was?* The original homepage loads in German, but you can change the display to English. Searchable by product or company for 244,230 European companies as well as 51,500 export-orientated companies in France, Ireland and the UK. You can view the name and postcode for free, but there is a charge for a full display.

## Middle East

### Arab World Online Commercial Directory
### http://www.awo.net/awocomdirSearch.asp

Provides basic details on an unspecified number of Arabian companies. Searchable by keyword.

### AME Middle East Business Information
### http://www.awonet/awocomdirSearch.asp

Provides brief contact details and some links for 200,000 companies from 14 Middle East countries. Searchable by name, product and country.

## Latin America

### IPL Trade Directory http://www.latinmarkets.com/

Database of over 40,000 companies in Mexico and Central America.

Searchable by keyword or by a variety of criteria using the advanced search. It should be noted that this site does not seem to have been updated since December 1998.

# USA

As with the UK, there is a wide range of national directories for the USA to search on the web. The open market in terms of telecommunications has spawned a range of US telephone directories, which have been supplemented by additional sources produced by commercial bodies. The following are just a few of the many sources than can be consulted:

## American Export Register http://www.aernet.com/

Basic information on 45,000 USA exporters. You need to register (free) to view data on individual companies.

## BigBook http://www.bigbook.com/

Produced by Superpages and covering 11 million US companies. Searchable by name, category and address (searching by specific state is a requirement).

## BigYellow http://www.bigyellow.com/

Data on 11 million US companies. Searchable by company name, type and address (searching by specific state is a requirement).

*InfoUSA* **http://www.infousa.com/**

> Similar in size to *BigYellow*. Searchable by category, name and address (state required).

*Switchboard* **http://www.switchboard.com/**

> Perhaps the most useful of the national directories in that you can search the whole of the country rather than being forced to search by state. Coverage is in the region of 10 million companies.

# Financial information

> Once upon a time it was possible to divide sites into those that gave accounts and those that provided equity data such as historical share prices. However, the growth in 'portals' – ie sites that seek to be all-embracing – has meant that financial information is a more all-encompassing name for such a category.
>
> The vast majority of sites in this category have been classified as 'international', since although they almost all have a heavy US bias in terms of coverage, they are not strictly limited to US data.

# United Kingdom

*Companies House* **http://www.companies-house.gov.uk/**

> The official site for records filed by all registered UK companies. This link provides only basic information on the company such as registered office address and date of accounts filed. For detailed accounts you need to use *Companies House Direct*, for which a subscription is required.

*HemScott* **http://www.hemscott.co.uk/**

> A useful source that includes a range of information on UK companies including key financials, major shareholders and contact details. For selected companies there are also interim and annual reports. Additional data is available for those using the Hemscott.net as their ISP.

# International

*CAROL* **http://www.carol.co.uk/**

> Although sometimes thought of as being only for UK information this site also provides links to accounts of Asian, European and US annual reports. Although the non-UK sections suggest you can only search by industry, you can in fact browse by company as well.

*ft.com* **http://www.ft.com/**

> An extensive site which provides, among other information, key background and financial data for up to three years on over 20,000 listed companies. There is also a facility for ordering electronically from over 3,500 company annual reports, which are then dispatched by post.

*Hoovers* **http://www.hoovers.com/**

> Provides snapshots on 15,000 companies world-wide (although the majority are within the USA) as well as links to an additional 37,000 companies. There is also additional information on another 8,000 for subscribers.

## *Justquotes* **http://www.justquotes.com/**

Another portal that provides everything from company profiles, financial statements, charts and equity prices through to broker reports and recommendations. Covers mainly US quoted companies, but some major overseas companies are included.

## *Report Gallery* **http://www.reportgallery.com/**

Holds reports on over 2,000 listed companies, albeit with an American bias.

## *StockMaster* **http://www.stockmaster.com/**

Similar (if less detailed) data to *JustQuotes*.

## *Wright Investor's Service* **http://profiles.wisi.com/**

An excellent source for profiles on quoted companies. Coverage is heavily USA-biased, although some larger companies in other countries are covered, including a reasonable number within the UK. Searchable by name, country or industry.

# USA

## *10K Wizard* **http://tenkwizard.com/**

A commercial source providing not only free access to 10K data on *EDGAR* (see below) but also enhanced display and alerting services, usually for a charge.

## *EDGAR* **http://www.sec.gov/edgarhp.htm**

The official database for all companies filing with the Securities and
Exchange Commission, which are principally quoted companies.
Unlike their UK counterparts, US companies are not obliged to file
their annual report to shareholders, but instead provide a more detailed
document known as a 10K. All documents available on *EDGAR* can be
printed or downloaded free of charge.

# News information

One of the most evident impacts of the web in terms of business
information has been the proliferation of news sources available to the
researcher. From the early innovations of push technology utilized by
such resources as *Pointcast* and *NewsEdge*, there are now a multitude of
news resources available, with many of the search engines and browsers
themselves offering you your own personalized 'news'. The problem
with many of the free sources that currently exist today is that they
either prevent or restrict specific company searches, or their coverage of
sources is somewhat restricted. This applies both to the newspapers
available on the web and to 'aggregators' – ie organizations that draw
in news feeds from external organizations.

# Aggregated news sources

The sources listed under this category provide information from a
range of sources, often with the facility for receiving alerts via e-mail.
We have deliberately excluded both search engines and the directories
(eg *Yahoo!*) who all provide their own personalized newspages based on
a very small number of sources. While aggregated news sources are
useful as a quick and simple research tool, one must be always aware
that the coverage of resources can often be selective, both in terms of

title and even in terms of content within such sources. This applies particularly to those providing free information. Their other main weakness is that few provide a facility for carrying out historical searches on companies (the *ft.com* site being the exception to the rule).

## *ft.com* **http://www.ft.com/**

Still one of the important sites on the web for news information. As well as current news you can search for earlier stories using **http://www.globalarchive.ft.com/**. Note that some of these articles require payment before the full content can be displayed.

## *Individual* **http://www.individual.com/**

Formerly *NewsPage*, this source allows you to search by company or keyword (the latter normally proving more reliable). Data is drawn from 40 different news sources.

## *NewsNow* **http://www.newsnow.co.uk/**

Provides newsfeeds from a variety of sources (principally UK) and updated every five minutes. Companies can be searched only by keywords.

## *Research Index* **http://www.researchindex.co.uk/**

No indication from the site how this compares with the printed equivalent, but a useful tool for searching a range of predominantly UK sources. There is a specific company search, but only headlines are displayed for each article. There is also a useful link to UK newspapers sites.

*Storyfinder* **http://www.pa.press.net/storyfinder/**

> A useful source for UK news. Produced by the Press Association, this site draws newsfeeds from over ten different sites. Searchable by keyword or company, but only for 'up-to-date stories'.

# Newspapers

> Most national and major regional newspapers have a presence on the web. However, their usefulness for company news is usually for current stories since few have an ability to search by company on a historical basis. The sources listed below give a useful starting point for searching by specific title, region or industry.

*E&P Media Links* **http://emedia1.mediainfo.com/emedia/**

> Allows one to search by magazines or newspapers within specific regions.

*Journalism UK* **http://www.journalismuk.co.uk/**

> Aimed at UK journalists this site provides a selective set of links to journals and newspapers.

*Newo News Resource* **http://newo.com/news/**

> Provides an alphabetical listing of countries through which you can browse for specific newspapers.

# Other useful sources

> There is a wide range of additional sources on the web that can be used

for identifying sources useful for company research. Metasites are one example of such tools. These are sites that do not normally provide data themselves but instead provide specific links to other sites. In other words, their strength (or weakness) is the value of the links they provide.

# United Kingdom

Many of the sources listed under 'international' can be equally good for searching for UK companies. The sources listed below are those that have been identified as specific to the UK.

### *Bird-Online UK* http://www.bird-online.co.uk/

Provides a searchable list of UK sites by category and keyword, including company research and company directors. There is also a database of consultants and training providers as well as companies seeking business partners/agents.

### *UK Company Researcher* http://www.ukcompanyresearcher.com/

Listing of sites providing UK company information by various categories, including region, industry, news and accounts.

# International

The sites listed below represent just a handful that exist on the web as a guide to company information. Limitations of space mean that search engines have had to be excluded from this category, although they of course complement the list of resources given in this chapter (see Chapter 2). Many are now starting to include directories within their sites allowing the searcher to drill down by subject. *Open Directory,* one of the main sources for such directories, is listed among these sources. It can be accessed either directly or via an increasing number of search engines. *Yahoo!*, its better-known competitor, is also listed, and while *Yahoo!* is still seen as the most desirable directory for obtaining a listing, the author's view is that it does not always seem as current or as relevant as *Open Directory* (though others may have their own view!).

## *BUBL LINK* http://link.bubl.ac.uk/business

A catalogue of Internet resources designed for, and funded by, the academic community in the UK. There are a number of sub-categories in business that are worth exploring.

## *Business Information on the Internet* http://www.rba.co.uk/sources/index.htm

Karen Blakeman's site *Business Information on the Internet* is a useful starting place for company information on the web. Among others it includes a stock market and company financials section, as well as company and telephone directories, and news sources.

## *Business Information Sources on the Internet* http://www.dis.strath.ac.uk/business/index.htm

Sheila Webber's site *Business Information Sources on the Internet* is one of the oldest and best-known sites for finding company information. It includes sections on company directories (arranged by specific regions), company profiles and financial information, and news sites. A very useful and extensive source, its only weakness being the infrequency of updates.

## *CeoExpress* **http://ceoexpress.com/**

A useful site that presents a list of searchable categories from its homepage. Some useful links to some major sources of company information, but its US bias is evident from the poorer international links. Still worth a visit, though.

## *Corporate Information* **http://www.corporateinformation.com/**

Another extremely useful source for company information, this provides an international set of links to company information as well as a more extensive set of links to sites covering the USA, Canada, Germany, France, Italy, Japan and the UK. The main criticism of this site is that the links seem to be listed in random order.

## *CRUISE (Cranfield University Internet Site Explorer)* **http://www.cranfield.ac.uk/cils/library/subjects/busmenu.htm**

One example of a simple but useful set of links for company information from a university site, this includes categories on annual reports and company information.

## *DIALOG* **http://openaccess.dialog.com/business**

Still one of the major business hosts, now offering direct access to selective content via the web. Payment is required for displaying and printing such data.

## *DowJones* **http://dowjones.wsj.com/**

Provides a selected amount of information free, with further data made available via the *Dow Jones Interactive* site. A nice touch is the way it combines website data with newsfeeds when searching by company. Strong US coverage but weaker for other countries.

### *International Business Resources on the WWW* http://www.ciber.msu.edu/busres.htm

Another useful university site, but this time from the US perspective and compiled by the Michigan State University. Perhaps not as easy to navigate as the *CRUISE* site (see above), but more extensive in its set of links.

### *Open Directory* http://www.dmoz.org/

A recent directory for the web, and one that seems to be a direct competitor for *Yahoo!* Not yet as comprehensive as the latter, although currency seems somewhat better. Now being used as the source of directory data in many search engines, including *AOL*, *Netscape* and *AltaVista*.

### *Yahoo!* http://www.yahoo.com/

Still the best-known directory on the web, and particularly useful for its company websites links as well as its directories. However, some of its links seem a bit long in the tooth now, and it still betrays a US bias in its overall content. There are also regional sites (including **http://www.yahoo.co.uk/**), but bear in mind that many of these links are still from the USA.

# The future of company information on the web

Although the above listing provides only an introductory guide to sites providing company information, it does demonstrate the increasing importance of the web for assisting users in such research. Indeed, the growth of websites providing company information presents both a challenge and a threat to traditional commercial publishers. Some such as *Kompass* and *Hoovers* have attempted to tackle this by continuing to offer both the print and electronic versions of directories, but at the same time only allowing access to selective free data on their website. Others such as *Hemmington Scott* have decided that an Internet service provider approach is more advantageous, and users wishing to obtain enhanced data from the latter must sign up to the *Hemscott* ISP site.

In the case of electronic hosts such as *DIALOG* and *Lexis-Nexis* the situation is more complex. Web publishing has meant that many companies are no longer reliant on their data being hosted on large mainframe computers, and already a number of these publishers have ended their ties with such hosts. This is particularly the case where the growth of free access to information has meant that many publishers now wish to compete by offering a combination of free and fee-based information directly from their own sites. Although all hosts own (or co-own) a certain amount of content on their site, they are dependent on many other publishers as well. The decline in access to such information suggests that the large hosts will be forced to concentrate on a smaller number of data sources, with the emphasis on detailed, high-quality data not available through traditional web or printed sources. Given the number of hosts that still exist, and the duplication of resources that is already evident, commercial logic suggests that in an overcrowded market we may see a number of mergers over the next few years, as well as a number of withdrawals from this sector. Evidence of this problem is already being manifested in the increasing cross-alliance and mergers taking place, the recent Reuters–Dow Jones merger being just one example.

Perhaps what is less clear is the future of free information on the web. While basic information is always likely to remain free, there must be some question mark over more detailed company data. Peter Scott

(1999), Chief Executive of Hemmington Scott, in an interview reported in *Information World Review* in September 1999, highlighted the labour-intensive nature of information-gathering, which clearly reflects a resource implication for many websites. At present, however, the strategy for many companies remains one of providing free information to draw visitors to their site, thus establishing some perceived 'market share'. The problem has been compounded by the intense competition in this sector, which has led some publishers to rely on other activities to subsidize such free information, while new start-up companies have relied on generous venture-capital backing. All the indications are that such provision of free and detailed company data remains unsustainable in the long term unless continually funded through external sources. Since advertising does not seem to offer an adequate income stream for such activities, the likely scenario is for a potential shake-out of this market over the next two to three years, with only a small number of larger companies surviving to provide detailed free company information on the web. This does not in itself suggest the demise of such free information on the web. However, what it does possibly offer to the surviving companies is a much greater control over what is provided free and what can be charged for. Ironically, this would be the converse of the current situation, where the consumer is almost spoilt for choice in terms of free sources.

# Conclusion

This chapter has attempted to provide a brief but pertinent summary of the sources that exist on the web for company information. For librarians and others involved in information provision, the sites listed give an indication of the wealth of information that exists on this topic. However, as ever, this medium represents just one piece in the jigsaw of information retrieval. The future challenge for information professionals will be as much about recognizing the weaknesses of specific web resources as it is about knowing of their actual existence.

# References

Coll, J and Murray, L (1999) UK company directories on the web, *Business Information Review*, **16** (1), 51–6.

Scott, P (1999) Breaking the chains, *Information World Review*, (September), 25.

# URLs mentioned in this chapter

*AME Middle East Business Information*
http://www.awonet/awocomdirSearch.asp
*American Export Register* http://www.aernet.com/
*Arab World Online Commercial Directory*
http://www.awo.net/awocomdirSearch.asp
*Asian Sources* http://www.asiansources.com/
*ASKALEX* http://www.askalex.co.uk/
*BigBook* http://www.bigbook.com/
*BigYellow* http://www.bigyellow.com/
*Bird-Online UK* http://www.bird-online.co.uk/
*BT PhoneNet* http://www.bt.com/phonenetuk
*BUBL LINK* http://link.bubl.ac.uk/business
*Business Information on the Internet*
http://www.rba.co.uk/sources/index.htm
*Business Information Sources on the Internet*
http://www.dis.strath.ac.uk/business/index.htm
*CAROL* http://www.carol.co.uk/
*CeoExpress* http://ceoexpress.com/
*Companies House* http://www.companies-house.gov.uk/

*Corporate Information* http://www.corporateinformation.com/

*CRUISE (Cranfield University Internet Site Explorer)*
    http://www.cranfield.ac.uk/cils/library/subjects/busmenu.htm

*DIALOG* http://openaccess.dialog.com/business

*DowJones* http://dowjones.wsj.com/

*E&P Media Links* http://emedia1.mediainfo.com/emedia/

*EDGAR* http://www.sec.gov/edgarhp.htm

*Electronic Yellow Pages* http://www.eyp.co.uk/

*Europages* http://www.europages.com/

*ft.com* http://www.ft.com/

*ft.com* http://www.globalarchive.ft.com/

*Global Source* http://www.globalsources.com/

*Global Yellow Pages* http://www.yellowpages.webguest.com

*HemScott* http://www.hemscott.co.uk/

*Hoovers* http://www.hoovers.com/

*Individual* http://www.individual.com/

*Infobel* http://www.infobel.com/

*InfoUSA* http://www.infousa.com/

*International Business Resources on the WWW*
    http://www.ciber.msu.edu/busres.htm

*IPL Trade Directory* http://www.latinmarkets.com/

*Journalism UK* http://www.journalismuk.co.uk/

*Justquotes* http://www.justquotes.com/

*Kellys* http://www.kellys.co.uk/

*Kompass* http://www.kompass.com/

*Mbendi* http://www.mbendi.co.za/

*Newo News Resource* http://newo.com/news/

*NewsNow* http://www.newsnow.co.uk/

*Open Directory* http://www.dmoz.org/

*Orient Business Express* http://www.accessasia.com/obehome.htm

*Report Gallery* http://www.reportgallery.com/

*Research Index* http://www.researchindex.co.uk/

*Scoot* http://www.scoot.co.uk/
*StockMaster* http://www.stockmaster.com/
*Storyfinder* http://www.pa.press.net/storyfinder/
*Switchboard* http://www.switchboard.com/
*Telephone Directories on the Web* http://www.teldir.com/
*10K Wizard* http://tenkwizard.com/
*The Biz* http://www.thebiz.co.uk/
*ThomWeb* http://infospace.com/uk.thomw/
*Trade UK* http://www.tradeuk.com/index.html
*UK Business Finder* http://www.infospace.com/uk/
*UK Company Researcher* http://www.ukcompanyresearcher.com/
*UK Index* http://www.ukindex.co.uk/
*UK Web Directory* http://www.ukdirectory.com/
*Webscot* http://www.webscot.co.uk/
*WLW Online* http://www.wlw.de/
*Wright Investor's Service* http://profiles.wisi.com/
*Yahoo!* http://www.yahoo.co.uk/
*Yahoo!* http://www.yahoo.com/
*Yell: UK Yellow Pages* http://www.yell.co.uk/ukweb/

# 5

# UK Government websites for business

*Keith Rose*

## Introduction

The Internet has become an increasingly important source of UK Government information over the past few years. In *Modernizing government* (Cm4310), available at **http://www.citu.gov.uk/moderngov/ whitepaper/4310.htm**, the UK Government made a commitment to being able to carry out a quarter of its transactions electronically by 2002, rising to 100% by 2008. More recent statements by ministers show a drive to exceed these targets. One of the main ways in which this is being realized is through a greater use of Internet technology by central government departments to deliver services and information. This is underpinned by the development of departmental intranets and of the interdepartmental Government Secure Intranet to improve the information flow within and between departments. More details, including the text of the white paper, are on the Cabinet Office's *Central Information Technology Unit* site at **http://www.citu.gov.uk/**. CITU is the central information point on developments in this field, and produces six-monthly bulletins on how far these targets are being reached.

This chapter looks at those websites produced by the UK Government which are likely to be useful to a business information researcher. The number of these has greatly increased in recent years, although the coverage still lacks the depth provided by the US, Canadian and Australian governments. Almost all these resources are world wide web resources – there are no 'official' newsgroups, and only a few closed e-mail lists.

We shall first consider general ways of locating UK central government information on the world wide web, and then look at how various websites go some way towards fulfilling business needs for information on government regulations and business support, as well as for general intelligence on government activities.

# Starting points

There are several main ways of finding UK Government websites of particular importance to business, from where other sites may be uncovered. All the general search engines give reasonable coverage of these sites. Most central government websites and many local government sites are in the **.gov.uk/** domain. A brief search for this domain on some popular search engines gave 381,725 hits on *Northern Light*, 163,346 on *AltaVista*, 390,000 on *Google* and 114,600 on *Hotbot*. The differences may be due to the different ways in which a variety of engines define a hit. Using a search on one of these can be one strategy for drawing together references to a policy that may span the interests of several departmental sites.

However, it is unsafe just to search for URLs in this domain, as a number of important sites are outside it. Exceptions include some of the more commercial sites, such as the new *British Trade International* site, which are in the **.com/** domain. Ministry of Defence sites are mostly **mod.uk/**, while further away from the centre, many police forces are **police.uk/** and NHS trusts **nhs.uk/**. Some non-governmental bodies are in other domains: the *Bank of England* is at http://www.bankofengland.co.uk/, while the *Arts Council* is at http://www.artscouncil.org.uk/. *The Defence Evaluation and Research Agency* is the only occupant of the .gb/ domain, at http://www.dra.hmg.gb/. So if you don't find the site you want from searching on +url:gov.uk, you may need to broaden your search, including any UK Government-specific terminology to distinguish them from any sites belonging to other governments.

You may encounter another difficulty if you try to guess the URL. Some parts of departments are increasingly putting up sites with URLs unrelated to that of the home department. Thus http://www.isi.gov.uk/ and http://www.consumer.gov.uk/ are run by the *Information Society Initiative* and *Consumer Affairs* sections of the *Department of Trade and Industry*. This is where gateway sites come into their own.

*Yahoo!* has an alphabetical list of departments at http://www.yahoo.co.uk/Regional/Countries/UnitedKingdom/Government/Departments/. However, this is only a selective list of 148 sites, and at the time of writing excludes, for example, the National Assembly for Wales site.

# UK Government sites

The main central point for finding UK Government websites is at http://www.open.gov.uk/, maintained by the Central Computer and Telecommunications Agency (CCTA), which was updated in September 1999. It forms one recognized central portal to the other sites. It has links not only to central government departments, but also to local authority sites and non-departmental sites belonging to departmental bodies.

If you know which department covers the subjects you need to know, use the alphabetical departmental index to find its home page. If you know the general subject, try using the topic index, which divides the departmental sites up by subject: this is much improved from the previous 'functional index'. If it is not clear who deals with what you're after, try using the search engine, which covers all the pages of the departmental sites. It gives more relevant results if you give it more terms. CCTA also hosts a number of departmental sites, such as DETR, so you may notice some common features on these sites.

# Main departments

While all Government departments produce information that is relevant to some businesses at some time, the following are the main departments that hold the most business-related material. All have details of their ministers and recent press releases, which include the text of official ministerial speeches. They frequently have the full text of green papers and other consultation documents sponsored by the department. Other features vary: you may be able to locate the official dealing with your area in one department, but not another; you may be able to order printed publications online from one department, but not from another. Exactly what is available changes as sites are updated: have a look and see.

## Department of Trade and Industry http://www.dti.gov.uk/

The DTI home page was redesigned in October 1999. Look here for information on the various business support schemes which the department sponsors, information on management best practice, exporting, import licences, energy industries, industrial relations and industrial tribunals, consumer affairs and the Office of Science and Technology. There is a separate page for ministerial speeches. The 'press releases' link takes you to the top of the *Central Office of Information* site at **http://www.nds.coi.gov.uk/**, from where you have to go to the DTI section. The site has a search engine and an A–Z index of pages.

## Treasury http://www.hm-treasury.gov.uk/

The home page of the Treasury, with economic news, details of the last two budgets, general government economic policy, and key economic indicators. This site can get very busy on budget day.

## Foreign and Commonwealth Office http://www.fco.gov.uk/

The FCO site takes more advantage of Internet technology than many other UK Government sites. It has details of UK foreign policy, assistance to exporters and advice to travellers to various countries, as well as visa requirements for visitors to Britain and contacts for British embassies and overseas missions. You can personalize the site if you want notification of news or to have updates to travel advice notes for your chosen countries e-mailed to you.

## Customs and Excise http://www.hmce.gov.uk/bus/home/

This has separate sections for public and business users. Under business, there are separate sections on VAT, customs duty and excise duty, each with relevant publications, forms and consultation papers. There is also a separate section on Intrastat trade statistics.

## Inland Revenue http://www.inlandrevenue.gov.uk/

This site contains the text of various tax leaflets and forms, and details of tax rates. There is a section giving advice on self-assessment.

## *Department of Environment, Transport and the Regions* http://www.detr.gov.uk/

The DETR site, with government policy and regulations in these areas. The home page is set out in a ring, with the department's wide range of activities arranged clockwise from 'About DETR' to 'wildlife and countryside', via 'construction', 'local transport', 'regeneration', 'shipping' and others. As with DTI, 'press releases' is a link to the top of the CoI site.

## *Office of National Statistics* http://www.ons.gov.uk/

This has links to ONS press releases, which contain the most recent announcements of official data such as the retail price index, and to *Statbase* at **http://www.statbase.gov.uk/** – a free (and growing) collection of 686 datasets of official statistics on a wide range of fields. There are also links to the ONS publications catalogue, with more detailed statistics, and the National Statistics Information and Library Service.

# Regulations

Much central government activity is concerned with producing and administering regulations that apply to many everyday activities. You can increasingly find the full text of government regulations on the relevant websites. Often the more basic pamphlets are available online in full text, while a contact is given for more detailed guidance, but this can be inconsistent between departments. The format also varies, some being in HTML, some in text, and some as .PDF files. *Direct Access Government* at **http://tap.ccta.gov.uk/dagii/welcome.nsf** is a central site linking to the various regulatory pages of different departments, searchable by department or subject.

# Taxation

For details on indirect and direct taxes, check the *Inland Revenue* site at **http://www.inlandrevenue.gov.uk/**, where all their booklets are published. There are also details of local tax offices. In the *Modernizing government* white paper (1999) there is a commitment to developing tax returns submitted over the Internet by 2000, and there are details of progress towards this on the site.

For VAT rates, check the *Customs and Excise* site at **http://www.hmce.gov.uk/bus/vat/index.htm**.

For tax and National Insurance rates, check *Inland Revenue* at **http://www.inlandrevenue.gov.uk/rates/index.htm**.

# Companies

The *Companies House* site at **http://www.companieshouse.gov.uk/** has the full text of the various 'notes for guidance' – frequently asked questions on company formation, what the legal requirements on companies are, and a weekly updated list of disqualified directors. Electronic access to company annual returns is available to password holders at *Companies House Direct* at **http://www.direct.companieshouse.gov.uk/**, and images of documents can be ordered for delivery by fax or e-mail. Electronic submission of company annual returns to companies house is planned from 2002.

# Import/export

Details of customs and excise duties are at the *Customs and Excise site* at **http://www.hmce.gov.uk/bus/excise/index.htm**.

Details of the various restricted goods for which export licences are required, and online application forms, are at the *Export Control Organization* site **http://www.dti.gov.uk/export.control/home.htm**, as well as a searchable list of the requirements by country, and sanctions currently in force.

# Environment, and health and safety

Several of the DETR subsites are concerned with different environmental regulations. *Environmental protection policy* is at **http://www.environment.detr.gov.uk/**, while wildlife and countryside issues are at **http://www.wildlife-countryside.detr.gov.uk/**.

The *Environment Agency* at **http://www.environment-agency.gov.uk/** has news, environmental risk assessment regulations, and details of their enforcement policy.

The *Health and Safety Executive* at **http://www.open.gov.uk/hse/hsehome.htm** has guidance for both employers and employees on best practice in health and safety, and reports on recent investigations: when accessed in early 2000, they were highlighting their interim report on the Paddington rail crash.

The *Air Accident Investigation Branch* at **http://open.gov.uk/aaib/aaibhome.htm** has the text of formal reports into all air accidents in the UK.

# Consumer protection

There is a central site at **http://www.consumer.gov.uk/** sponsored by the consumer affairs section of the DTI, which acts as a gateway to other consumer protection sites, such as *Office of Fair Trading* at **http://www.oft.gov.uk/**, and the various regulators of privatized utilities, such as *Oftel* at **http://www.oftel.gov.uk/**, which deals with the telecommunications industry.

# European regulations

An increasing number of regulations now apply throughout the European Union, and you will need to go to EU sites to find out the full details.

The overall EU home page is at **http://europa.eu.int/**, but with such a large site it is better to go straight to the search engine at **http://europa.eu.int/geninfo/query_en.htm**, or if you are fairly clear as to the directorate general responsible, go to the European Commission home page at **http://europa.eu.int/comm/index_en.htm**. Each DG has its own subsite with a fairly uniform structure, with contacts, activities and key documents, but the search engine may find pages on DG subsites not clearly linked to the DG home page.

If you have an account, you can search the *Celex* database at **http://europa.eu.int/celex/celex_en.html** for directives and regulations since 1953, available in both HTML and word formats. Alternatively, you can use *Eurlex* at **http://europa.eu.int/eur-lex/en/index.html** to check for recent directives and other regulations, or the priced document delivery service, *Eudor*, at **http://www.eudor.com/** to search for documents since 1995 (including the sometimes elusive .com documents), which can then be paid for as requested and delivered in TIFF fax format. Receiving them as faxes can be quicker and easier than receiving and manipulating them as files.

# Support

Central government departments also work to support and develop British businesses. Much of this centres on the DTI and, for exporting, FCO, but other departments are involved with their particular sectors – for instance, MAFF for agriculture and food, or DCMS for the arts.

# Export

Central government help for exporters, big and small, is detailed at the *British Trade International* site at **http://www.britrade.com/**, with a searchable database of overseas trade fairs, individual 'market menus' for various export markets, information on the export market for various industrial sectors, and online ordering of the 'hints to exporters' series of booklets (some of these are also online in full text). It also includes the homepage of the *Export Market Information Centre* at **http://www.britrade.com/emic/**. EMIC maintains a detailed list of overseas sites, with business information by country and by industry.

Firms looking for specific export sales leads should go to *Trade UK* at **http://www.tradeuk.com/trade.html**, which holds databases of export leads gathered by overseas posts and firms wishing to export. Firms can enter their details online to join the database and get further information. .

The *Foreign and Commonwealth Office* site at **http://www.fco.gov.uk/** has details of UK embassies abroad, FCO advice to travellers, and other services.

The *Export Credit Guarantee Department* site at **http://www.ecgd.gov.uk/** has details of their support services for the financing of exports, mainly exports of capital goods.

# General

The various DTI sponsor divisions for different sectors of the economy are at **http://www.dti.gov.uk/support/index.htm**, grouped by sector in a long scrollable list. Each has links at least to the contacts within the department and major support programmes; some have more information available.

# Regional assistance

The *Invest in Britain Bureau* at **http://www.dti.gov.uk/ibb/** gives guidance and support to overseas firms seeking to set up plants in Britain, with news and frequently asked questions. Similarly, in Wales the *Welsh Development Agency* at **http://www.wda.co.uk/**, in Scotland *Scottish Enterprise* at **http://www.scotent.co.uk/**, and in Northern Ireland the *Northern Ireland Industrial Development Board* at **http://www.idbni.co.uk/index.htm**, give support to relocating firms.

The nine Government Offices in England coordinate the activities of DTI, DETR and DfEE in their areas, and are the first port of call for firms in those areas seeking assistance. The Government Office pages vary in format and in the structure of their URLs, but contain similar information. For instance, *GO West Midlands* at **http://www.go-wm.gov.uk/** has sections on the region, frequently asked questions, useful West Midlands addresses and their annual report. *GO – London* at **http://www.open.gov.uk/glondon/browser.htm** has sections on the various components of the Government Office: housing, planning, transport, regional regeneration and London government. These are closely allied to the autonomous *Business Link* network, whose national home page is at **http://www.businesslink.co.uk/**. The Scottish and Welsh equivalents are *Local Enterprise Companies* at **http://www.scotent.co.uk/** and *Business Connect* at **http://www.bc.wales.com/**. The *enterprise zone* site at **http://www.enterprisezone.org.uk/**, sponsored by DTI and Business Links and run by *DIALOG*, lists sites of interest to smaller businesses, including relevant government agencies.

# Innovation

## *DTI Innovation Unit* **http://www.innovation.gov.uk/home.htm**

This Unit seeks to stimulate innovation in UK industry. Its site includes case studies, information on partnerships, and the text of the annual innovation lecture.

The *Information Society Initiative* is at **http://www.isi.gov.uk/**. ISI tries to bring firms together who are active in creating the IS. Its site gives access to online guides, details of local support centres, and best practice guidelines in all aspects of creating the information society.

## Patent Office **http://www.patent.gov.uk/**

The Patent Office site has straightforward explanations of the different branches of intellectual property rights (if that's possible!) and has copies of their leaflets for inventors, application forms, and details of services, including paid-for searches.

## UK Foresight Programme **http://www.foresight.gov.uk/**

The Office of Science and Technology are the sponsors of this site, which aims to develop a vision of the future, and bring together the knowledge held by people in business, science and government. The site has details of the work of the various 'foresight panels' in different topics.

# Information

This section looks at those sites that give more general information about central government activities and Government policy in various matters.

# On Parliament

These are not strictly 'central government' sites, but much central government activity centres around and serves Parliament, so you may need to include Parliamentary information to get a complete picture:

## Activities in the House

The *UK Parliamentary WWW service* at **http://www.parliament.uk/** has links to sites giving information on Houses of Commons and Lords, and committees of both.

The *Hansard Commons* site at **http://www.parliament.the-stationery-office.co.uk/pa/cm/cmhansrd.htm** has the complete text of Commons *Hansard* from the beginning of the 1996–7 session, updated daily while Parliament is in session, The previous day's proceedings are available after 12.30pm. It is arranged in reverse date order, with the current week's debates first. The site's search engine can search for either keywords in a debate or speakers, and can be limited by date range and record type. The entry for each day is divided into a series of roughly equal pages which include the column numbers from the printed version. The *House of Lords proceedings* site at **http://www.parliament.the-stationery-office.co.uk/pa/ld/ldhansrd.htm** functions similarly.

You can find forthcoming business in both Houses for the next week, plus membership of Commons committees and state of the parties in the *House of Commons Weekly Information Bulletin – Commons* at **http://www.parliament.the-stationery-office.co.uk/pa/cm/cmwib.htm**. It also includes the progress of bills in the current session, with dates of first and second readings – useful if you need to trace the debate on a particular stage of a bill.

More general UK political news is at the *BBC UK politics pages* at **http://news.bbc.co.uk/hi/english/uk_politics/default.htm**, which include links to live transmissions when Parliament is in session, and background information on MPs. You could also have a look at the *UK*

*Politics* site at **http://www.ukpol.co.uk/**, sponsored by Politico's bookshop and much-expanded over earlier versions. This includes similar information from a slightly different angle, mixing parliamentary, departmental and party-political information. Those after a more academic analysis of policy could try the *ESRC Whitehall project pages* at **http://www.ncl.ac.uk/~npol/whitehall/index.html**. These contain papers considering the 'changing nature of central government in Britain', with briefings on aspects of policy and the history of policy development.

## Scottish Parliament and Welsh Assembly

*Scottish Parliament* at **http://www.scottish.parliament.uk/** includes details of MSPs, parliamentary business, and links to other Scottish Parliamentary sites.

*National Assembly for Wales* at **http://www.assembly.wales.gov.uk/** includes a 'who's who', press releases, details of activities and links to other Welsh Assembly sites.

# On departmental activities

Most departments have 'what's' new' pages, which you can bookmark to check on recent developments (see above), or find by using the **open.gov** index. Press releases, with announcements about new initiatives and the departmental contacts, are usually on departmental sites, and also on the *Central Office of Information* site at **http://www.nds.coi.gov.uk/**. This holds press releases for most departments since 1 January 1998, listed in alphabetical order by department and then chronologically. It is possible to view today's and yesterday's press releases, and run a search on either all or selected departments. Departments vary in whether they maintain a separate list of press releases or link through to the CoI site. If there is a separate list, you may need to check it as well as the CoI list, for completeness. If you have only vague details about a press release, or if you want to go back before 1998, you may still find it easier and quicker to use a paid service that includes the CoI's Hermes database.

If you are after EU announcements or the text of commissioners' speeches, check these on *Rapid*, the commission's 'spokesmans' service' at **http://europa.eu.int/rapid/start/welcome.htm**, logging in as 'guest'.

# Publications

With the liberalization of government publishing over recent years, you may have to look in several places to track down a particular publication. Central government publications may be issued by individual departments, or through the Stationery Office. Where a publication is produced jointly with a non-departmental body, it may not appear on the department's site at all, but only on that of the other body. Parliamentary publications, such as Acts and Command Papers, are always published by the Stationery Office.

Parliamentary and crown copyright is administered by the non-privatized remnant of HMSO. *HMSO* at **http://www.hmso.gov.uk/** has advice on the interpretation of Crown and Parliamentary copyright, 'Dear Librarian' letters and links to official publications. It also holds the text of all Acts of Parliament since the 1996 session, Statutory Instruments and local Acts since 1997.

The privatized *Stationery Office* site at **http://www.tso-online.co.uk/** has details of new and forthcoming titles, listed in the online version of 'The Daily List', and a search engine for all their publications in stock, with a shopping basket for online ordering. It also acts as a gateway to websites for subscribers linked to publications such as the *Civil Service Yearbook* at **http://www.csy.co.uk/** and *London Gazette* at http://www.london-gazette.co.uk/.

To locate publications if they don't immediately appear on TSO, try *British Official Publications Current Awareness Service* at http://www.soton.ac.uk/~bopcas/, a searchable database of HMSO and departmental official publications published since 1995, based in the Ford Library collection at the University of Southampton. The full database is open to subscribers only, but the preceding six months' publications can be browsed for free. Another password-access-only commercial service is *UK Official Publications* at http://www.ukop.co.uk/ – Chadwyck Healey's searchable database of documents published by the Stationery Office and departments since 1980.

Recent departmental publications are usually available online from the department's site. For older material, and those still only in hard copy, departmental publications lists are usually available from each department's site, with details of ordering. These will usually include only those which are currently in print. Publications out of print should have been deposited with the British Library, so you could also try BL OPAC97 or BLAISE-LINE to trace a loan copy.

You may find that different sites offer different amounts of information on a particular publication. For example, the text of a white paper may be available both from the Stationery Office and from the sponsoring department's sites, but supporting documents and summaries may only be available from the departmental site.

The white paper on Crown copyright, Cm 4300 (*The future management of Crown Copyright*, 1999), included a commitment for each department to produce 'information asset registers' detailing their publicly available but unpublished information, such as databases, with details of access. The work to produce these has only just started, however: details on progress to date and, eventually, links to the IARs are on the *Inforoute* site at http://www.inforoute.hmso.gov.uk/. Keep an eye on it for developments.

# Conclusion

In this chapter, I've only been able to skim the surface of the increasing volume of information that UK central government is now making available on the web. More is being added all the time, so keep an eye on **open.gov.uk** and your favourite departmental sites.

# References

*The future management of Crown Copyright*, Cm 4300, The Stationery Office, (March 1999).

*Modernising government*, Cm 4310, The Stationery Office, (March 1999).

# URLs mentioned in this chapter

*Air Accident Investigation Branch*
    **http://open.gov.uk/aaib/aaibhome.htm**
*Arts Council* **http://www.artscouncil.org.uk/**
*Bank of England* **http://www.bankofengland.co.uk/**
*BBC UK politics pages*
    **http://news.bbc.co.uk/hi/english/uk_politics/default.htm**
*British Official Publications Current Awareness Service*
    **http://www.soton.ac.uk/~bopcas/**
*British Trade International* **http://www.britrade.com/**
*Business Connect* **http://www.bc.wales.com/**
*Business Link national network* **http://www.businesslink.co.uk/**
*Celex* **http://europa.eu.int/celex/celex_en.html**
*Central Information Technology Unit* **http://www.citu.gov.uk/**
*Central Office of Information* **http://www.nds.coi.gov.uk/**
*Civil Service Yearbook* **http://www.csy.co.uk/**
*Companies House* **http://www.companieshouse.gov.uk/**

*Companies House Direct* http://www.direct.companieshouse.gov.uk/
*Consumer Affairs* http://www.consumer.gov.uk/
*Customs and Excise* http://www.hmce.gov.uk/bus/excise/index.htm
*Customs and Excise business pages* http://www.hmce.gov.uk/bus/home/
*Customs and Excise VAT rates*
     http://www.hmce.gov.uk/bus/vat/index.htm
*Defence Evaluation and Research Agency* http://www.dra.hmg.gb/
*Department of Environment, Transport and the Regions*
     http://www.detr.gov.uk/
*Department of Trade and Industry* http://www.dti.gov.uk/
*DTI Innovation Unit* http://www.innovation.gov.uk/home.htm
*DTI sponsor divisions* http://www.dti.gov.uk/support/index.htm
*Direct Access Government* http://tap.ccta.gov.uk/dagii/welcome.nsf
*Enterprise Zone* http://www.enterprisezone.org.uk/
*Environment Agency* http://www.environment-agency.gov.uk/
*Environmental protection policy* http://www.environment.detr.gov.uk/
*ESRC Whitehall project pages*
     http://www.ncl.ac.uk/~npol/whitehall/index.html
*European Union* http://europa.eu.int/
*European Union search engine*
     http://europa.eu.int/geninfo/query_en.htm
*Eudor* http://www.eudor.com/
*Eurlex* http://europa.eu.int/eur-lex/en/index.html
*European Commission* http://europa.eu.int/comm/index_en.htm
*Export Control Organization*
     http://www.dti.gov.uk/export.control/home.htm
*Export Credit Guarantee Department* http://www.ecgd.gov.uk/
*Export Market Information Centre* http://www.britrade.com/emic/
*Foreign and Commonwealth Office* http://www.fco.gov.uk/
*Government Office London*
     http://www.open.gov.uk/glondon/browser.htm
*Government Office West Midlands* http://www.go-wm.gov.uk/

*Hansard Commons* http://www.parliament.the-stationery-office.co.uk/pa/cm/cmhansrd.htm

*HMSO* http://www.hmso.gov.uk/

*House of Commons Weekly Information Bulletin – Commons* http://www.parliament.the-stationery-office.co.uk/pa/cm/cmwib.htm

*House of Lords proceedings* http://www.parliament.the-stationery-office.co.uk/pa/ld/ldhansrd.htm

*Health and Safety Executive* http://www.open.gov.uk/hse/hsehome.htm

*Information Society Initiative* http://www.isi.gov.uk/

*Inforoute* http://www.inforoute.hmso.gov.uk/

*Inland Revenue* http://www.inlandrevenue.gov.uk/

*Inland Revenue rates* http://www.inlandrevenue.gov.uk/rates/index.htm

*Invest In Britain Bureau* http://www.dti.gov.uk/ibb/

*Local Enterprise Companies* http://www.scotent.co.uk/

*London Gazette* http://www.london-gazette.co.uk/

*Modernizing Government* (Cm 4310) http://www.citu.gov.uk/moderngov/whitepaper/4310.htm

*National Assembly for Wales* http://www.assembly.wales.gov.uk/

*Northern Ireland Industrial Development Board* http://www.idbni.co.uk/index.htm

*Office of Fair Trading* http://www.oft.gov.uk/

*Office of National Statistics* http://www.ons.gov.uk/

*Oftel* http://www.oftel.gov.uk/

*open.gov.uk site* http://www.open.gov.uk/

*Patent Office* http://www.patent.gov.uk/

*Rapid* http://europa.eu.int/rapid/start/welcome.htm

*Scottish Enterprise* http://www.scotent.co.uk/

*Scottish Parliament* http://www.scottish.parliament.uk/

*Statbase* http://www.statbase.gov.uk/

*Stationery Office* http://www.tso-online.co.uk/

*Trade UK* http://www.tradeuk.com/trade.html

*Treasury* http://www.hm-treasury.gov.uk/

*UK Foresight Programme* http://www.foresight.gov.uk/

*UK Official Publications* http://www.ukop.co.uk/

*UK Parliamentary WWW service* http://www.parliament.uk/

*UK Politics* http://www.ukpol.co.uk/

*Welsh Development Agency* http://www.wda.co.uk/

*Wildlife and countryside issues at DETR* http://www.wildlife-countryside.detr.gov.uk/

*Yahoo! alphabetical list of departments*
http://www.yahoo.co.uk/Regional/Countries/UnitedKingdom/Government/Departments/

# 6

# The Internet for small and medium-sized enterprises

*Diana Grimwood-Jones*

## Introduction

The focus of this chapter will be web-based information designed to help smaller businesses to run more efficiently, or to ease some of the practical problems that can arise every day, or for when companies are seeking to expand but are unsure where to start, and are looking for advice and guidance. In other words, the emphasis is on *information for business* rather than *business information* in the classic sense. It is geared to information workers within small business environments, or people who work in an advisory capacity with small businesses, though there is no reason why interested managers of small businesses cannot use it on a self-help basis.

Firstly, we need a definition of what a small business is. The SME (small and medium-sized enterprise) has no universally recognized definition, and is in no way a homogeneous group – turnover can vary hugely between companies of the same physical size in different industry or service sectors. As a rough rule of thumb, we can regard a *small business* as employing fewer than 200 staff. This does not rule out national or even transnational organizations (potentially global if they are web-based) but small businesses will tend to have in common some of the following broad characteristics:

- a lack of, or restricted, in-house IT management and support
- staff who fulfil a number of functions, even at senior level
- a focus on hard bottom-line issues – operational rather than strategic
- restricted information resources (where they exist at all)
- lack of time, money (or awareness) for developing information-seeking skills.

Although many SMEs, particularly at the upper-size level, or the more technologically advanced, will have very adequate information provision, this chapter will assume at best a patchiness in Internet access, use and experience.

# Defining the information need

Information products designed specifically for the smaller business have been slow to develop in all formats, though in the early 1990s the possibilities offered by CD-ROM publishing and its growing use by end-users heralded an expansion in the range of electronic information available. By the mid-1990s, Allan Foster (1995) was noting the growing business information industry presence on the Internet, and the large providers were all developing innovative products to make use of it. Foster's article includes a selective guide to key business Internet sites. Of the 20 sites listed, only four are British, and only one of these, Millennium's Internet *Digipages* at **http://www.milfac.co.uk/milfac**, is specifically aimed at SMEs. Most of the major categories of business information – business news, journals, accounting and taxation, marketing, finance, economics and banking, management, entrepreneurship and international business – are dominated by US products for use in large corporate environments.

At the same time, there was some interest in seeing where SMEs fitted into this picture. A fairly typical survey carried out by Mercury Business Intelligence (reported in *What's New in Business Information*, March, 1995) found that the majority of small businesses were disinclined to venture onto the information superhighway – well over half the companies surveyed at that time did not even possess a modem. Their most common business requirements were for company reports and credit checks, directory enquiries, legal information, marketing and market research. This information was accessed by phone, fax and post, and via a range of personal contacts, which included library services; however, these traditional information sources were considered to be slow, out of date and of relatively low quality.

In an attempt to bridge the gap between SMEs on the one hand, and information providers and intermediaries on the other, there have been various initiatives involving SMEs on both a European and a national level that have had a significant electronic information component – for example, the Department of Trade and Industry's Information Society Initiative, and its constituent programme Electronic Networking for Small Businesses, were based on the idea that, if UK companies were to stay competitive in rapidly changing global markets, they must be able to make effective use of the new international electronic networks that would offer easy and rapid access to essential information.

The creation of a network of Business Links in England between 1993 and 1996 (and their equivalents in Scotland, Northern Ireland and Wales) has served to sharpen the focus on the kinds of information needed by, and supplied to, the SME community. The *Business Link Services Guide* (1997) defines its purpose as to 'help businesses and their advisers obtain the information they need to make better decisions, develop new products and services, penetrate new markets, write persuasive business plans, and comply with the law'. From the first, the *Guide* insisted that the Business Link information service must provide access to a comprehensive range of online databases that would include:

- a news and current affairs database
- a company and product sourcing database
- Companies House and credit information
- a grants and finance database
- databases relevant to target sector businesses.

It should also provide access to regional and national services relevant to customer needs. This list still serves as a useful guide to SME preoccupations. A detailed examination of Business Links and information delivery to SMEs carried out by Patricia Stoat and Angela Abell (1995) makes clear that they lack the time skills and know-how to make use of external information. Indeed, 'information' in itself has little value to SMEs, who need a mix of data, interpretation and analysis of data and advice for action. In other words, small firms do not separate out 'information' from the solution to the problem. Their most valued sources of information are internal, or within business networks, and regional and local information is of critical importance.

The picture of SME information need and use is brought up to date in a recent report on a British Library-funded research project into the use of the Internet as an information resource for small and medium-sized enterprises, carried out by the University of Strathclyde and the Library Information Technology Centre (Allcock and others, 1999). The aims of the project (which included companies in Scotland and England) included identifying the types of Internet resource that are found useful by SMEs. Usage of the website set up for the project indicated that the most heavily used section of the site was *Companies*, followed by management and legal issues, advice agencies, news, specific industries and general reference. This accords broadly with earlier surveys and with the kinds of questions handled by Business Link information staff.

Although there remain a number of barriers to SME use of the Internet as end-users – including technical barriers, search difficulties, and lack of time and training – lack of the relevant information itself is no longer a problem: the volume of information specifically targeted at smaller businesses has increased hugely over the past couple of years. The next section will look at some of the currently available 'one stop' sites (gateways with links to a multiplicity of other sites of interest, or 'shopping malls' of information and advice on a range of business topics) that have been developed to serve the burgeoning small business and SOHO (small office, home office) community.

# Gateways and other 'one stop' sites
## Department of Trade and Industry

A good starting point for UK businesses of all sizes is the *DTI* website at **http://www.dti.gov.uk/**. As a department, the DTI aims to promote enterprise, innovation and increased productivity by encouraging the capacity of business (including SMEs) to grow, to invest, to develop skills, to adopt best practice and to exploit opportunities abroad, recognizing the development of the knowledge economy and taking account of regional differences. One area of the site offers help specifically for small businesses and new business, but other areas, including help in improving business performance, business expansion, innovation and technology, and help with regulations, might be equally applicable. There are links in the text to appropriate initiatives, schemes and services – for example, the Small Firms Loan Guarantee Scheme, which guarantees loans for small businesses with viable business proposals which have tried and failed to obtain a conventional loan through lack of security, and the Smart scheme, which provides grants to individuals and SMEs to review, research or develop technologies leading to commercial products. Help is also available for a wide range of specific industries, including agriculture, biotechnology, construction, design, electronics, engineering, tourism, arts and sports. The site also offers links via drop down menus to 39 key DTI sites (including ACAS, Companies House, the Patent Office and Trade UK) and nine key Government sites.

# The Enterprise Zone

Closely linked to the DTI site is *The Enterprise Zone*, launched by the Department in late 1997 and now managed by DIALOG at **http://www.enterprise-zone.org.uk/**. The home page offers buttons on a range of functions – finance, sales and marketing, legal, business start-up, HR, training and export – which in turn link to quantities of relevant sites. A click on finance will lead you not only to business angels and sources of venture capital, but also sites of interest as a taxpayer or employer; sales and marketing covers finding new customers (with links including *Yellow Pages*, *Trade UK National Exporters Database*, ICC and Business Parks), advertising and promotion, business opportunities (including a link to tenders on the web) and Industry Information, which has a host of industry specific links. An online chat button gives access to topical online interviews with the great and the good in public life. There is a 'link shopper' service for office product procurement, which describes itself as 'UK's largest office store for business buyers'. If, after all this, you find your favourite site isn't listed, there is a 'submit a site' facility for proposed additions.

## Business links

Both the main DTI site and *The Enterprise Zone* (among others) provide a link to the main *Business Links* website. This can be accessed directly at **http://www.businesslink.co.uk/**. Details are given of the various services available from a Business Link, and the site incorporates a directory of Business Links, which can be accessed via a map if you're unsure of the Business Link nearest to you. Other features include a facility for viewing the *Business Link Bulletin* and (if you are an organization involved in business support activities) subscribing to *Business Focus*. This site, and other UK-Government sponsored sites for small business, are changing with the launch of the new Small Business Service (part of whose remit has been to take forward the Business Link network) from 1 April 2000. The DTI *Consultation Paper* on the Small Business Service, setting out its key tasks, is available at **http://www.dti.gov.uk/sbs/consult/Summary.htm**

## Local Chambers of Commerce

The local Chamber of Commerce is a vital resource for many smaller businesses. The national network of approved Chambers of Commerce can be accessed via the *British Chambers of Commerce* site at **http://www.britishchambers.org.uk/**. The site also provides a news service and bulletin board, and links to services such as the *Exportzone*, which provides guidance on all aspects of breaking into new markets overseas or developing an existing export operation.

## The Strathclyde/LITC project

The Strathclyde/LITC project involved a substantial website development, hosted on the Strathclyde server. Responsibility for maintaining the links within this has now passed to the Glasgow

Chamber of Commerce, and the home page of what is now branded the *Chamber Business Information Centre* can be found at **http://www.glasgowchamber.co.uk/dis/index.html**. Any snobbish non-Scots should forget their prejudices and check this site out. It is a really excellent collection of links to online resources, covering general reference (currency rates, dictionaries, maps, patents and standards, share prices, travel and time and weather), business news (Scotland, UK and international) advice and opportunities, managing your business (covering accountancy, employment, marketing, etc), companies, industries (a small but growing selection, to which the events industry is newly added), other business lists, internet guides and advice, people and leisure. An added-value feature of this resource is the often quite detailed site description, so that you can browse the potential usefulness of particular sites without having to visit them first.

# Biz.net

A new entrant into the 'one stop' small business marketplace is Virgin's *biz.net* service at **http://www.virginbiz.net/**. Described as 'the complete online small business service. The support you'll get here makes up your virtual management team – use it to plan and grow your enterprise', it is certainly impressive. Its style is typically simple and forthright: the section 'manage your business' covers money, law, people, sales and 'biznews', with the emphasis on practical business issues. For example, click on '*people*' and you are offered subsections headed 'be a boss', 'keep it legal', 'in the firing line', 'people forum' and 'IT forum' – a good mix of information and the opportunity to ask for assistance or exchange information with others. The 'biznews' section is worth noting as it focuses on news of specific interest to small business, and is updated from around the country every five minutes. Sector-specific headlines are also available, and via 'departmental news' you can get up to date on current issues in marketing, credit, accounting, the Internet and business. Other facilities offered include the possibility of creating your own website, discussions and events, and information geared to where you are in the business lifecycle: start-up, growing or moving.

## BusinessZONE

Sift Group plc is a company specializing in the development and management of virtual business communities at **http://www.sift.co.uk/**. One of these is *BusinessZONE*, 'the everyday resource for SOHO and SME professionals on the Internet', at **http://www.businesszone.co.uk/**. The home page provides some dozen headlines linked to top business news stories, and a free company information search facility. A menu lists news, links, databases, directory, presszone, search, help and any answers. a click on '*links*' will take you to a page offering general business links (to investment, business resources, business software, travel, publications, weather, shopping, sports) and an Internet monitor: 'headline' content from business-related websites from the previous month. Following the link from business resources leads you to two pages of selected free and priced resources, including those specifically related to small business (eg Business Bureau UK, Microsoft's Small Business page, The Small Business Advisor, Yahoo! Small Business Information) and those of more general interest (eg Britannica Online, Company Annual Reports Online, the CBI, US Business Data). The databases link from the home page focuses on providing a search facility to Companies House data through the zone's direct interface with ICC. Details are also provided of relevant databases available through DataStarWEB. The *Directory* link takes you to *Accounting Web*, described below.

# Other communities

Another Sift community with more general interest is *EUbusiness* at **http://www.eubusiness.com/** for those interested in the impact of European Union legislation on their businesses. Sift is now developing the site to build in advanced database technology.

A relatively new service from British Telecom is *Connect to business* at **http://www.btconnect.com/**. Some of the channels (which include travel, legal and regulatory, IT and communications) are a bit thin, but money and finance is worth checking out.

Most of the sites listed above are focused on the UK. Clearly, some of the biggest and most sophisticated are USA-biased, and can be good sources of general and international business information. One of these is *The Small Business Directory* at **http://www.bizmove.com/directory/directorymain.htm**, which covers such topics as knowledge base (starting, managing, buying and selling a business), making money with your site, software (including software libraries and popular downloads), newsgroups and business opportunities. The site offers search facilities for software to buy, and for books (through *Amazon*).

# Search engines and other information resources

All the major search engines offer access to small business information, but have a heavy American bias. Probably the best regarded is *Yahoo!*, whose main small business site at **http://smallbusiness.yahoo.com/** manages to cram a lot of information into a small space and clear layout. Topics offered include technology, human resources, international business and trade; other parts of the site offer package tracking, services, conventions and shows, a business guide (how to build a business online), featured business tools, featured articles and small business solutions. There is also a free-text search facility. If you are only interested in the UK, go to the *Yahoo! UK Small Business Guide* at **http://www.yahoo.co.uk/Business_and_Economy/ Small_Business_Information/** and select UK only or Ireland only. Subdirectories include business opportunities, business plans, credit merchants, employment law and organizations.

It you're looking for instant access to a large volume of non-specific information, a good general site is *refdesk.com* at **http://www.refdesk.com/**. Although some features are geared to a North American audience (eg e-mail your congressman; Canada postal look-up) there are links to a huge amount of more generally useful information, including dictionaries, exchange rates, international phone directories, stocks in real time, and – should you need it – the complete works of Shakespeare. There are also links to the main news services, and to the principal US and international newspapers and business press.

If you are a librarian, you can take advantage of a subscription service called *KnowUK* at **http://www.knowuk.co.uk/** that provides key information about the people, institutions and organizations of the United Kingdom. Produced by Chadwyck-Healey, it is not a compilation of links to information elsewhere, but draws together in a single source some of the most heavily used reference materials in a library, eg *Who's who, The municipal year book* and *The statesman's yearbook*. The main topic areas are biographical information, community and voluntary information, education, government, health, information sources, media, national events, religion, travel and leisure. Libraries can request a free two-week trial of the product.

Last but not least in terms of useful collections of information, it is well worth checking the index to the free online newsletter *Free Pint* (main site at **http://www.freepint.co.uk/**; index with activated hyperlinks at **http://www.freepint.co.uk/issues/99index.htm**). This fortnightly publication has now built up a good range of subject-specific articles, many of which are relevant to business – for example, business and accounting, competitive intelligence, electronic commerce, engineering, financial information, intranets, market research, patents, and trade associations. Each article contains an evaluated selection of key sites.

# European sites

The European Union (EU) has, over the years, made various attempts to encourage greater participation by SMEs in European-funded programmes. The official EU website is *Europa* at **http://europa.eu.int/**. The home page provides access to news (including press releases from EU institutions, a calendar of events and official euro rates), institutions such as the European Parliament, the European Court of Justice and the European Investment Bank, policies and basic information on the European Union (including access to an assortment of official documents, legal texts and other sources of information). An interesting new service is *Dialogue with Business, the One Stop Internet Shop for Business* at **http://www.europa.eu.int/business/en/index.html**. This is aimed at companies wanting to do business in Europe, and needing advice on how to certify their product, find a business partner in the EU, or bid for public contracts, or who just want a source of information on the Single Market. Sections include key issues (public procurement, intellectual property rights, technical harmonization, funding opportunities), Single Market rules (including community and national legislation and the official journal), personalized advice and feedback (business advice from Euro Info Centres, the euro etc) and practical information. This last offers links to fairs and exhibitions, the *Europages* business directory of 500,000 companies in 30 European countries, access to the business press in all EU member states, a translation service, a short message service and 'business links': a daily updated list to the web's best global business sites from 70 countries.

Another key European site is *CORDIS* (Community Research & Development Information Service) at **http://www.cordis.lu/**. The EU's research activities are mostly implemented under five-year research, technological development and demonstration (RTD) programmes, and the *CORDIS* domain serves as the gateway to detailed web services covering the current Fifth Framework Programme, 1998–2002 (FP5), and the previous Fourth Framework Programme. Its newly redesigned home page (previewed at the London Online show, December 1999) will make the many *CORDIS* services easier to access. Companies wishing to tender for projects have an increasing range of useful tools to help them: *CORDIS* provides central access to all calls for proposals and tenders, together with accompanying documentation and materials launched under FP5, a partners search facility, a proposal preparation tool, contract preparation materials, an intellectual property rights helpdesk, individual programme infodesks and sources of support in the various member states. The ERGO pilot service provides a gateway to national research and development information services.

A good starting point for SMEs is the 'innovation in practice' button on the home page. This takes you to a page offering guided tours, innovation services and other useful services. The guided tours (downloadable PDF files) cover topics such as turning an idea into a project, and using *CORDIS* as a tool for technology transfer. The innovation services section offers links to a range of useful information and contacts – for example, details of the *Innovation/SMEs programme* (the specific European Commission programme for small business) at **http://www.cordis.lu/innovation-smes/home.html**, and SME specific measures. As access to finance is a particular concern, another good site on the list to visit is *Financing Innovation* at **http://www.cordis.lu/finance/home.html**, which includes information for innovators (including access to finance from venture capitalists and informal investors), information for investors, policy issues, and practical information and tools. This last provides links to an event calendar, calls for tender and a contacts list giving access to a number of relevant organizations. Contacts available through the innovation services section include the network of Innovation Relay Centres (IRCs) and SME National Contact Points in EU and other European states. Other useful services to which access is provided from the 'innovation in practice' page include *Europa*'s *Dialogue with business*, *BC-NET* (the *Business Cooperation Network*) and *TASBI* (*Trans-Atlantic Small Business Initiative*) a joint US/European initiative to encourage partnerships between European and American small and medium-sized enterprises.

A different view of innovation is provided through the *Research and Innovation in the Regions* service, accessed from the *CORDIS* home page or directly from **http://www.cordis.lu/regions/home.html**. This service enables individual regions to promote their research and innovation infrastructures, services and activities. Specific regions within the UK that are already making use of this service are East Midlands, North East, Scotland and Wales. The *Regions* service is under active development at the time of writing, and will contain a strong focus on information sources and networks, including ready access to FP5 National Contact Points, Innovation Relay Centres, Euro Info Centres and the Business and Innovation Centres Network.

# Sites for specific business functions

The sites described above will cover, between them, most if not all the information required to start up, manage and expand a small or medium-sized enterprise. This particular section is not designed to be yet another 'one-stop shop', but it was thought useful to provide a shortlist of key sites for day-to-day business issues.

# News and current affairs

The *Financial Times* is a must-have. It is at **http://www.ft.com/** and incorporates a three-year archive which can be very useful when researching particular large companies. Also bookmark the *BBC Business News* site at **http://news.bbc.co.uk/hi/english/business/default.stm**, which recently received an enthusiastic five-star rating from Demon as an 'unmissable' site with a lot to offer small businesses.

# Company and product information

All the familiar hardback directories are available on the web – for example, *Yellow Pages* at **http://www.yell.co.uk/** (1.6 million UK companies, searchable by business type, company name or location), *Kelly's directory* of 12,000 companies at **http://www.kellys.reedinfo.co.uk/** and Thomson's *In Business* directory of 2 million UK firms at **http://www.inbusiness.co.uk/**. For international listings, try *Kompass* at **http://www.kompass.com/**, *Telephone Directories on the Web* at **http://www.contractjobs.com/tel/**, a listing of yellow pages sites worldwide, or *WorldPages* at **http://www.worldpages.com/global.html**, with links to 230 directories from over 100 countries. *Millennium Facilities* at **http://www.milfac.co.uk/milfac/**, an early entrant into web-based services for SMEs, offers details of over 60,000 UK companies both on and off the Internet. You can search by name or sector, or register your own company free of charge. For other aids to market research, see Chapter 7 of this book and the section on export assistance below.

## *Companies House* and credit information

*Companies House* at **http://companieshouse.gov.uk/** offers direct access to all the latest UK-registered company accounts and data, and has an e-mail enquiry service. Late payers, bad debtors and suppliers going out of business are all among the problems that can have a disastrous effect on a small business, so the facility for checking a company's credit rating before dealing with them can save a lot of grief. ICC offers *Juniper* (details at **http://193.133.118.15/juniper/juninfo.htm**), an online service containing in-depth analysis on over 5.3 million British limited companies and unincorporated businesses (sole traders and partnerships). A recent offering with a small business focus from *Experian* at **http://experian.com/**, which has to be the least informative business information site on the web) is the *Non-Limited Businesses Database*, containing such information as county court judgements, credit ratings, risk band, payment trends etc for 2.2 million small businesses, sole traders and partnerships.

# Sources of grants, finance and business opportunities

The possibilities of funding – grants, preferential loans and other financial assistance – can make all the difference to a small business at critical points in its development such as start-up, expansion or a move to new premises. Two of the most popular products are now available over the web. EPRC Ltd, the commercial arm of the *European Policies Research Centre* based in Strathclyde University at **http://www.eprcltd.strath.ac.uk/eprcltd/**, maintains *InfoGrant*, which provides details of the grants and other financial assistance schemes available to businesses in the UK. The other is *Grantfinder* at **http://www.grantfinder.co.uk/**, which claims to be the most comprehensive database of UK and EU funding, including grants, loans, subsidies and other incentives. *Grantfinder* offers a range of support services, including help desks and application assistance to clients making a grant application.

For everything you could ever want to know about franchises, visit the *British Franchise Association* site at **http://www.british-franchise.org.uk/**, which includes access to a directory of accredited companies and advisors, and details of associated organizations around the world.

If your company sees e-commerce as a business opportunity but doesn't know where to start, it is worth visiting the *Hotwired* site at **http://www.hotwired.lycos.com/webmonkey/e-business**, which includes tutorials on e-commerce and market research on the web, e-storefront options, advertising on the web and building the customer relationship once you've got going.

## Managing your business

Advice on all UK business (and personal) tax matters is available on the *Inland Revenue* site at **http://www.inlandrevenue.gov.uk/**. For VAT information see the *Customs and Excise* site at **http://www.hmce.gov.uk/**.

Local authorities offer a huge range of services and incentives to small business, as well as being vital sources of planning, regulatory and other information. A comprehensive directory of local government websites (covering all county, metropolitan, unitary, borough and district authority sites) is available at **http://www.tagish.co.uk/tagish/links/localgov.htm**. A list of town and parish council sites is also available.

If you're looking to move to new premises, check out *The Property Mall* at **http://propertymall.com/**, which covers the UK commercial property market, or *Estates Gazette Interactive* at **http://www.egi.co.uk/**, which covers news and developments in the property markets, and also offers subscriber access to the London Office Database covering property in the City, West End and Docklands. To staff your new offices, the main recruitment agencies are all accessible on the web. A good starting point is *Work* from the *UKPlus* home page at **http://www.ukplus.com/**, which links to selected recruitment agencies and to the Federation of Recruitment and Employment Services.

If your business requires legal advice, there is a lot of it available on the web. The main *Law Society* site at **http://www.lawsoc.org.uk/** includes guidance on finding a solicitor. Its specific service to business, *Lawyers for your Business* (backed by Business in the Community, the Federation of Small Businesses and the Forum of Private Businesses) at **http://www.lyfb.lawsociety.org.uk/**, offers a series of step-by-step guides to employment law, property matters, contracts, health and safety, raising money for a business and structuring a business, and maintains a library of frequently encountered legal pitfalls.

# Trade associations

Trade associations can be invaluable sources of information and advice, though they have been slow to take up the opportunities offered by the web. A general business association, the *Federation for Small Businesses* at **http://www.fsb.org.uk/**, is the UK pressure group for the small business sector. Its home page includes a useful listing of current relevant news stories.

The DTI's Information Society Initiative has included the formation of *TANC* (the *Trade Association Network Challenge*) to encourage trade associations to make more creative use of the Internet. The *TANC* home page at **http://www.brainstorm.co.uk/TANC/Welcome.html** includes a link to the *Directory of Trade Associations*, the web's most comprehensive UK trade association directory. Access to a wider selection of trade associations, in which the UK and Irish ones are flagged as such, is through *Yahoo!* on http://uk.dir.yahoo.com/Business_and_Economy/Organisations/ Trade_Associations/.

# Export assistance

British Trade International, a government organization that brings together the work of the Foreign and Commonwealth Office and the DTI in support of British trade and investment overseas, has a website packed with practical information on market research, arranging visits to countries or bringing key people to the UK, and dealing with cultural or language problems, at **http://www.brittrade.com/**. Links are also provided to the *Trade UK Export Sales Leads* and *Trade UK National Exporters Database*. Other practical information is offered by the *British Chambers of Commerce*, who manage the Export Marketing Research Scheme (EMRS). (Their site is referred to briefly above at **http://www.britishchambers.org.uk/**.)

# Patents and trademarks

The big name in Internet-delivered patent and trademark information is *Micropatent* at **http://www.micropat.com/**. For patent searching for small-scale or occasional use, it offers a daily subscription facility for full-text or front-page research using their USA, Europe, PCT (WIPO) and Japan databases, whilst *MarkSearch PRO* claims to have trademark information available within hours of receipt of updates from the USPTO.

# Sites for individual SME sectors

Many business sectors have a very high percentage of members who are small firms, sole traders or partnerships. Information available to these on the web varies considerably; on the whole, the service sectors are better provided for than the traditional industry sectors. Some sectors are addressed in detail in individual chapters in this book; in the space available, this section can only highlight a few examples, to illustrate some of the possibilities that the web provides.

Details of all the Sift Group virtual communities are available at **http://www.sift.co.uk/communities/index.html**. These include the *AccountingWeb* directory of accountants at **http://www.businesszone.co.uk/directory.index.html** (listing is free), which provides contact details, details of firm websites, specialisms and the range of services offered. *TrainingZONE* at **http://www.trainingzone.co.uk/**, which is for training and HR professionals, includes directories of training and consultancy, venues, suppliers and company data, whilst *TravelMole* at **http://www.travelmole.com/** is aimed at travel journalists, tour operators, hotels and other travel professionals, and aims to keep track of developments (from news stories to relevant websites) for people working in the travel industry.

The legal profession is very well served on the web. There is a Sift legal community – *LawZONE* at **http://www.lawzone.co.uk/** – which aims to provide 'the best online community for the legal profession and allied fields'. Two of the many other sites to note are Delia Venables' *Portal to Legal Resources in the UK and Ireland* at **http://www.venables.co.uk/**, which provides up-to-date links to sites and resources in the UK, Ireland and overseas, details of barristers and solicitors, legal newspapers and journals, and legal technology (including legal software and IT suppliers, and guides to the Internet for lawyers), and *InfoLaw* at **http://www.infolaw.co.uk/**, which has a slightly different focus and includes sections on government, parliament and the courts, legal resources (including a list of legal resources by practice area, and *LawFinder* access to primary law on the web), and goods and services for UK lawyers.

Another exceptionally well-served group is architects, via the many services offered through *RIBA* (start at **http://site.yahoo.net/about-riba/**). The main *RIBA* domain has 30 mini-sites, each with its own home page. These include client and practice services, electronic services, regional services and services for the press and TV. From the *RIBA Library* site, a *Links* button leads to 49 pages of links to electronic lists and discussion groups, directories, awards, education, environment, maps and much more, representing in total a quite staggering amount of information.

Finally, here is an example from materials technology that demonstrates what collaboration can achieve. The World Centre for Materials Joining Technology wanted to increase its penetration of the SME market, and went to the DTI for advice. The outcome was a joint programme, resulting in *JoinIT* at **http://www.twi.co.uk/**, a web service for engineers working in SMEs that provides direct answers to technical questions, and information on research, training and consultancy.

Given the speed of content development on the web, it can only be a matter of time before similar successes are made available to benefit the small business community specifically.

# References

Allcock, S and others (1999) *Business information on the Internet: use of the Internet as an information resource for small and medium-sized enterprises: final report*, British Library Research and Innovation Report 136, British Library Research and Innovation Centre.

*Business Link service guide* (1997) Edition 2. N. Pl., British Chambers of Commerce, Department of Trade and Industry. Local Government Association and the TEC National Council, 1997.

Foster, A (1995) Using the Internet for business information, *Business Information Review,* **12** (1), 2–17

Stoat, P and Abell, A (1995) *Business Links*, Library & Information Briefings 61, South Bank University.

*What's New in Business Information* (1995) 'Small firms snub online data', *What's New in Business Information*, **4**, 1995, 25–6.

# URLs mentioned in this chapter

*AccountingWeb* http://www.businesszone.co.uk/directory.index.html

*BBC Business News*
http://news.bbc.co.uk/hi/english/business/default.stm

*Biz.net* http://www.virginbiz.net

*British Chambers of Commerce* http://www.britishchambers.org.uk/

*British Franchise Association* http://www.british-franchise.org.uk/

*British Trade International* http://www.brittrade.com/

*Business directory* http://www.inbusiness.co.uk/

*Business Links* http://www.businesslink.co.uk/

*BusinessZone* http://www.businesszone.co.uk/

*Chamber Business Information Centre*
http://www.glasgowchamber.co.uk/dis/index.html

*Companies House* http://companieshouse.gov.uk/

*Connect to business* http://www.btconnect.com/

*Consultation Paper* http://www.dti.gov.uk/sbs/consult/Summary.htm

*CORDIS* http://www.cordis.lu/

*Customs and Excise* http://www.hmce.gov.uk/

*DIALOG* http://www.enterprise-zone.org.uk/

*Dialogue with Business, the One Stop Internet Shop for Business*
http://www.europa.eu.int/business/en/index.html

*Digipages* http://www.tagish.co.uk/tagish/links/localgov.htm

*DTI* http://www.dti.gov.uk/

*Estates Gazette Interactive* http://www.egi.co.uk/

*EUbusiness* http://www.eubusiness.com/

*Europa* http://europa.eu.int/

*European Policies Research Centre*
     http://www.eprcltd.strath.ac.uk/eprcltd/

*Experian* http://experian.com/

*Federation for Small Businesses* http://www.fsb.org.uk/

*Financial Times* http://www.ft.com/

*Financing Innovation* http://www.cordis.lu/finance/home.html

*Free Pint* http://www.freepint.co.uk/

*Free Pint* http://www.freepint.co.uk/issues/99index.htm

*Grantfinder* http://www.grantfinder.co.uk/

*HotWired* http://www.hotwired.lycos.com/webmonkey/e-business

*InfoLaw* http://www.infolaw.co.uk/

*Inland Revenue* http://www.inlandrevenue.gov.uk/

*JoinIT* http://www.twi.co.uk/

*Juniper* http://193.133.118.15/juniper/juninfo.htm

*Kelly's directory* http://www.kellys.reedinfo.co.uk/

*KnowUK* http://www.knowuk.co.uk/

*Kompass* http://www.kompass.com/

*Law Society* http://www.lawsoc.org.uk/

*Lawyers for your Business* http://www.lyfb.lawsociety.org.uk/

*LawZONE* http://www.lawzone.co.uk/

*Micropatent* http://www.micropat.com/

*Millennium Facilities Digipages* http://www.milfac.co.uk/milfac

*Portal to Legal Resources in the UK and Ireland*
     http://www.venables.co.uk/

*refdesk.com* http://www.refdesk.com/

*Research and Innovation in the Regions*
     http://www.cordis.lu/regions/home.html

*RIBA* http://site.yahoo.net/about-riba/

*Sift Group* http://www.sift.co.uk/

*Sift Group* http://www.sift.co.uk/communities/index.html

*SMEs programme* http://www.cordis.lu/innovation-smes/home.html

*Telephone Directories on the Web* http://www.contractjobs.com/tel/

*The Property Mall* http://propertymall.com/

*The Small Business Directory*
http://www.bizmove.com/directory/directorymain.htm

*Trade Association Network Challenge*
http://www.brainstorm.co.uk/TANC/Welcome.html

*TrainingZONE* http://www.trainingzone.co.uk/

*TravelMole* http://www.travelmole.com/

*UKPlus* http://www.ukplus.com/

*WorldPages* http://www.worldpages.com/global.html

*Yahoo! UK Small Business Guide*
http://www.yahoo.co.uk/Business_and_Economy/Small_Business
_Information/

*Yahoo!* http://smallbusiness.yahoo.com/

*Yahoo!*
http://uk.dir.yahoo.com/Business_and_Economy/Organisations/
Trade_Associations/

*Yellow Pages* http://www.yell.co.uk/

# 7

# Market research resources

## *Jill Bradley*

## Introduction

Market research is the collection and evaluation of data to understand customers' needs and to assist suppliers in planning to meet those needs. It is used by commercial organizations, whose existence depends on accurately meeting customers needs, but increasingly market research is also used by various government departments, the healthcare sector, charities and other non-profit-making organizations to help them to focus their efforts in the right direction. It is also used to find out the needs, opinions and attitudes of staff within an organization and to canvass public opinion on current topics of interest.

Here is a definition of market research offered by the Market Research Society, which is the leading British professional body for market researchers:

Market research is the means used by those who provide goods and services to keep themselves in touch with the needs and wants of those who buy and use those goods and services.

# Basic market research techniques

## Desk research

The use of published sources to provide background data on a market or a framework for more specific research can be an effective, quick and relatively cheap method for collecting and analysing secondary data to begin the research process. This may include internal data on sales, production and distribution, statistics and reports produced by government, trade and professional bodies, company information, journal and news articles, and published survey reports produced by commercial research companies. It is within this area of market research that the Internet can offer the widest scope of material and where it is becoming increasingly useful.

## Quantitative research

When secondary data is unavailable, lacks authority or is not specific enough to meet the research needs, quantitative research steps in. It involves the use of a questionnaire to collect detailed information from a representative sample of relevant individuals; the data is then tabulated, analysed and interpreted to produce a report of the findings. Methods for the collection of data for qualitative research include: face-to-face interviews, telephone interviews, postal self-completion interviews and hall tests, which are usually used for product tests. Qualitative research is usually carried out by a professional market research company on behalf of a client, and the results would be confidential to that client. The Internet can be used to find contact details of market research companies and to check that they are reputable members of the professional associations. The company's own websites may also be used to check what sort of projects they have undertaken in the past, and this together with lists of current clients may help to indicate their areas of expertise.

# Omnibus questions

An omnibus is a regularly conducted quantitative survey with a specific target group. A set number of people is interviewed on each occasion. Omnibuses can be conducted monthly, quarterly or even weekly and it is possible to buy individual questions to be asked during one or more wave of interviewing. In addition to the bought questions there will usually be various demographic questions which will allow your own questions to be analysed.

This is an ideal option for the situation when you need answers to a few questions but want to sample a fairly large group of people. The set-up costs for a quantitative study would be disproportionally high, so buying some questions on a relevancy omnibus can be a very cost-effective way to obtain your data. *MRWEB* at **http://www.mrweb.com/** contains a list of major omnibus surveys. These are classified by subject and will give you information about target sample, frequency of omnibus, number of interviews conducted and contact data.

# Qualitative research

Qualitative researchers will say that, while quantitative research tells you what people do, qualitative research tells you why they do it. Information is collected on individuals' attitudes through in-depth interviews or group discussions using a discussion guide rather than a questionnaire. This type of research yields less structured data than quantitative research, and because sample sizes are so small, no accurate figures can be derived from the data. However, its open-ended approach is useful in providing an insight into the attitudes and motivations which underlie and affect behaviour and buying patterns. The Internet can be used to find reputable and experienced qualitative companies in the same way as it can be used to find quantitative researchers.

# Data collection on the Internet

Increasingly the Internet is beginning to be used as the actual medium for conducting primary market research. As less than a third of the adult population of the United Kingdom has access to the Internet, and their profile is not representative of the population as a whole, this is somewhat limited in scope at the moment, but as the density of computer ownership increases it is likely to become more common.

The Internet is of course an ideal medium for collecting information about Internet users specifically. This can used for quantitative surveys using a web-based questionnaire to conduct interviews. In this case interviewees are recruited by e-mail, either by means of pop-ups which appear when an individual logs on to a chosen website, or by banners running on relevant websites.

There are also some attempts being made to conduct qualitative research over the Internet using virtual focus groups or e-mail focus groups. The advantage of this approach is that you can conduct a focus group without participants needing to travel to a central point for the meeting. Using this technology it is possible to have a focus group which includes individuals in different countries and even different continents.

# Market research resources on the Internet

## Evaluating material

Many people are wary of information obtained through the Internet, and there is often a strong feeling that it is less authoritative, less accurate and more prone to error, perhaps even containing deliberately false information. Some scepticism is certainly called for in the assessment of information from the Internet, as the accessibility of the Internet as a publishing medium does make it vulnerable to erroneous and misleading information sources. However, the same skills which are used for assessing printed material and more conventional electronic sources can be used to judge Internet content:

## The authority of the provider

Sites which originate from some professional body or from a respected publisher are no more likely to contain errors than printed material from the same sources. On the other hand, personal sites produced by individuals may be interesting but need to be cross-checked with some other source before their contents are accepted as factual.

## Possible bias

If a site is produced by an organization or individual who may have a hidden agenda, its content may be slanted to some degree or other.

## Currency

Often sites are put up onto the Internet in a flurry of enthusiasm and then, once the initial impetus is over, there is nobody with the time or inclination to update them. Thus much of the material available on the Internet is old and fairly worthless. However, the regularity with which a site is updated will give some indication of the value placed upon it by the originating organization and hence the amount of time and attention to detail which has been invested in its creation and upkeep.

# Some useful sites

There are some sites which are specifically directed towards market research sources in general. This type of site gives a good overview of available material, so a few good examples of these are given below.

## MRWeb http://www.mrweb.com/

Run by a market research consultant and web design and Internet consultancy company, this site is free for users and is funded by advertisers. It is intended to be an online resource for market research companies and professionals, but would be a useful kick-off point for anybody interested in the subject.

*MRWeb* offers a series of useful links to use for desk research; these are classified by industry sector, which makes them particularly user-friendly. Other elements of the site which may be particularly useful to the non-professional are a list of market research companies with links to their websites and a directory of major omnibus surveys by subject.

## EMIC http://www.brittrade.com/emic/index.html

The British Trade International's free self-service library for exporters, *EMIC* is designed to help identify, select and research the export markets offering the most potential for British products or services. At the library there are various web commercial databases which can be used for research by visiting the library: Euromonitor, Dun & Bradstreet, EIU, World Markets Online. About 30 CD-ROM databases are also available for use within the library. In addition there are lists of other useful links for exporters at **www.brittrade.com/emic/guide.html**, which are classified by sector, geography or as a simple alphabetical listing.

## Market Search Directory http://www.marketsearch-dir.com/home.htm

This lists over 20,000 published market research surveys on markets worldwide. There is no actual data available but it will enable you to find if there is any published market research available which will cover your area of interest. Searching is free but there is a charge for obtaining contact details of the publisher of any report. A subscription to the service costs $310 and it is available as a CD-ROM for the same price.

# Search engines

These are probably the key to using the Internet for any kind of research. Favourites lists are useful for frequently accessed sites, but spending large amounts of time compiling an extensive collection of bookmarks can be counterproductive. The Internet changes so fast that keeping your bookmarks current is like painting the Forth Bridge – a never-ending task – so that it would seem to be more sensible to use the resources somebody else has produced. Most people have their own favourite search engine, which is often just the one they are used to using. While there is nothing wrong with this, it is worth investigating new search engines as they appear – different engines can be good at different tasks and coverage of subject areas vary from engine to engine. Just two search engines are given below (for further examples see Chapters 2 and 3).

## *IXQUICK* **http://ixquick.com/**

This is not strictly speaking a search engine at all but a meta search engine; it takes your search terms, translates the syntax then searches simultaneously across a number of major search engines. Sites are ranked according to the number of search engines that have the site in their top ten for that search. As different search engines use different algorithms to rank sites this helps to smooth out individual search engine bias.

## *AltaVista* **http://www.altavista.com/**

This search engine can be useful for finding new subject areas before compiling a favourites list. Its coverage is excellent, so it is good for broad searching and for offbeat subjects, but you can be overwhelmed by too many hits. There is a strong US bias but it is possible to restrict your search to the UK. *AltaVista* allows some structured searching. Search abilities are still fairly primitive compared with online and CD-ROM systems, but this search engine allows a more sophisticated search than most of the other engines currently available.

# Market research publishers

Don't expect to find much free market research data on the Internet – it is labour-intensive and expensive to produce and no company whose business is selling data can afford to give it away free. However, many of the market research publishers now have web pages, so the Internet can be a good place for checking the availability of published research, and a lot of them will offer free samples from some of their more recent reports. This selection does not aim to be exhaustive, but provides just a few examples of the type of site available.

## *MAID* **http://www.maid-plc.com/**

Owned by DIALOG Corporation, this is a host system rather than a publisher, so it offers access to a very wide range of published material worldwide. The advantages *MAID* offers include: the scale and scope of material available through one interface; the very flexible and sophisticated indexing and search capability; and finally the facility for purchasing small sections of reports or even single tables. However, the disadvantage is that there is a substantial subscription to access the system, as well as charges for the specific data retrieved. This service would be worth considering if you planned to do substantial amounts of desk research across a variety of subject areas, but is likely to be too expensive for the casual or occasional user.

## *Mintel* **http://www.mintel.co.uk/**

This company is well known for its published market research reports, which specialize in the UK consumer and retail markets. For a visitor this site lists the available reports with prices and ordering information; if you wish to register with the site, you can buy and view reports directly.

## *Euromonitor* **http://www.euromonitor.com/**

This site belongs to a well-established and respected market research publisher, who is a leading provider of global consumer market and business intelligence.

Their published market research spans the major markets of Western Europe, North America and Japan, as well as the emerging markets of Asia, Latin America, the Middle East, Eastern Europe and Africa.

They publish about 400 off-the-shelf market reports each year and 30 statistical reference handbooks and information source directories.

Products are available electronically, via CD-ROM and the Internet. The website enables users to find detailed information about their products and services. From this site you can also buy sections from the latest reports on a pay-per-view basis.

## *Datamonitor* **http://www.datamonitor.com/**

The site of a well-established and respected market research publisher, it lists their available reports, with ordering and pricing information. They specialize in market analysis reports covering the following areas:

automotive and transport, consumer, energy industry, financial services market, healthcare products, medical equipment, and technology.

## *Keynote* http://www.keynote.co.uk/

Yet another well-established and respected market research publisher, whose reports cover a very wide variety of UK product sectors, they have bought Market Assessment who publish MAPS reports, and together they publish 400 titles covering the industrial, consumer and service sectors. This site lists their available reports, with ordering and pricing information, and for keynote reports the table of contents and executive summary are available free.

## *Verdict* http://www.verdict.co.uk/

A niche market research publisher specializing in the UK retail market. In this area they are experts, producing a range of reports which include factual material but also detailed analysis. In addition they produce *Retail Verdict UK*, which is a monthly newsletter analysing retail trends and new developments from a strategic viewpoint. The newsletter contains a broad mix of features on topics such as company profiles, market analyses and reviews of new store developments and concepts. For up-to-date news they provide a daily news summary of all the retail stories breaking in the UK national press each day. All 14 UK national daily newspapers are read for retail news and summarized in the 3–4 pages of news stories, which are available to subscribers on the website by 9am each morning.

## *Frost and Sullivan* http://www.frost.com/

Frost and Sullivan is a market consultancy company that also produces published reports on its website. It is possible to register as a subscriber and to receive industry insight newsletters – there is no charge for this service.

# Market research organizations

## *Market Research Society* **http://www.marketresearch.org.uk/**

The MRS is the UK professional body for market researchers. Its site is expanding and it contains some useful general material on market research. However, the major annual publication of the MRS is their *Research Buyers Guide*: a directory which provides research buyers with crucial information on companies and consultants offering market research and related services throughout the UK and Eire. It includes details of research markets, services and locations, contact names and an overview of each organization's activities, and it is currently available only on paper. Similarly, their journal titles and conference proceeding are paper-based, which unfortunately limits the usefulness of this website.

## *British Market Research Association* **http://www.bmra.org.uk/**

The BMRA is the UK trade association for the industry. The site contains a list of members, which is a very useful starting point for finding market research companies, but the information given for each entry is quite limited. The BMRA also has a service called Selectline, which is a database allowing companies to be selected who offer specific services. There is some information about Selectline on the website, but searches are done by BMRA staff and the results are passed to the enquirer – as yet there is no facility for direct searching on the site. Selectline can be used to identify sources of specific types of market research service and it is free to enquirers. However, it should be approached with caution as the research companies pay for entry into the database. This means that coverage is extremely patchy, with many reputable companies having no presence.

### *ESOMAR* http://www.esomar.nl/

The worldwide association for market research professionals has a very extensive website, which contains much useful information. ESOMAR has 6000 personal members and 1500 organizational members across 100 countries, so this is an ideal place to start if you wish to commission market research outside the UK. The *ESOMAR* site has a listing of market research companies which is searchable by country, by methods used and by industry specialization. There is also an extensive listing of the national professional associations for many countries.

## Market research companies

The BMRA site (see above) includes a list of all of its member companies, which includes websites and e-mail addresses where available; this is available at **http://www.bmra.org.uk/bmra.html**.

For a wider geographical coverage you can use the links provided by the *ESOMAR* site (see above). The directory is available at **http://www.esomar.nl/directory.html**.

Listed below are sites of a few of the bigger UK companies:

### *Taylor Nelson Sofres* http://www.tnagb.com/

One of the world's leading marketing information groups. Separate international divisions specialize in IT, Internet, telecommunications, business and financial services, healthcare, consumer goods and panels, automotive, media and marketing services. There are international offices across Europe, the Middle East, America and Asia Pacific.

## *Mori* **http://www.mori.com/**

Mori is the eighth-largest UK market research agency, with 15 offices in 13 countries worldwide and a presence in 35 countries including business partners.

## *Ipsos-RSL* **http://www.rslmedia.co.uk/**

A UK-based market research company within the French-owned Ipsos Group, Ipsos-RSL provides full service research, offering both quantitative and qualitative facilities in local markets as well as international coordination. Ipsos-RSL Media, which is one of the three companies which make up Ipsos-RSL, comprises three specialist divisions serving the research needs of the media industry.

# Population and demographic statistics

In order to put market research statistics into perspective it is often necessary to include background information about the total population the market is drawn from; this is usually called the universe.

For example, let's imagine there is a product which is bought by 1% of the population of the USA and also by 10% of the population of Finland. The product has a much bigger share of the market in Finland than it has in the USA. However, the total population (the universe) of the USA is 260.6 million, while in Finland it is 5.1 million. This means that the 1% share of the market in the USA is over 2 million sales, while in Finland a 10% market share is only half a million sales. In relative terms the company has a larger presence in Finland than in the USA but in actual terms the US sales are much larger.

There are many sources of statistics available on the Internet, including official government figures. Some recommended sources for demographic and general statistics are given below:

## *National Statistics* **http://www.statistics.gov.uk/**

This website contains the latest comprehensive range of official UK statistics and information about statistics, as well as providing free access to a selection of recently released publications in downloadable PDF format.

The site is organized around 13 themes (broad subject areas), which makes it easier to find information quickly.

## *UNICEF* **http://www.unicef.org/pon96/contents.htm**

This site concentrates on social statistics and reports but it also contains a section of statistical profiles worldwide, which are grouped into continents. It is an easy and authoritative source for population figures for individual countries.

## *OECD* **http://www.oecd.org/statistics/**

This site contains statistics on OECD member countries. The data includes: demography, health, national accounts, labour, agriculture, industry, services, transport, taxation, energy, environment, direct investment, trade, aid, education, science and technology, and many other indicators.

## *Bureau of Labor* **http://stats.bls.gov/**

A rich source for authoritative statistical information on the USA.

*Eurostat* **http://europa.eu.int/com/eurostat/Public/datashop/print-catalogue/EN?catalogue=eurostat**

Eurostat is the statistical arm of the European Union. Its website covers the European market in some detail and includes statistics on population, economy, industry, transport, agriculture and trade.

# Country information

The sites listed above contain much useful material on individual countries, but there are other sites which are structured to allow a much broader picture to be gained for background material on one specific country. This may include not only statistical material but also commentary and description. Here is a selection of such sites:

*CIA World Factbook* **http://www.odci.gov/cia/publications/pubs.html**

An invaluable source of basic but free information on virtually every country in the world, this contains statistics and brief text on the geography, people, economy, political situation and communications infrastructure for each country covered.

## European sites

The four sites at **http://www.statistics.gov.uk/ukin_figs/default.asp** (UK), **http://www.insee.fr/fr/home/home_page.asp** (France), **http://www.statistik-bund.de/e_home.htm** (Germany) and **http://petra.istat.it/** (Italy) are produced by the government statistical body of each country. They contain a basic statistical review of major aspects of the population, industry and economy of that country. These figures tend to be fairly up to date, and thanks to their sources they can be considered extremely reliable.

### MBendi http://www.mbendi.co.za/index.htm

This site is intended to assist companies and business people around the world to do business in Africa. It contains information on the business opportunities and challenges in the countries of Africa, the major companies and organizations, and various industry sectors within the region.

### Brazilinfo http://www.brazilinfo.net/

An extensive Internet guide to Brazil covering information about business, geography and the population.

### Latin Focus http://www.latin-focus.com/

This site contains information on Argentina, Brazil, Chile, Columbia, Mexico, Peru and Venezuela. It is less detailed then the Brazil site listed above, but it does include economic forecasts for Latin America as a whole as well as information on the individual countries.

### Hong Kong Trade Development Council http://www.tdctrade.com/

The Council was set up to promote Hong Kong's trade in goods and services. Its aim is to develop Hong Kong's role as an information hub, as a sourcing and business centre in Asia Pacific, and as the gateway to Chinese mainland. This site has useful information on the economy of the region, and also contains business and industry news.

# Industry information

Each industry sector will have its own resources and websites available.

A good starting point is to use keywords in one of the search engines to locate relevant starting sites, which will often include lists of other related resources. Increasingly, portals that are subject-specific are appearing. These are a boon to any Internet-based researcher, providing as they do a ready access point to subject areas.

Professional and trade associations usually have websites, and although these may vary in quality they can prove to be a very useful source of information about the industry in general. Some organizations will also provide statistics and information on companies operating within their area.

Most major companies now have quite extensive websites, which usually include electronic copies of their annual reports, together with information about their product ranges and the markets they service. In addition to their value as a source of competitive information about the company itself, they may be used to form a picture of the industry as a whole. Caution must be exercised in using the information in this way, but in some cases the top few companies will command a substantial part of the total market, so that an analysis of these companies will give a rough indication of the progress of the major part of that industry.

It would be impossible to cover even a minor selection of industry-specific sites, so the links included below cover just a few examples of this type of site:

## *NUA* http://www.nua.net/surveys/

This excellent site includes brief summaries of published Internet surveys, and it is very useful for obtaining trend information and Internet penetration figures. It is organized into categories and also includes a keyword search facility.

## *MPSI Database* http://www.bbi.co.uk/vehicle/info/

A specialist site for data retrieval, field research, evaluation and forecasting of new motor vehicle (passenger cars and commercial) registrations. A free sample on the website includes year-2000 forecasts of car registrations for all major European countries, both for private cars and by fleet size for company cars.

## *Information Society Initiative* http://www.isi.gov.uk/isi/govbenchframe.htm

In order to benchmark the UK's progress towards the Information Age in comparison with our major competitors, the DTI has sponsored research into levels of ownership, usage and understanding of information and communication technologies (ICTs) by companies of all sizes and sectors in the benchmarked countries. Electronic versions of these studies are available on the website.

## *IDG* http://www.idg.net/

This site contains lots of snippets of information on the computer industry.

## *Newspaper Association of America site* http://www.naa.org/marketscope/analysis/retail/

A good starting point for anyone wanting to find information on the retail industry.

## *KNAUF expo* http://www.knauffiberglass.com/hot/cif97.html

Here you will find detailed statistics on the USA construction market.

# Conclusion

The Internet can be used for finding out general information about the market research process and how surveys should be set up and conducted. It is also a very useful source for information about specific market research companies and could be used to locate reputable organizations to conduct primary research on your behalf. However, without doubt the main strength of the Internet as a market research resource is the wealth of information available to assist in the desk research process.

In one chapter it is only possible to give a brief flavour of the types of sites which may be useful, so this is by necessity an eclectic choice of those sites that the author has found useful. If you talked to other market research professionals, they would no doubt compile a somewhat different list. This simply reflects the varied and somewhat chaotic nature of the Internet as it is today.

# URLs mentioned in this chapter

*AltaVista* **http://www.altavista.com/**
*Brazilinfo* **http://www.brazilinfo.net/**
*British Market Research Association* **http://www.bmra.org.uk/**
*British Market Research Association* **http://www.bmra.org.uk/bmra.html**
*Bureau of Labor* **http://stats.bls.gov/**
*CIA World Factbook* **http://www.odci.gov/cia/publications/pubs.html**
*Datamonitor* **http://www.datamonitor.com/**
*EMIC* **http://www.brittrade.com/emic/guide.html**
*EMIC* **http://www.brittrade.com/emic/index.html**
*ESOMAR* **http://www.esomar.nl/**
*ESOMAR* **http://www.esomar.nl/directory.html**
*Euromonitor* **http://www.euromonitor.com/**
*Eurostat* **http://europa.eu.int/com/eurostat/Public/datashop/print-**

catalogue/EN?catalogue=eurostat

*Frost and Sullivan* http://www.frost.com/

*Hong Kong Trade Development Council* http://www.tdctrade.com/

*IDG* http://www.idg.net/

*Information Society Initiative*
http://www.isi.gov.uk/isi/govbenchframe.htm

*Ipsos-RSL* http://www.rslmedia.co.uk/

*IXQUICK* http://ixquick.com/

*Keynote* http://www.keynote.co.uk/

*KNAUF expo* http://www.knauffiberglass.com/hot/cif97.html

*Latin Focus* http://www.latin-focus.com/

*MAID* http://www.maid-plc.com/

*Market Research Society* http://www.marketresearch.org.uk/

*Market Search Directory* http://www.marketsearch-dir.com/home.htm

*MBendi* http://www.mbendi.co.za/index.htm

*Mintel* http://www.mintel.co.uk/

*Mori* http://www.mori.com/

*MPSI Database* http://www.bbi.co.uk/vehicle/info/

*MRWeb* http://www.mrweb.com/

*National Statistics* http://www.statistics.gov.uk/

*Newspaper Association of America*
http://www.naa.org/marketscope/analysis/retail/

*NUA* http://www.nua.net/surveys/

*OECD* http://www.oecd.org/statistics/

*Statistical department of French Government*
http://www.insee.fr/fr/home/home_page.asp

*Statistical department of German Government* http://www.statistik-
bund.de/e_home.htm

*Statistical department of Italian Government* http://petra.istat.it/

*Statistical department of UK Government*
http://www.statistics.gov.uk/ukin_figs/default.asp

*Taylor Nelson Sofres* http://www.tnagb.com/

*UNICEF* http://www.unicef.org/pon96/contents.htm
*Verdict* http://www.verdict.co.uk/

# 8

# E-commerce - an overview

## Martin White

## Introduction

E-commerce is certainly big business for market research companies, consultancies, conference organizers and publishers. Newspapers such as the *New York Times* now have regular e-commerce sections, and most business magazines (*Fortune* is a very good example) have regular stories on the latest e-commerce start-up company and the millions that the owners will soon be worth. The market forecasting industry has always had to fight off an image of over-estimating market demand, but as with the case of mobile telephones, the e-commerce market has grown at rates that were beyond even their most optimistic forecast.

The problem that they face is defining just what *is* e-commerce. In its broadest definition it is commercial activity conducted over a telecommunications network, leading to the purchase of goods or services. This definition includes those transactions in which one element is carried out over a network, but other elements, in particular the transfer of funds, are carried out through different channels, such as telephone, fax, or a paper order. This wide variation makes it very difficult to quantify the scale of e-commerce, either in terms of the number of transactions, or their value. However it is important to bear in mind that the very high growth rates that are currently being forecast are from a very low initial base. The US Department of Commerce has commented that even with the current forecasts for the US e-commerce market, the value of the transactions is probably less that 1% of the total value of all purchasing in the USA.

Conducting business electronically is not new. In the mid-1980s in particular, there was considerable interest in the development of Electronic Data Interchange (EDI) services as a way in which the complex paper-work involved in purchasing goods across national boundaries could be simplified. Even in the mini-computer environment, the problems of developing applications software to handle the wide range of document formats presented enormous problems, especially given the fact that most countries did not recognize electronic documents as having any legal status. Telecommunications costs were very high, as this was the era before deregulation of telecommunications services in Europe had had any significant effect outside the UK. The end result was that although there were some success stories, notably in the automobile industry, the growth in EDI was much slower than anticipated.

In an historical context it is also important not to forget that there was one very important and successful e-commerce service, and that was (and still is) the Minitel service in France, with food, wine, travel tickets and many other products being advertised and sold over the system. The Bildschirmtext videotex service in Germany was less successful, but did provide a platform for electronic banking services.

The arrival of the Internet, and the development of web technology and standards, has changed everything. The question of standards is especially important for traffic to be able to cross national boundaries. The globally accepted standards of the Internet and the web have created a global market, enabling companies to justify investment in e-commerce on the basis of a market potential of hundreds of millions of purchasers.

# Market segmentation

There are two fairly distinct market sectors, the business-to-consumer sector (often given the abbreviation B2C) , and the business-to-business sector (B2B). This chapter is primarily concerned with the business-to-business sector, but some comments on the consumer sector are relevant. The way in which consumers make purchasing and payment transactions varies considerably from country to country, and especially between the USA and Europe. This has to do with the way that the banking systems operate, the extent to which shopping is a social event, and the importance of mail order, which is much more popular in the UK and Germany than in the USA and Canada, for example. There are also national variations in the relative importance of price, brand reputation and requirement for personal/customized service. All these present considerable problems for companies seeking to develop e-commerce applications for the consumer market in Europe, with the additional complications of language, and taxation and product liability issues.

This raises a very important issue, which affects both consumer and business transactions, and that is in the case where a dispute arises, which court has the jurisdiction to hear the dispute, and which law will the court apply to determine the rules applicable to that dispute? If a CD-player is purchased by a French national living in Germany from a supplier in the UK, and the product does not meet the specification laid down in the brochure, then does the purchaser sue in Germany, France or the UK?

The main types of products purchased in the consumer market are books, CDs and travel reservations, with groceries starting to be the next major market segment, especially in the UK. The most visible company in the consumer sector is of course Amazon, which is moving from books to CDs, videos, and many other products. The rate of growth of the company has been quite dramatic, and yet profits have been almost invisible. Despite the volume of trading in books through not only Amazon but other suppliers in the UK market such as Books Online, the major bookshop chains are continuing to invest in new superstores, with upwards of 200,000 titles in some of their London stores. Certainly, some of the smaller bookshops are now under considerable pressure from electronic services, and without doubt there are going to be major structural changes in retailing over the next few years.

After all the e-commerce hype of 1999 and the resulting very high valuations on dot.com companies, the market underwent a major upheaval in May 2000 as industry analysts, mainly in the USA, started to worry about just when these dot.com companies were going to start to make a profit. Even Amazon has not escaped scrutiny, and in the UK there was the very public collapse of Boo.com, which was selling clothing and related accessories over the web.

# Business-to-business e-commerce

Business-to-business e-commerce has attracted rather less attention from the press, except perhaps the success stories of Dell and Gateway, among others, who have developed significant sales of PCs and other IT equipment from their websites. One of the reasons for the success of this route has been the ability of the supplier to provide a highly customized service to a purchaser without having to hold substantial stocks of every possible configuration of PC. A purchaser can use the website to decide on the best configuration against price, place the order, and then the supplier effectively manufactures to order.

What is happening here is that the entire supply chain is being changed to take advantage of the benefits of e-commerce, rather than just providing an electronic means of concluding the purchase.

The majority of companies do not start up a total e-commerce operation from scratch. The usual route is to start with an electronic brochure on the website, perhaps with an e-mail box for queries. The next step is often to make the site even more interactive, with detailed product descriptions and perhaps the ability to purchase by credit card. Then the volume of transactions becomes such that these orders need to be integrated into accounting and stock management systems, and this is where things start to get difficult if the company has not taken a strategic view of the opportunities and the problems. This is because, as was indicated above, e-commerce will change the relationship not only between the company and its customers, but also between the company and its suppliers, including support activities. Products and services sold globally require global support, and a help-desk that just operates on UK office hours will create substantial ill-will. The purchase is not over until the customer is satisfied that the product meets their needs.

One of the outcomes of this progressive 'adoption ladder' is that any forecasts about e-commerce need to be considered very carefully to understand just what is being measured. Although some of the new dot.com companies only trade electronically, these represent a very small percentage of business transactions in any country.

An important consideration that companies need to address to take the maximum advantage of e-commerce is the attitude of the board of directors to the procurement and purchase functions. This is the flip side of the e-commerce opportunity. All too often the main objective of the purchasing department is to obtain the lowest price for an acceptable product. Rarely are customer support issues taken into account, for example. There may be an extreme reluctance to allow a purchase department to use an e-commerce solution, and this may stem from the department itself, concerned that its role may be under threat. Certainly new procedures and guidelines have to be developed, especially where a company has ISO 9001 quality management procedures that may rely on formal sign-offs for purchasing and other activities. None of this can happen without commitment from the board, and therefore from the shareholders, who may have to be sold further investment in IT systems.

Within the overall heading of B2B e-commerce four categories of electronic relationships are emerging. These are based around the recognition that purchasing is either carried out on a long-term and systematic basis, or on an ad hoc basis as a particular need arises. In either case the purchases are either of manufacturing inputs or of what are referred to as maintenance, repair and operations items (MRO), of which the best example is office supplies. One of the most interesting developments of late 1999 and early 2000 has been the way in which companies that have formerly been competitors (such as Ford and Chrysler) have now joined together to create electronic trading exchanges. A possible issue here is whether or not these exchanges are infringing competition law. The borders between the categories are somewhat blurred.

# Standards

The issue of standards to enable partners in a supply chain to exchange structured documents, such as orders, shipping information and invoices, has been one of the major problems in establishing an open electronic commerce environment. The original purpose of the development of highly structured message formats for Electronic Document Interchange (EDI) applications was to facilitate computer-to-computer communication of high volumes of what would originally have been paper documents. Although EDI is used extensively in a number of major manufacturing and transportation sectors, such as the automobile industry, there is now keen interest in seeing if the future for this type of exchange is through XML standards over an extranet.

Extensible Markup Language (XML) is a subset of the ISO Standard Generalized Markup Language, and without going into detail here it provides a platform-independent method of exchanging data between databases. For more detailed information there is a website at **http://www.xml.org/**, and there is also a Microsoft implementation, *BizTalk*, at **http://www.biztalk.org/**. One important initiative is the eCo Interoperability Framework that has been developed by members of *CommerceNet* (**http://www.commercenet.com/**).

The eCo Interoperability Framework consists of two parts: the Architecture Specification and the Semantic Recommendations. These two portions can be used together or independently. The eCo Architecture has a 7-layer structure that enables businesses to describe electronic marketplaces from the highly abstract level of a network of marketplaces down to the level of individual protocols used to exchange business documents. It describes a set of interfaces that must be implemented to communicate at each of those levels. The architecture is extensible at each layer, including the capability to specify or define a set of transaction protocols.

The eCo Semantic recommendations document offers a set of recommendations for creating business documents in the form of Document Type Definitions (DTDs) and DTD Schemas so that those documents will be highly interoperable with other online businesses.

The rate at which XML-based interoperability develops is dependent on the extent to which the eCo and BizTalk proponents themselves start to talk a common language. The only certainty is that XML will be at the heart of any eventual standard, and as such it is important to be familiar with the implementation of XML.

# The information requirements of e-commerce

Any decision to purchase is not taken lightly. There is always a requirement to ensure that all available sources of the product are identified, and that the trade-offs that are inevitable between functionality, price, performance and support are made on an informed and objective basis. Potential suppliers could be based almost anywhere in the world, so reliance on UK directories of suppliers may be misplaced. There may be a requirement to look at relevant standards and regulations, and identify case histories of companies with similar problems. All this information has to be assessed in relation to the needs of the company itself.

The result is that the requirement to be able to integrate internal and external information is now of crucial importance to the business. This was seen as a role for an intranet, but most intranets still have only a very limited input of external information other than in a few information-intensive sectors such as pharmaceuticals. To meet the need for integrated information there is now considerable interest in the development of what are variously called enterprise portals, or vertical portals, the latter term now being contracted to 'vortals'. In the past, the problem was the lack of software tools to provide this integration in a cost-effective way, offering each employee the ability to customize content integration. However, corporate portal applications, sometimes referred to as enterprise information portals, are now emerging. These are software applications that are able to integrate information from a wide range of internal and external resources, delivering the information through a browser-based interface that each employee can customize to suit his or her specific requirements. There are now over 60 vendors in this market, among them companies such as Autonomy, Brio, Hummingbird, Plumtree and Viador. Many of the major diversified IT companies are also entering this market, including IBM, Microsoft and Oracle.

# Regulatory issues

Many regulatory issues still have to be addressed, at both national level and international level. These include the validity of electronic signatures, acceptable encryption and security procedures, and the resolution of the tax implications of e-commerce. The main forum for the debate and resolution of the international issues is the OECD, which organized a major conference in Ottawa in 1998 and a further conference in Paris in late 1999 to see what progress had been made. The overall answer was some, but slowly.

Tax issues are especially difficult to resolve, but given the potential loss of revenues to the countries involved, the need to find solutions is recognized as very urgent. The concept of off-shore banking to reduce tax liabilities is well recognized, but the scale of e-commerce tax revenues will undoubtedly be significantly greater. In the case of Value Added Tax, there are different levels in most of the EU member states. Switzerland has quite a low rate of tax, currently only 6.5% compared with an average of around 15–20% elsewhere in Europe, and depending on how the tax regulations are framed, Switzerland may end up being a tax haven for e-commerce. The global nature of the Internet, and therefore e-commerce, has reduced the ability of individual countries to set tax regimes that are optimized for national economic and political purposes.

The taxation issue is however part of a more significant problem and that is the problem of legal jurisdiction, especially where there is a need to go to court over product liability or failure to conform to a contract. Let us say that a customer in the UK purchases a car from a garage in the Netherlands using a website based in Germany but over a network that is based in the USA. If there is a fault with the car, in which country should the customer take action for redress? The view of the European Commission at present is that the customer should be able to sue in the UK, but this represents a major problem for the owner of the website, and the owner of the garage. The progress of the discussions on juris-diction should be followed closely, as this issue is potentially far more of a threat to the development of electronic commerce than any other.

# In conclusion

This brief article can do no more than point up some of the main trends and issues in the development of e-commerce. The companies that are probably most under threat from e-commerce are the medium-sized companies. The majority of the larger multinational companies have already committed themselves to e-commerce, and have the resources to cope with the challenges and the opportunities. Small companies have less in the way of established legacy systems to adapt or re-engineer to cope with the requirements of e-commerce.

In between these two groups are companies that face very significant problems in changing their own business processes, and those of their suppliers and customers, to take advantage of the reduced transaction costs of e-commerce solutions.

In spite of all the column centimetres now devoted to e-commerce in newspapers, magazines, consulting reports and market surveys, we need to recognize that e-commerce is still in its infancy. There are probably going to be some spectacular failures over the next couple of years, and it is important to learn lessons from both the successes and the failures. It seems likely that fundamental regulatory and legal issues on electronic contracts, data protection, digital signatures, legal jurisdiction and taxation are going to take much longer to solve than interoperability and the design of effective e-commerce websites. As a result it may not be until 2001/2002 that we move beyond the somewhat experimental Phase 1 of e-commerce into a more mature market environment.

# Reference

Kaplan, S and Sawhney, M (2000) E-Hubs – The new B2B Marketplace, *Harvard Business Review*, **78** (3), 97–103.

# Resources

I have been highly selective in the resources I have listed here, mainly because new reports are being published every week, and websites that seemed to be very useful suddenly stop being updated.

# Books and reports

There are now a great many books on e-commerce issues, but an excellent introduction to the issues, with an emphasis on the technology of e-commerce is *The E-business (R)evolution* by Daniel Amor, published by Prentice Hall in 2000. Daniel Amor is a senior consultant on the staff of Hewlett Packard in Germany, and so writes from a European perspective. Although not specifically on e-commerce the issues of managing information are discussed in detail in *Competing with Information*, edited by Donald Marchard, Professor of Information Management and Strategy at the IMD business school in Lausanne, and published in 2000 by John Wiley & Sons Ltd.

# Organizations

In September 1999 the Performance and Innovation Unit of the Cabinet Office published 'e-commerce@its.best.uk' as an introduction to the principles of e-commerce, and the issues that affect the development of e-commerce in the UK. Though now already a little dated it is a good introduction. Copies can be obtained from **http://www.cabinet-office.gov.uk/innovation**, and it is worth getting the CD-ROM version as there are some useful appendices that do not appear in the printed report. The site of the UK Government's e-envoy is **http://www.e-envoy.gov.uk/**.

The OECD has done a great deal to highlight and address the issues of electronic commerce, though the various publications and reports are spread all over the website (**http://www.oecd.org/**) so an adroit use of the search facility is required. The papers from the 1998 Ottawa conference are excellent and there are new papers supporting a conference organized by the OECD in Paris in October 1999.

In the UK, e-centreUK is the trading name of the Association for Standards and Practices in Electronic Trade – EAN UK Ltd, which was launched in 1998 as a result of the merger of the Article Number Association and the Electronic Commerce Association. There is a good list of links on the site (**http://www.e-centre.org.uk/**) to UK, European and international organizations.

The Information Society Programme Office, which is sponsored by the European Commission, has a substantial electronic commerce section on its site (**http://www.ispo.cec.be/**).

## Current awareness

The NUA Internet Survey service (**http://www.nua.ie/**) and *E-commerce Times* (**http://www.ecommercetimes.com/**) are two effective ways of keeping up with developments. The daily e-mail news alert service from *E-commerce Times* is good because it is selective and provides credible analysis on the stories it covers, though there is a US bias to the content. The NUA service provides a weekly update of surveys on Internet market developments, including e-commerce.

# Portal sites

There are a number of sites that try to list every other e-commerce site that there is, but of them all I would recommend *Roger Clarke's Electronic Commerce Pages* (**http://www.anu.edu.au/people/Roger.Clarke/EC/index.html**) where quality takes precedence over quantity. Coming in a close second are both the US and UK *CommerceNet* sites (**http://www.commerce.net/** and **http://www.commercenet.org.uk/** respectively).

The Economist Intelligence Unit launched a new e-business site (**http://www.ebusinessforum.com/**) at the beginning of May 2000, and an initial assessment suggests that this will be an important resource for global information on e-business issues. Unlike other EIU sites there is no subscription charge for this particular site.

The *Netmarketmakers* (**http://www.netmarkettmakers.com/**) site has links to a number of reports from US market research and consulting companies and a few brokers' reports. Overall this is a good starting point for US information.

Another site with a wealth of resources on web marketing and e-commerce issues is that developed by Ralph Wilson (**http://www.wilsonweb.com/**) which claims to have over 1500 links to articles and papers on e-business.

# IT companies

Although many IT companies have e-commerce information on their sites, the two best exponents of the art are IBM and GE Information Services. In particular the IBM Institute for Advanced Commerce (**http://www.ibm.com/iac/about.html**) has some very good white papers on the site, but the main IBM site is also well set out. The GE Information Services site (**http://www.geis.com/**) is almost as good, with some well-prepared white papers.

A comprehensive list of corporate portal companies can be found on the *Intranet Focus* website (**http://www.intranetfocus.com/**) and product descriptions of many of the applications are in the directory section of a corporate portals site developed by Business Intelligence Ltd (**http://www.bi-portals.com/**).

## Management consultancies

The major management consulting practices, notably KMPG (**http://www.kpmg.com/**), Arthur Andersen (**http://www.ac.com/**) and Booz Allen all cover e-commerce issues, with good articles on the subject appearing in the *Strategy and Business* publication from Booz Allen (**http://www.strategy-business.com/**). The reports prepared by these companies often only remain on the site for a relatively short period of time, so it is advisable to check these sites on a regular basis. The Delphi Group is a US-based IT market strategy company which has set up a site specifically for B2B information, and this can be found at **http://www.oneclickb2b.com/**.

## URLs mentioned in this chapter

*Arthur Andersen* **http://www.ac.com/**
*BizTalk* **http://www.biztalk.org/**
*Booz Allen* **http://www.strategy-business.com/**
*Business Intelligence Unit* **http://www.bi-portals.com/**
*Cabinet Office* **http://www.cabinet-office.gov.uk/innovation**
*CommerceNet UK* **http://www.commercenet.org.uk/**
*CommerceNet USA* **http://www.commerce.net/**
*Delphi Group* **http://www.oneclickb2b.com/**
*e-centreUK* **http://www.e-centre.org.uk/**
*E-commerce Times* **http://www.ecommercetimes.com/**

*Economist Intelligence Unit* http://www.ebusinessforum.com/
*Extensible Markup Language* http://www.xml.org/
*GE Information Service* http://www.geis.com
*IBM Institute for Advanced Commerce*
  http://www.ibm.com/iac/about.html
*Information Society Programme Office* http://www.ispo.cec.be/
*Intranet Focus Ltd* http://www.intranetfocus.com/
*KPMG* http://www.kpmg.com/
*Netmarketmakers* http://www.netmarketmakers.com/
*NUA Internet Survey* http://www.nua.ie/
*OECD* http://www.oecd.org/
*Ralph Wilson* http://www.wilsonweb.com/
*Roger Clark's Electronic Commerce Pages*
  http://www.anu.edu.au/people/Roger.Clarke/EC/index.html
*UK Government e-envoy* http://www.e-envoy.gov.uk/

# 9

# Insurance resources

*Jane Heath*

## Introduction

Insurance provides for the transfer of risk – that is to say, it protects a company or an individual against financial loss arising from unexpected or unlikely events. Insurance is frequently linked to risk management, since a company will want to identify and assess risk exposures, and to take measures to prevent costly insurance claims. Similarly, individuals should run their lives so as to avoid claims on their policies (for example, by driving safely). Insurance companies and brokers will advise on risk management, and become involved in initiatives such as driver training and security tracking devices. The insurance policy compensates for financial loss if such events do nevertheless occur. Life insurance is somewhat different in that it provides for an extremely certain event (death). The insured pays a regular premium, which will lead to the payment of a sum of money when the policy matures. This can be on the policyholder's death (thus ensuring financial security for his or her dependents) or at the end of a specified term of years. Life insurance is therefore a vehicle for personal saving, and in fact nearly all life insurance premium income comes from policies which have a savings element.

In the UK the insurance market consists of the domestic market, which arranges insurance for individuals and organizations, and the London market, which supplies insurance and reinsurance for internationally traded risks (such as marine and aviation). The London market consists of Lloyd's and a number of UK and foreign-owned insurance companies. In recent years the structure of the market has changed as a result of consolidation. Several large UK and European insurance companies and insurance brokers have merged, with the result that some well-known names have disappeared, and there are now hardly any quoted insurance brokers in the UK. There have also been 'bancassurance' mergers between banks and insurance companies, creating financial services conglomerates. In the future the insurance environment is likely to change further with new players coming into the market.

Regulation will also affect the rate of change. The responsibility for supervising insurance companies has recently passed from the Department of Trade and Industry to HM Treasury. Some supervisory functions for insurance will be carried out by the new Financial Services Authority. Insurance brokers are regulated at present by the Insurance Brokers Registration Council, but this is due to be abolished and replaced by a self-regulatory body.

In addition, e-commerce is presenting challenges and opportunities for the UK insurance community. Insurance professionals are already highly computer-literate. A survey by the Department of Trade's Information Society Initiative (*Moving into the information age*, 1999) showed that 79% of insurance businesses used PCs with modems, the Internet or external e-mail. This compares with the average of 71% for UK businesses in general. Insurance sites are now appearing in the UK which offer electronic trading. This is most noticeable for personal insurance but it is also beginning for commercial business as well, despite the traditional view that insurance transactions are too complicated for the web (especially because of the legal implications). This may still turn out to be the case, but even if e-commerce does not take off for insurance business as hoped, there will still be great possibilities for development in three areas: the management of information, increased efficiency in gathering and disseminating information, and the simplification of processes and documentation involved in insurance transactions.

Insurance industry professionals need a wide range of information to enable them both to provide a service to their customers and to run a viable business. Typically they want statistics of claims experience, numbers and types of policies sold, information on sources of business, risk exposures for particular industries, and statistics for mortality and morbidity. They also want details of competitor companies and their strategies, products and financial results. As indicated above, these may well not be the traditional players. However, the amount of in-depth information for insurance available on the world wide web, particularly on the free sites, is fairly limited.

The main body for providing statistics for the industry is the Association of British Insurers, and these are available on the website (see below), but only to member insurance companies or to others on payment of a high subscription fee. There are some statistics and reports available elsewhere, but you have to work hard to find them. Official statistics are of course a valuable source for insurance professionals, but again detailed figures are only likely to be available on subscription, and the other problem is that, while you can get figures for motor accidents from this source, it will not tell you the proportion of these events which were insured, or the number of insurance claims arising. Company sites, although those for quoted companies contain financial details, are often dull. They tend to be be little more than online brochures, with an occasional article or report thrown in (although there are some honourable exceptions, eg Swiss Re). There are few links to other useful sites for the user seeking information on insurance. Similarly, some industry associations have informative sites, but others just have a guide to services for members with a press release section.

In all fairness, companies have been making an effort in a constantly changing environment to update their sites, and to add to their difficulties some who were half-way through the process had to go back to square one when they merged with a large company with a site of its own. Given the speed at which developments happen in this area there will undoubtedly be new and revamped sites appearing in great numbers over the next few months.

Another feature is that in insurance as in other areas many of the sites you find have a strong US bias. Figures from the SafeTnet Insurance Guide show that of a total of 8712 insurance websites 6448 (74.01%) were US; the UK, in third place after Canada, had 480 (5.51%). Since insurance is a global business many of these will have some relevance to UK users, but there is a limit to the usefulness of sites which list mainly US companies or US state regulators

# Insurance and risk management – portals and general sites

Below are a few of the major sites (for individual publications such as *Insurance Day*, please see below under Insurance News and Publications).

## *Association of British Insurers* **http://www.abi.org.uk/**

The ABI is the main trade body for the UK industry, and is the main source for statistics on the UK insurance market. It also produces analyses of the industry and consumer leaflets. The free pages contain consumer advice, and an extensive range of statistics and reports on the UK insurance market is obtainable on subscription. Full access is only available to members, as the site contains some confidential information.

### The Chartered Insurance Institute http://www.cii.co.uk/

The main professional institute and examination body for the insurance industry. There are details of courses and qualifications, news about the CII and information about the well-stocked library. Interesting planned developments are the provision of online course texts (training videos can already be obtained) and *CII Library Online*, which will enable users to view and print information from the library database. Other useful features are a glossary of insurance terms and an excellent directory of insurance and insurance-related websites (on the library pages).

### Dataclarity Worldwide Insurance Links Database http://www.dataclarity.co.uk/

This proclaims itself as 'portal to insurance on the Internet' but is essentially an extremely comprehensive directory of links to all types of company and organization involved in insurance world-wide, although there is also an 'added value sites' section, which has links to glossaries, weather sites, legal sites and others.

### Global Reinsurance News Service Network http://www.globalreinsurance.com/

This has news on reinsurance and insurance. The marketplace section includes listings of captives, loss adjusters, consultants and brokers. For companies brief profiles are included as well as an archive of articles.

### Global Risk Management Network http://www.grmn.com/

As well as news, this site provides a databank of special reports, a discussion forum and Swiss insurance company Winterthur's extensive collection of links to insurance and other sites. *International Risk Management* and *The Review* can also be viewed here.

## Insurance Industry Internet Network **http://www.iiin.com/**

A comprehensive directory of links to companies, brokers, law firms and other services world-wide. Listings are alphabetical only – there is no regional listing. Also, as this is a directory of links, companies without a website will not be listed.

## Insurance Services Network **http://www.isn-inc.com/**

Includes information on insurance markets – available and compulsory covers, how the market operates etc – in over 50 countries world-wide.

## Lloyd's **http://www.lloydsoflondon.co.uk/**

This site has very comprehensive information on the Lloyd's insurance market. Information includes directories of Lloyd's brokers, agents and underwriters – underwriters are listed by type of cover as well as alphabetically. Publications include *Lloyd's Global Results*. Also available in *Lloyd's MarketView* are financials for underwriting syndicates and managing agents. *MarketView* is in effect a links page, but is particularly well designed in that it has icons for news, financials, products, people and contacts which link to the relevant pages on the syndicates' websites. Lloyd's has launched a new service on this site called *MotorView,* which is a brief guide to motor cover offered by syndicates – it does not go beyond this at present although Lloyd's describes it as interactive.

## Nottingham University Centre for Risk and Insurance Studies **http://www.nottingham.ac.uk/unbs/cris/**

This contains a limited amount of UK market statistics, together with information on how to obtain their more detailed studies.

### RSX — The International Insurance Portal http://rsx.co.uk/

This site has been set up by Wire Ltd, an insurance systems specialist. It is a directory of insurance-related sites, including brokers, claims managers, country information and information by peril or risk. One useful feature is its 'risk management by industry' section, which gives statistical and other information by industry. The 'property risks' section has extensive lists of sites on weather and climate, as well as natural phenomena such as earthquakes and volcanoes. Much more UK-oriented than some services, but even here some of the sites are American because there is nothing available for other markets.

### Swiss Reinsurance Company http://www.swissre.com/

Swiss Re have an extensive list of research reports on insurance – the Sigma series, which includes a yearly report on insurance markets world-wide, and others. These can all be downloaded free of charge.

## Insurance news and publications

Some of the sites below are electronic versions of publications well known to insurance professionals, while others are services created specifically for the web. Insurance publications are new entrants, many having come on to the web as recently as 1999.

### Business Insurance — Corporate Risk Management, Employee Benefits and Managed Health Care News http://www.businessinsurance.com/

This is an American magazine but covers markets world-wide and is widely read in the UK, particularly for its spotlight reports on market sectors, eg the annual survey of insurance brokers. It contains a searchable archive of the full editoral content of the last two weeks' issues. The full archive from 1994 is available on subscription (discounted for print subscribers). Other services include a web links page, a discussion forum, and a section of articles on IT issues.

## *Financial Regulatory Briefing* http://www.frb.co.uk/

A searchable collection of articles and press releases from a large number of financial sector organizations.

## *ft.com* http://www.ft.com/

You can now view the FT's company news by industry sector, and there is a section for financial services, with insurance news at the bottom. You can also, of course, do a keyword or sector search on insurance in the global archive, and save the search for future use.

## *Info-on-Insurance* http://info-on-insurance.com/info-on-insurance/index.mv

An insurance site with emphasis on Europe. Free registration gives you short summaries of the last three months' insurance stories, by country – very useful if you don't want to be swamped by US stories. It is a little irritating that stories are in forward chronological order, so you have to scroll right down to the bottom to see the latest. There is a database of stories by company. It is hosted by FutureVantage, a consultancy based in Basel, which lists as one of its main activities the provison of insurance and banking information via the Internet.

## *Insurance Age Electronic* http://www.insuranceage.com/

This publication aimed at brokers has current and archive news sections. The market focus section provides a current awareness service on new products. There is also a links directory of insurance companies and organizations.

## Insurance Day http://www.llplimited.com/idahome.shtml

This site is available online on payment of a subscription. There are separate subscriptions for the current editions and the archive, but they can be combined at a discounted price.

## Insurance Newslink http://www.insurancenewslink.com/

Headlines only are presented in the initial result, and you click on the headline to produce a brief abstract. Stories are organized into a wide variety of headlines, thus permitting precision browsing, and you can also search. There is a long archive – in some categories there are stories going back to the early 1990s, which makes this site useful if you want an aide-mémoire of developments in insurance over the last few years. Subscription site.

## Insurance Times http://www.insurancetimes.co.uk/

Online access to this week's and last week's issues of the magazine. The site includes the insurance handbook, which is a find-an-insurer service for special risks. Entries are arranged by category. If you register you can also get daily news on insurance – general, product, technology, people and global news.

## The Miller Insurance Group http://www.millerinsurance.co.uk/

This broker site includes an abstract news service with a daily update and an searchable archive of up to 30 days. Abstracts are categorized by type, country, company and publication.

### Post Online **http://www.postmag.co.uk/**

This has recently become available online, and is free for direct subscribers to the paper copy. Other users have limited access on registration. The site has the current issue together with a searchable archive. Other features are an 'ask the experts' service, a discussion forum and industry links to insurers, brokers, associations and others. Planned services are databases of insurance companies and legal or specialist service providers.

### Professional Broker Online **http://www.broking.co.uk/**

Full access to the current issue and archive is available on registration. This, together with *Reinsurance Online* below, is a sister publication to *Post Magazine*, and some of the information is common to all three sites.

### Reinsurance Online **http://www.re-world.com/**

As with *Post Magazine*, online access is for subscribers to the paper copy (either *Reinsurance* or *Post*).

# Companies and organizations

## Associations

- *Association of British Insurers* at **http://www.abi.org.uk/** (see above).
- *British Insurance Brokers' Association* at **http://www.biiba.org.uk/**
- *Chartered Institute of Loss Adjusters* at **http://www.cila.co.uk/**
- *The Chartered Insurance Institute* at **http://www.cii.co.uk/** (see above).
- *International Underwriting Association* at **http://www.iua.co.uk/** formed by the merger of the London and International Insurance

and Reinsurance Association (LIRMA) and the Institute of London Underwriters (ILU).

➟ *Life Insurance Association* at **http://www.lia.co.uk/**
➟ *Loss Prevention Council* at **http://www.lpc.co.uk/**

# Bookshop

## *Witherbys* **http://www.witherbys.com/**

A specialist insurance bookshop, the site has a full list of publications, organized into categories to allow browsing. Each entry has publication details; some have screen shots of the front cover. There is an online ordering facility (similar to that of Amazon).

# Insurance brokers

These are the sites of the principal insurance brokers operating both in the UK and world-wide. Most of these sites have extensive information about their products, services, people and also financial results where they are required to file publicly available accounts.

➟ *The Aon Corporation* website at **http://www.aon.com/**
➟ *Bradstock Insurance Brokers* at **http://www.bradstockcover.co.uk/**
➟ *British Insurance Brokers' Association* at **http://www.biiba.org.uk/index.html**
➟ *Heath Group PLC* at **http://www.heathgroup.com/**
➟ *Jardine Lloyd Thompson* at **http://www.jltgroup.com/**
➟ *Lambert Fenchurch* at **http://www.lambertfen.com/**
➟ *MMC Marsh & McLennan* at **http://www.marshmac.com/**
➟ *The Miller Insurance Group* at **http://www.millerinsurance.co.uk/** (see also above).

➠ *Willis* at **http://www.williscorroon.com/**

# Insurance companies

Like insurance brokers, companies use their sites primarily to provide information on the company and its products and services:

➠ *Allianz Group* at **http://www.allianz.com/**
➠ *American International Underwriters* at **http://aiu.aig.com/aiu/**
➠ *AXA Group* at **http://www.axa.com/**
➠ *BUPA* at **http://www.bupa.co.uk/**
➠ *CGU PLC* at **http://www.cgugroup.com/**. This site includes extensive information on natural disasters.
➠ *Direct Line* at **http://www.directline.co.uk/** includes brief figures on the motor and home insurance markets.
➠ *FM Global* at **http://www.fmglobal.com/** has useful guidance on risk management for commercial insurance buyers, such as how to construct a disaster plan, and establishing a risk management strategy.
➠ *Friends Provident* at **http://www.friendsprovident.com/** is a life insurance company.
➠ *Gerling* at **http://www.gerling.com/**
➠ *Independent Insurance* at **http://www.independent-insurance.co.uk/**
➠ *Legal and General* at **http://www.landg.com/**
➠ *Norwich Union* at **http://www.norwich-union.co.uk/**
➠ *Prudential Corporation* at **http://www.prudentialcorp.com/**
➠ *Royal and Sun Alliance* at **http://www.royal-and-sunalliance.com/**
➠ *Swiss Re* at **http://www.swissre.com/** (see also above).
➠ *Winterthur* at **http://www.winterthur.com/** and **http://www.winterthur-int.co.uk/** (the UK site includes *WinfoLinks*, a very useful directory of web links).

➠ *Zurich Financial Services* at **http://www.zurich.com/**

# International bodies

## *Comité Européen des Assurances* **http://www.cea.assur.org/**

Representative body for European insurance. Research papers can be ordered online by credit card, and position papers are free.

# Specific topics

## Alternative risk transfer

### *Artemis — The Alternative Risk Transfer Portal* **http://www.artemis.com/**

This site includes news (current and a four-year archive), feature articles on alternative risk transfer, directories of companies and a glossary.

### *Catastrophe Risk Exchange* **http://www.catex.com/**

Electronic trading is now taking place via this site. The public site has background on how the market operates.

### *London International Financial Futures and Options Exchange* **http://www.liffe.com/**

Detailed information on trading and products, statistics, news.

# Captives

## *Bermuda Insurance Market* **http://www.bermuda-insurance.org/**

This site includes a section on captive insurance, which has statistics on the relative sizes of captive domiciles, and also a guide – an explanation of what captives are, how to set one up in Bermuda, and solvency and reporting requirements. There is also a directory of companies.

## *Captive Insurance and Alternative Risk Transfer Resources at captive.com* **http://www.captive.com/**

Directories of captives: single-parent (with names of parents), and group captives (including risk retention groups and pools).

## *Guernsey Financial Services Commission* **http://www.gfsc.guernseyci.com/**

In the insurance section there are questions and answers on setting up an insurance company in Guernsey, statistics and a list of authorized insurers (no links).

## *Industrial Development Agency (IDA) Ireland* **http://www.idaireland.com/**

A general guide to business and investment which, under the financial services section, has details of Dublin's International Financial Services Centre, including listings of captive insurance companies.

# Credit insurance

## *Euler Trade Indemnity* **http://www.tradeindemnity.com/**

Euler Trade Indemnity is an insurance company specializing in credit management. The site has advice and explanations, economic analysis and reviews, and you can also place a debt online.

# Education and training

## *The Chartered Insurance Institute* **http://www.cii.co.uk/**

See above.

## *The Insurance Institute of London* **http://www.iilondon.co.uk/**

The Institute gives its aim as the raising of professional knowledge of insurance professionals working in London, and the provision of assistance to members in their career development. The site has an archive of lecture texts and details of forthcoming events and meetings.

## *Loss Prevention Council* **http://www.lpc.co.uk/**

The leading authority on loss prevention and control, together with its subsidiary organization the Fire Prevention Association. There is a catalogue of courses.

# Insurance law

There are few free sites specific to UK insurance law, but several of the leading law firms specializing in insurance make their publications available online.

### *Cameron McKenna* **http://www.cmck.com/**

The site includes a free electronic information service from Cameron McKenna's publication. Users select topics of interest and can then either browse the chosen topics or search the full archive. They are also sent news on their topics by e-mail.

### *Clifford Chance* **http://www.clifford.chance.com/**

Newsletters and service guides can be viewed.

### *Clyde & Co* **http://www.clydeco.com**

This site has a resource section with articles, bulletins and archives. Unlike the sites above, however, it is not searchable.

### *Kennedys* **http://www.kennedys-law.com/**

Access to the firm's publications is via a section called 'the Law'. One useful subsection is The Woolf Compendium, a fairly detailed guide to the new civil procedure rules.

## Life insurance

### *Cover Magazine* **http://www.cover-mag.co.uk/**

Specialist magazine on life and health insurance for UK advisers. Features include product surveys, directories of providers and information on state benefits (the site's tables of benefits would appear not to be dated, but provide a link to the *Benefits Agency* site, which makes checking the current rates easy).

### Life Insurance Association http://www.lia.co.uk/

Primarily a description of the association and its activities, together with details of membership benefits, and of qualifications, training and continuing professional development.

### LIMRA International http://www.limra.com/

This international membership research organization includes a strong UK membership. There are research updates but these are only available to members. Other information includes details of courses, meetings and publications. There are discussion forums in a registered members' section.

### The UK in Figures http://www.statistics.gov.uk/stats/ukinfigs/pop.htm

A selection of official statistics giving population and vital statistics.

### World Health Organization http://www.who.int/

The basic health indicators section has figures on health, mortality and life expectancy for all WHO member states. There are also more detailed statistics in, for example, the *WHO Cancer Mortality Databank*.

## Rating agencies

### AM Best http://www.ambest.com/ and http://www.bestreview.com/

A well-known insurance research and ratings organization. Insurance company ratings can be obtained, and there is also a glossary, and insurance news (headlines only). There are links to *Best's Review*, where you can see the latest issue and some articles from previous issues.

*Moody's* **http://www.moodys.com/**

*Standard & Poor's* **http://www.standardandpoors.com/ratings/**

> Both these sites, which provide special ratings for insurance companies, display their ratings on their websites free of charge. Each has a guide to their rating systems.

# Regulatory bodies

*Financial Services Authority* **http://www.fsa.gov.uk/**

> The new body set up by the Government to be the single regulatory authority for the financial sector in the UK, the FSA will take over responsibility for insurance companies from HM Treasury. The site describes the FSA's supervision regime in detail, and provides lists of authorized institutions. Consultation papers on the progress towards the new regulatory regime can be downloaded.

*General Insurance Standards Council* **http://www.gisc.co.uk/**

> The GISC is the new independent self-regulatory body for the general insurance industry. The site has details of board membership, an explanation of GISC's purpose and activities, and contact points.

*Insurance Ombudsman* **http://www.theiob.org.uk/**

> As well as offering advice to consumers on how to make a complaint against an insurer, the text of the last three annual reports is given and the quarterly bulletins. Case summaries are published in the bulletin, and there is an index of these.

# Research organizations

## *RIRG* http://www.rirg.com/

> A consultancy specializing in services to corporate insurance buyers. The site is a guide to its services, publications and conferences.

# Risk management

## *Arson Prevention Bureau* http://www.arsonpreventionbureau.org.uk/

> The Bureau was set up in 1991 by the ABI and the Home Office to combat what was seen as a growing problem. As well as information on the Bureau's work there is a wide range of statistics on such topics as the incidence of arson, fatal and non-fatal casualties, large losses, and the types of building targeted.

## *ECS Underwriting* http://www.ecsuw.com/

> The company specializes in environmental risk management. The site includes policy documents, sample claims and exposures, details of covers, questionnaires to enable users to get an idea of what covers they need, and a glossary of environmental terms.

## *Hartford Steam Boiler* http://www.hsb.com/

> Information on risks and issues, including checklists of precautions to take to avoid losses, specific engineering risks, available covers and reading lists of papers on engineering risks.

## *RIMS (Risk and Insurance Management Society, Inc)* http://www.rims.org/

> Includes summaries of articles from *Risk Management Magazine* for the

the last three months, with details of the reprint service, and details of conferences.

## *RiskINFO* **http://www.riskinfo.com/**

Links to commercial sites with information on particular types of risk.

## *RMIS-Web The Risk Management – Insurance Information Systems Website* **http://rmisweb.com/**

Reviews and articles on risk information systems, and also directories of providers of systems and consultants.

# Specialist search engines

## *FinanceWise* **http://www.financewise.com/**

A search engine for financial services. Registration (free) is required, and you then search from a personal home page.

## *FIND* **http://www.find.co.uk/**

The UK financial services directory search engine. There is a category for insurance, and other categories include investments, banking and savings, and information services.

## *Yahoo!Finance* **http://www.finance.yahoo.com/**

Includes insurance, with a daily news service.

# Discussion forums/mailing lists

Generally there are not many forums or mailing lists available in the field of insurance, and those that do exist tend to be centred mainly on the USA.

## *Across the Millennium* **http://www.acrossthemillennium.co.uk/**

A forum for brokers which is backed by the Institute of Insurance Brokers.

## *Global Risk Management Discussion Forum* **http://www.grmn.com/pages/discuss/forum.asp**

Has more entries from European users than other forums listed here.

## *Risk Forums* **http://www.riskforum.com/**

This is within the *RiskINFO* site at **http://www.riskinfo.com/**. It is an interactive conference for insurance and risk management and safety professionals. There is also a mailing list.

## *RISKMail* **http://riskmail.lsu.edu/**

A forum for professionals and researchers in the fields of risk management and insurance.

# References and further reading

Kluwer (looseleaf) *Handbook of insurance*, Kluwer Publishing.
Maynard, Paul (1998) The brokers' challenge, Focus: Zurich Insurance Company (Third Quarter 1999).

Moving into the information age: a sectoral benchmarking study (1999) Department of Trade and Industry, Information Society Initiative, available at

http://www.isi.org/

# URLs mentioned in this chapter

*Across the Millennium* http://www.acrossthemillenium.co.uk/

*Allianz Group* http://www.allianz.com/

*AM Best* http://www.ambest.com/

*AM Best* http://www.bestreview.com/

*American International Underwriters* http://aiu.aig.com/aiu/

*The Aon Corporation* http://www.aon.com/

*Arson Prevention Bureau* http://www.arsonpreventionbureau.org.uk/

*Artemis – The Alternative Risk Transfer Portal* http://www.artemis.com/

*Association of British Insurers* http://www.abi.org.uk/

*AXA Group* http://www.axa.com/

*Bermuda Insurance Market* http://www.bermuda-insurance.org/

*Bradstock Insurance Brokers* http://www.bradstockcover.co.uk/

*British Insurance Brokers' Association* http://www.biiba.org.uk/

*British Insurance Brokers' Association*
   http://www.biiba.org.uk/index.html

*BUPA* http://www.bupa.co.uk./

*Business Insurance – Corporate Risk Management, Employee Benefits and Managed Health Care News* http://www.businessinsurance.com/

*Cameron McKenna* http://www.cmck.com/

*Captive Insurance and Alternative Risk Transfer Resources at captive.com*
   http://www.captive.com/

*Catastrophe Risk Exchange* http://www.catex.com/

*CGU PLC* http://www.cgugroup.com/

*The Chartered Insurance Institute* http://www.cii.co.uk/

*Chartered Institute of Loss Adjusters* http://www.cila.co.uk/

*Clifford Chance* http://www.clifford.chance.com/

*Clyde & Co* http://www.clydeco.com/

*Comité Européen des Assurances* http://www.cea.assur.org/

*Cover Magazine* http://www.cover-mag.co.uk/

*Dataclarity Worldwide Insurance Links Database*
        http://www.dataclarity.co.uk/

*Direct Line* http://www.directline.co.uk/

*ECS Underwriting* http://www.ecsuw.com/

*Euler Trade Indemnity* http://www.tradeindemnity.com/

*FinanceWise* http://www.financewise.com/

*Financial Regulatory Briefing* http://www.frb.co.uk/

*Financial Services Authority* http://www.fsa.gov.uk/

*FIND* http://www.find.co.uk/

*FM Global* http://www.fmglobal.com/

*Friends Provident* http://www.friendsprovident.com/

*ft.com* http://www.ft.com/

*General Insurance Standards Council* http://www.gisc.co.uk/

*Gerling* http://www.gerling.com/

*Global Reinsurance News Service Network*
        http://www.globalreinsurance.com/

*Global Risk Management Discussion Forum*
        http://www.grmn.com/pages/discuss/forum.asp

*Global Risk Management Network* http://www.grmn.com/

*Guernsey Financial Services Commission*
        http://www.gfsc.guernseyci.com/

*Hartford Steam Boiler* http://www.hsb.com/

*Health Group PLC* http://www.heathgroup.com/

*Independent Insurance* http://www.independent-insurance.co.uk/

*Industrial Development Agency (IDA) Ireland*
        http://www.idaireland.com/

*Info-on-Insurance* http://info-on-insurance.com/info-on-insurance/index.mv

*Insurance Age Electronic* http://www.insuranceage.com/

*Insurance Day* http://www.llplimited.com/idahome.shtml

*Insurance Industry Internet Network* http://www.iiin.com/

*The Insurance Institute of London* http://www.iilondon.co.uk/

*Insurance Newslink* http://www.insurancenewslink.com/

*Insurance Ombudsman* http://www.theiob.org.uk/

*Insurance Services Network* http://www.isn-inc.com/

*Insurance Times* http://www.insurancetimes.co.uk/

*Jardine Lloyd Thompson* http://www.jltgroup.com/

*Kennedys* http://www.kennedys-law.com/

*Lambert Fenchurch* http://www.lambertfen.com/

*Legal and General* http://www.landg.com/

*Life Insurance Association* http://www.lia.co.uk/

*LIMRA International* http://www.limra.com/

*Lloyd's* http://www.lloydsoflondon.co.uk/

*London International Financial Futures and Options Exchange*
    http://www.liffe.com/

*Loss Prevention Council* http://www.lpc.co.uk/

*MMC Marsh & McLennan* http://www.marshmac.com/

*The Miller Insurance Group* http://www.millerinsurance.co.uk/

*Moody's* http://www.moodys.com/

*Norwich Union* http://www.norwich-union.co.uk/

*Nottingham University Centre for Risk and Insurance Studies*
    http://www.nottingham.ac.uk/unbs/cris/

*Post Magazine* http://www.postmag.co.uk/

*Professional Broker Online* http://www.broking.co.uk/

*Prudential Corporation* http://www.prudentialcorp.com/

*Reinsurance Online* http://www.re-world.com/

*RIMS (Risk and Insurance Management Society, Inc)*
    http://www.rims.org/

*RIRG* http://www.rirg.com/

*Risk Forums* http://www.riskforum.com/

*RiskINFO* http://www.riskinfo.com/

*RISKMail* http://riskmail.lsu.edu/

*RMIS-Web The Risk Management – Insurance Information Systems Web Site* http://rmisweb.com/

*Royal and Sun Alliance* http://www.royal-and-sunalliance.com/

*RSX – The International Insurance Portal* http://rsx.co.uk/

*Standard & Poor's* http://www.standardandpoors.com/ratings/

*Swiss Re* http://www.swissre.com/

*Swiss Reinsurance Company* http://www.swissre.com/

*The UK in Figures* http://www.statistics.gov.uk/stats/ukinfigs/pop.htm

*Willis* http://www.williscorroon.com/

*Winterthur* http://www.winterthur.com/

*Winterthur* http://www.winterthur-int.co.uk/

*Witherbys* http://www.witherbys.com/

*World Health Organization* http://www.who.int

*Yahoo! Finance* http://www.finance.yahoo.com/

*Zurich Financial Services* http://www.zurich.com/

# 10

# Accountancy resources

## Ben Heald

## Introduction

Accountancy, the term used to describe the profession of an accountant, essentially comprises the control and recording of financial transactions. Many people need the help of an accountant to complete their tax returns and most businesses use accountants to help them control their finances. Particularly in the UK and in other countries where the British influence has been strong (principally the Commonwealth countries), training as an accountant is seen as a general training for business, with accountants not only pursuing their training whilst working for a company, but also going on to work in industry and commerce, often in senior executive positions.

The professional accountancy bodies play a significant role as they control who qualifies as an accountant. There are five main UK bodies:

- the Association of Chartered Certified Accountants (ACCA)
- the Chartered Institute of Management Accountants (CIMA)
- the Chartered Institute of Public Finance and Accountancy (CIPFA)

- the Institute of Chartered Accountants in England & Wales (ICAEW)
- the Institute of Chartered Accountants of Scotland (ICAS).

Without going into the somewhat tortuous detail about why there are five bodies (when just one would be far more convenient for almost everyone who is not an accountant), some background is necessary to understand how these bodies differ.

The ICAEW has the largest number of qualified accountants (116,000), but if you include students in training (and it is important to remember that some students spend a long time trying to become an accountant) then the ACCA is the largest, with a total of 75,000 qualified accountants and 165,000 students world-wide.

Both ACCA and CIMA operate on an international scale, and are growing much faster than the other bodies thanks to the hunger for a professional qualification across the developing world.

ICAS and CIPFA are much smaller, with ICAS focused on Scotland and CIPFA focusing on the public sector.

Finally, it is worth pointing out that there are further bodies that are either smaller or focused exclusively on students.

The accounting sector also includes thousands of people who work in businesses that supply products or services to accountants, people who work in accounting firms and are not trained accountants, plus a large number of clerks and bookkeepers not pursuing a professional qualification. In the UK there are approximately 500,000 people working in the accounting sector.

As with any sector, when describing how accountants use the Internet or what resources are available, one needs to remember that accountants work in a wide variety of organizations and perform an even wider range of roles, from running the accounts of the UK to doing tax returns for the general public.

# How good is the Internet at providing information on accountancy?

For basic background information the Internet has a huge depth of information. All the professional bodies have sites where you can get spadefuls of information. After all, this is the easy part of using the Internet intelligently, viz reproducing standard marketing and background information literature! As with everything on the Net, the problem is that it's not all in one place and you're never sure what else there might be around.

Moving on to more specialized information, such as information on specific issues, articles and other information (that at least we know should be available electronically), the situation becomes more complicated. Much of this information is available in subscription form from various publishers. Whether it is available on the Internet depends on where the publisher is in terms of its Internet strategy. At the time of writing (July 2000) most of these publishers have not yet taken the plunge and made their material available online. There are some exceptions, such as Butterworths, who have begun to make available whole products electronically. Almost without exception, though, the publishers have realized that all their information will soon be delivered over the Internet. There are three significant issues:

1   Will the material be made available on a subscription or a pay-per-view (PPV) basis?
2   Where will it be delivered: just on a publisher's site or more widely via the more frequently visited 'portal' or 'community' sites?
3   How will the information be packaged? For example, using the Internet much more flexibility is possible, so that an alerting news-breaking product can contain hyperlinks to more in-depth information.

The short answer is that the simplest thing to do initially is to make information available by subscription on a publisher's site with no reformatting of information. In the longer term you will find information being delivered from a multiplicity of sites in new user-friendly formats. For example, in time, if you want to ask an accountant a question, it will simply be a case of typing your question on your particular portal (Freeserve, say). This will then (taking advantage of links with an accounting portal such as *AccountingWEB*) issue alerts to accountants either in a particular area or with a particular specialism.  They will respond either by e-mail or by telephone direct to the questioner.

Another example would be news alerting services that are free but contain within them embedded links to paid-for or subscription information.

## Resources that people can use to find out more

In terms of finding out about the subject of accountancy, the best place to start is the sites of the professional bodies. However, there are a number of other important sites in the accounting space that, although focused on accountants, also provide a great depth of information for anyone else looking for information on either accountancy or accountants. So we shall now consider what the Government, the professional bodies, the software houses, the publishers, accountancy firms and new media have to offer.

## The Government

The Government has a clear mandate to disseminate its information more widely and more effectively: the Internet, used correctly, can help them meet both these objectives. The problem is that the Government moves slowly. Although all the relevant organizations have radically improved their sites, they are still essentially static, and rather uninviting, repositories of information.

The sites from the *Inland Revenue* at **http://www.inlandrevenue.gov.uk/** and *Customs & Excise* at **http://www.hmce.gov.uk/** both contain copies of consultation papers, press releases and downloadable forms. The year 2000 promises to be an interesting one as the Inland Revenue has committed itself to being able to accept tax returns over the Net for the 1999/2000 tax year. Taxpayers who both file their tax return and subsequently pay their tax bill online will qualify for a £10 credit. However, agents acting for taxpayers will not be able to file tax returns over the Net until April of 2001. There have been early problems with the system, but this is the start of the drive by the Government to get people to submit their returns via the Internet. The *Business and Accounting Software Development Association (BASDA)* at **http://www.basda.org/** is coordinating some of these new initiatives. The *Treasury* at **http://www.hm-treasury.gov.uk/** also maintains full details of all recent budgets.

*Companies House* at **http://www.companies-house.gov.uk/** is another government body that is radically changing the way it makes its information available. Although a small monthly fee is still charged, users can now download copies of company accounts for as little as £2.50. Companies House has also committed itself to allowing an increasing number of transactions to be completed via the Internet over the next few years.

# Professional bodies

In contrast with the other main professional bodies, the ICAEW has a number of sites: a public site at **http://www.icaew.co.uk/**, a members' site at **http://www.icaewmembers.co.uk/**, sites from its specialized faculties at **http://www.icaewfirms.co.uk/** (owned by Waterlow) and a site from its commercial arm: the *Accounting Business Group (ABG)* at **http://www.abgweb.com/**. This has resulted in a number of online brands that despite being linked can be confusing. The members' site, launched in December 1999, includes free Internet access in conjunction with Breathe. There is also a site that sits alongside the Institute's magazine *Accountancy*, which is to be found at **http://www.accountancymagazine.com/**.

The ACCA launched properly on the web in July 1998, with a site at **http://www.acca.org.uk/** that users could profile based on their location and interests. One of the interesting things they tried was using country-based domain names. For example users entering the site via the *Hong Kong* domain (at **http//www.acca.org.hk/**) see a version of the main ACCA site customized with Hong Kong news and events. The ACCA, together with their rivals CIMA, took the lead in delivering exam results by e-mail to their students around the world in January 1999. This has been a clear strategy for the ACCA – to use the desire of their students to find out their exam results to initiate what is intended to be ongoing electronic communication. The ACCA has recently launched *ACCAdemy* at **http://www.accademy.com/**, which is a partnership with the international tutors BPP to provide online learning possibilities for their huge number of students world-wide. More recently they have also announced an online procurement initiative with Barclays Bank.

*CIMA* at **http://www.cima.org.uk/** were serious about the web even earlier, with a site that included databases of members and exam exemptions in January 1998. In contrast with the ACCA, who dropped their discussion forums during 1999, the CIMA discussion areas are alive and well.

Sites from the other professional bodies are *CIPFA* at **http://www.cipfa.org.uk/** and *ICAS* at **http://www.icas.org.uk/**.

If you are interested in professional bodies in other countries, the best place to start is the *International Federation of Accountants (IFAC)* at **http://www.ifac.org/**.

# Accounting software houses

*Sage* at **http://www.sage.com/** is the dominant vendor of small business software in the UK. In the middle of 1999 it launched a small business portal targeted at the millions of business users globally that use their software. The site included news, weather, stock quotes and business information – all the things one takes for granted from the main portals. At the same time Sage is web-enabling its products, with the result that, as its users become better connected to the web, its client-based products become ever more strongly linked to the Sage business portal. It is interesting that Sage quickly dropped the business portal idea and is now focusing more on allowing its users to develop website solutions through its partnership with IBM. In the USA Sage has recently announced that a web-based version of its entry-level accounting package Peachtree is available for rent over the Internet for $10/month at **http://www.peachtree.com/**.

In February 2000, Pegasus was bought by *Freecom.net* at **http://www.freecom.net/** (a company that floated on AIM in November 1999 and that provides Internet shopping solutions for small businesses). *Freecom.net* has also recently bought *Systems Union* at **http://www.systemsunion.com/** (a leading SunSystems reseller). As with Sage, this combination will focus on selling web-enabled accounting and e-commerce solutions to businesses. In fact *Freecom.net* has recently announced that it will be changing its name to *Systems Union*.

Access Accounting has taken a similar approach with its *AccessWeb* product to be found at **http://www.accessweb.co.uk/**, which is a product designed to get users of Access's accounting software up and running with an e-commerce-enabled website.

*Digita* at **http://www.digita.com/** is another innovative house which is developing a consumer tax portal.

There is insufficient space to cover all the accounting software companies. Virtually all have got sites going, and to differing extents have downloads, demos, client testimonials and support groups online. Many of them have not really grasped the point that the Internet should primarily be used to service their current customers better, rather than achieving anything significant with the millions of people who are never going to find their sites in the first place. Perhaps the most interesting initiative currently is application services provision (ASP), which is the facility for software users to rent access in flexible ways to software over the web. For example, Solution6, one of the leading developers of practice management software for the major accounting and legal firms, is developing web-delivered desktop products that include Microsoft tools. The belief is that users of these products will be able to access this not just where all the software is correctly configured but wherever they have access to the Internet – for example, from home, on a train, in an Internet café or at an airport terminal. The parallel is with a networked office where user profiles are stored centrally, so that users can log on to any machine and work with their e-mail, their favourites etc.

The ICAEW has (in conjunction with Learned Information and AccountingWEB) put together a searchable database of over 12,000 software products. AccountingWEB also has an extensive directory of suppliers to the sector and these can be found at **http://www.accountingweb.co.uk/software** and **http://www.accountingweb.co.uk/suppliers**.

# Publishers

The publishers are perhaps not still in denial mode, but certainly haven't embraced the fact that close to half their audience are now using the web as a regular part of their work. Butterworths have recently launched their *TaxDirect* service at **http://www.butterworths.co.uk/**, which for £1200 a year means you have access to some very deep resources, whilst *Croner CCH* at **http://www.cch.co.uk/** and others have selected products available online. The publishers are struggling with both where to allow their content to be distributed, and whether to distribute it in bite-sized chunks. The Internet industry has clear advice for these people: 'Better to eat your own babies than let someone else do it!'

It's not just the traditional publishers who are struggling to know how to respond. The *Accounting Standards Board* (ASB) at **http://www.asb.org.uk/**, which issues the accounting standards that govern how accounts are prepared in the UK, only provides summaries of the standards on its site – you have to pay if you want to get hold of the full text. This is despite the fact that it is not a commercial operation. This will clearly change in the next couple of years.

For the smaller publishers it's a much simpler decision. The web offers them the opportunity to sell their content through some of the portal or community sites. For example, AccountingWEB are now reselling content from a number of smaller publishers such as Parkes Business Focus who publish background information on individual industries to help accountants understand their clients' businesses. Some other publishers' sites that you might wish to explore are *Thomson Tax* at **http://www.thomtax.co.uk/**, *Gee* at **http://www.gee.co.uk/**, the *International Accounting Standards Committee* at **http://www.iasc.org.uk/** and *Sweet & Maxwell* at **http://www.sweetmaxwell.co.uk/**.

# Accountancy firms

Small and medium-sized accounting firms still have a dilemma. On the one hand, it is difficult not to put a site together if your competitors are. On the other hand, there are few firms who can point to significant benefits, and the challenges of keeping a site up to date and relevant are quite tough, as is the challenge of getting clients to use the sites on a regular basis.

It is estimated that about 20% of the UK's accounting firms have now established a website (this figure is obviously skewed heavily towards the larger firms). The ICAEW publishes it's own online directory of firms at **http://www.icaewfirms.co.uk/**, as does *AccountingWEB* at **http://www.accountingweb.co.uk/accountants**.

There are plenty of individually interesting initiatives. A London firm Ascot Drummond, which specializes in computer contractors, now offers its clients web access to its accounting records at **http://www.ascotdrummond.co.uk/**.

AccountingWEB's *PracticeWeb* service at **http://www.practiceweb.co.uk/** allows its member firms to set up a bespoke site with generic business and tax content, for which they pay a monthly fee.

At the larger end of the spectrum, the sites from the big firms are large repositories of business knowledge: surveys, case studies, graduate recruitment information etc. Examples of these are: *Arthur Andersen* at **http://www.arthurandersen.co.uk/**, *Deloitte & Touche* at **http://www.deloitte.co.uk/**, *Ernst & Young* at **http://www.eyuk.com/**, *KPMG* at **http://www.kpmg.co.uk/** and *PricewaterhouseCoopers* at **http://www.pwcglobal.co.uk/**.

Accountancy professionals working for the larger firms will be getting much of their Internet content through managed intranets. For example, KPMG has set up K World. All the major firms have established these services. It remains to be seen how satisfied their users will be with the content of these 'walled gardens'. On the one hand, KPMG will struggle to make their intranets as good as the major business sites. On the other hand, to the extent that intranet owners restrict access to the wider Internet, business sites will be keen to work with them. It will no doubt become increasingly difficult for any large organization to prevent its staff having access to the Internet – at the very least, staff will expect and demand it.

# New media

The driver of change is the Internet industry. Money is still pouring into the development of Internet infrastructure and technology, and fuelling rapid innovation and development, which has led to the range of new services being offered. It will be fascinating to see what can be delivered when Internet access speeds increase in 2001. For example, professionals will increasingly be able to undertake continuing professional development online.

AccountingWEB is just one example of many new media businesses. In the USA, *Pro2Net* at **http://www.pro2net.com/** is another example of a professional community site.

*AccountingWEB* at **http://www.accountingweb.co.uk/** is a community of over 85,000 accountancy professionals based around a series of regular newswires to alert users to the latest developments in the profession. Users participate in online workshops, software support forums and polls, and have the opportunity to add their comments to any story on the site.

# Finding out more

There are a number of places where you can find out more. The ICAEW maintains an excellent general business links area at http://www.icaew.co.uk/menus/links/links.htm, whilst over 500 tax links are maintained on *AccountingWEB* at http://www.taxzone.co.uk/

# URLs mentioned in this chapter

*ACCA (Hong Kong)* http//www.acca.org.hk

*ACCA (UK)* http://www.acca.org.uk/

*ACCAdemy* http://www.accademy.com/

*AccessWeb* http://www.accessweb.co.uk/

*Accountancy* http://www.accountancymagazine.com/

*Accounting Business Group* (ABG) http://www.abgweb.com/

*Accounting Standards Board* http://www.asb.org.uk/

*AccountingWeb* http://www.accountingweb.co.uk/

*AccountingWeb* http://www.accountingweb.co.uk/accountants

*AccountingWeb* http://www.accountingweb.co.uk/software

*AccountingWeb* http://www.accountingweb.co.uk/suppliers

*AccountingWeb* http://www.taxzone.co.uk/

*Arthur Andersen* http://www.arthurandersen.co.uk/

*Ascot Drummond* http://www.ascotdrummond.co.uk/

*Business and Accounting Software Development Association (BASDA)*
    http://www.basda.org/

*CIMA* http://www.cima.org.uk/

*CIPFA* http://www.cipfa.org.uk/

*Companies House* http://www.companies-house.gov.uk/

*Croner CCH* http://www.cch.co.uk/

*Customs & Excise* http://www.hmce.gov.uk/

*Deloitte & Touche* http://www.deloitte.co.uk/

*Digita* http://www.digita.com/

*Ernst & Young* http://www.eyuk.com/

*Freecom.net* http://www.freecom.net/

*Gee* http://www.gee.co.uk/

*ICAEW* http://www.icaew.co.uk/

*ICAEW* http://www.icaew.co.uk/menus/links/links.htm

*ICAEW* http://www.icaewfirms.co.uk/

*ICAEW* http://www.icaewmembers.co.uk/

*ICAS* http://www.icas.org.uk/

*Inland Revenue* http://www.inlandrevenue.gov.uk/

*International Accounting Standards Committee* http://www.iasc.org.uk/

*International Federation of Accountants (IFAC)* http://www.ifac.org/

*KPMG* http://www.kpmg.co.uk/

*PracticeWeb* http://www.practiceweb.co.uk/

*PriceWaterhouseCoopers* http://www.pwcglobal.co.uk/

*Pro2Net* http://www.pro2net.com/

*Sage* http://www.peachtree.com/

*Sage* http://www.sage.com/

*Sweet & Maxwell* http://www.sweetmaxwell.co.uk/

*Systems Union* http://www.systemsunion.com/

*TaxDirect* http://www.butterworths.co.uk/

*Thomson Tax* http://www.thomtax.co.uk/

*Treasury* http://www.hm-treasury.gov.uk/

# 11

# Patent information

*Stephen Adams*

## Introduction

The patent literature provides many windows into the activities of a technology-based company. A proper grasp of its value will help the commercial or business information searcher in a variety of situations. A few examples are:

- monitoring the research activities of an individual company
- monitoring the research activities of an industry sector
- identifying research collaborations or key workers
- evaluating the geographic spread of a company's markets
- reviewing the intellectual property assets of a takeover or merger target.

The Internet has enabled very large quantities of information about patents, as well as the patent documents themselves, to be made widely available. From the searcher's point of view, the field is a complex one, and it is helpful to have at least a basic idea of the legal processes behind patenting before embarking upon the use of any source of patent data. **Appendix 1** at the end of this chapter provides a short overview of the main points.

The remainder of this chapter considers the range of sources available on the Internet, according to the information which they deliver to the user. The majority of Internet sources are free of charge to the user, but where this is not so, it is noted on the first occasion when the source is referred to. Specific prices are not stated, as these are subject to change without notice. Users considering registration with a commercial source should visit the home page of the supplier for current prices.

Throughout the text, the abbreviations IP and IPR are used to mean 'intellectual property' and 'intellectual property rights' respectively.

# General background sources

A number of helpful Internet sites have developed which provide a basic background to patents and patenting. These provide a more focused alternative to the generalized search engines or classified listings. A typical *Lycos* or *AltaVista* search will yield many thousands of hits on the term 'patent', but specialized patent portals help to circumvent this problem.

One of the longest-established portals is the *IP Mall* based at the Franklin Pearce Law Center (FPLC) in New Hampshire, USA, at **http://www.ipmall.fplc.edu/**. This provides a good selection of links to many other patent-related sites. Being based upon a law school, the coverage of legal materials, especially US law, is very good but other aspects such as information sources are less well done. There is a reasonable selection of simple FAQ documents, but again these represent a US viewpoint for the most part. When considering patent matters, this is particularly unfortunate since the US system is very much the exception to world-wide practice in many areas.

Two more recent additions are *IPMenu* at **http://www.ipmenu.com/** from the Australian law firm of Phillips, Ormonde & Fitzpatrick, which has a very extensive range of information from many countries, and *Mayall's IPLinks* at **http://www.mayallj.freeserve.co.uk/index.htm**, which has good coverage of the information aspects of patents.

It is increasingly being recognized that patent awareness should form part of the researcher's toolkit. The European Commission has created the *IPR Helpdesk* at **http://www.ipr-helpdesk/en/home.html**, which is designed to support its grant-holding researchers. This does not aim to replace detailed legal advice on individual cases, but does provide an excellent gateway into the local patent support organizations in the 15 member states of the EU, together with some good FAQ documents on patents.

Searchers wishing to obtain details on how to obtain a patent in a particular country will often find some information via the website of the appropriate national patent office. At the time of writing, over 60 offices world-wide have some form of site. The pages of the *US Patent and Trademark Office* at **http://www.uspto.gov/**, the *European Patent Office* (EPO) at **http://www.european-patent-office.org/**, the *Japanese Patent Office* (JPO) at **http://www.jpo-miti.go.jp** and the *World Intellectual Property Organization* (WIPO) at **http://www.wipo.org/** all have extensive collections of links to other offices, as do the portals listed above. However, it should be noted that some of these have only limited English-language content, since they are aimed primarily at informing national inventors.

Beyond official patent office pages, the websites of some regional or international organizations also contain information about the intellectual property regime within their locality. This often takes the form of summaries of existing or forthcoming law and procedures within each trading bloc. Examples include the *European Commission's Directorate-General for Enterprise*, which includes parts of the former DG.XV, at **http://wwweuropa.eu.int/comm/dgs/enterprise/index_en.htm**, the *Association of South-East Asian Nations* (ASEAN) at **http://www.asean.or.id/**, the *Commonwealth of Independent States*

(CIS) at, for example, **http://www.infcis.com/**, the Gulf Cooperation Council in the Middle East and the South American bodies *Mercosur* (see, for example, **http://www.mac.doc.gov/ola/mercosur/index.htm** or the Spanish service **http://www.mercosur-news.com.uy/**) and the Andean Community. *The World Trade Organization* (WTO) at **http://www.wto.or/g** has a significant interest in intellectual property rights, notably through the TRIPS Agreement. A further site worth mentioning is that of the *US Trade Representative* at **http://www.ustr.gov/**. This department issues periodical reports under the national US 'Special 301' legislation, monitoring for abuse of intellectual property rights amongst the USA's trading partners. These reports often provide excellent summaries of the current state of IP law around the world.

For a less legal viewpoint, there are several Internet-based periodicals or news areas for the patent professional and for the inventor. Confusingly, there are two sites called *Inventors' World*. The first is an inventor-oriented directory site at **http://www.inventorworld.com/**, whilst the second links to the magazine of the same name, although at the time of writing this appeared to have moved to a new site with a different URL. *Intellectual Property Magazine* at **http://www.ipmag. com/** also provides useful background reading. Recently, the long-established database producer *Derwent Information* at **http://www.derwent.com/** has started to include a 'guest column of the month', which contains views of well-respected patent professionals. This site also includes some FAQ material and access to a variety of surveys and publications in the field of patents.

# Locating help – people and organizations

In the UK it is no longer a legal requirement to employ a qualified patent agent in order to lodge application papers for a patent. However, the process of drafting a patent specification is a complex one, and many inventors still need to locate a local agent to act on their behalf. Registered attorneys belong to the *Chartered Institute of Patent Agents* (CIPA), whose website at **http://www.cipa.org.uk/** contains a searchable membership list. One of the best sources for European information is the searchable list of patent attorneys registered to practice before the *EPO* at **http://www.european-patent-office.org/reps/search.html**. The professional body of this group, the *European Patent Institute* (EPI) also has its own website at **http://www.epipatent.com/**. There is a corresponding list at the USPTO site for registered US attorneys. Some guidance on employing a patent agent can be found at the website of the UK *Institute of Patentees and Inventors* (IPI) at **http://www.invent.org.uk/**. British Government-sponsored websites for inventor support can be found at **http://www.innovation.gov.uk/home.htm** and the *National Endowment for Science, Technology and the Arts* (NESTA) site at **http://www.nesta.org.uk/**.

Some of the portals mentioned in the previous section have partial listings of attorneys, inventor organizations and patent offices; increasingly, the latter will have one or more e-mail addresses for contact and enquiries. The *WIPO* site at **http://www.wipo.int/** contains an excellent directory of the patent office addresses for the 100-odd countries belonging to the Patent Cooperation Treaty (PCT), but few details for non-signatory states. Two very extensive lists of people and organizations can be found at the websites of *J. W. Piper & Co* (a New Zealand-based attorney firm) at **http://www.piperpat.co.nz/index.html** and the South African firm of *Spoor & Fisher* at **http://www.spoor.co.za/**.

At the time of writing, it is quite difficult to identify exhaustive collections of information about patent-related academic or training courses, either from the legal or the information specialist's point of view. The *CIPA* site (see above) offers some information on careers in intellectual property work, including qualification-granting bodies, and the *IP Forum* based at *Manchester Business School* at **http://info.sm.umist.ac.uk/ipc** also contains details, although it is necessary to register for this site. Introductory courses on patent information are run by the *British Library* at **http://www.bl.uk/**. For online users, *Derwent Information* offer instruction on their range of products at **http://www.derwent.com/**, but these courses are usually associated with an online host and it is necessary to be a registered user with them before being able to attend.

# Legal texts

One of the advantages of delivering information in electronic form is the ability to provide rapid updating of complex texts, such as treaties, regulations and other legal documents. Patent practitioners now have available on their desktop a substantial selection of the full texts of relevant legislation.

As would be expected, the national patent office website is often the best place to start for this type of material. Thus the *EPO* site provides direct access to not only the European Patent Convention itself and the associated rules, but some of the case law in the form of the Decisions of the Technical Board of Appeal. All of these documents are freely searchable with extensive hyperlinked texts. In the USA, the corresponding legislation is Title 35 of the United States Code (35 USC), which is available at **http://www4.law.cornell.edu/uscode/35/**. The patent attorney's guidebook, the *Manual of Patent Examining Procedure* (MPEP), is also on the Internet at **http://patents.ame.nd.edu/mpep/mpep.html**.

There are several attempts to provide comprehensive coverage of world-wide legislation. The WIPO is progressively migrating the material which it formerly published on CD-ROM as the IP-LEX product to its website at **http://clea.wipo.int/**. The non-official *Spinoza* project at **http://www.unimaas.nl/~spinoza/iplib.htm** is an ambitious exercise to collect English-language editions of national patent legislative collections. The US attorney firm of *Oppendahl & Larsen* at **http://www.patents.com/** and the Danish firm of *VRN* at **http://www.vagn.dk/patent** also provide extensive links.

There is less in the form of periodical literature in the IPR field than in some other technical areas, presumably because a proportion of the content is in the form of 'house magazines' of the national patent attorney association, and is hence retained on closed access as a member benefit. A few IP periodicals, such *as Intellectual Property Today* appear in a reduced form, such as the most recent few issues at **http://www.lawworks-iptoday.com/**. The *Journal of Information Law & Technology* (*JILT*) at **http://elj.warwick.ac.uk/jilt/** or **http://bubl.ac.uk/journals/lis/com/jilt/** appears in web format. Certain other periodicals, such as the US Bureau of National Affairs publication *Patent, Trademark & Copyright Law Daily*, are available in machine-readable form via commercial databases, but not yet on the Internet.

# Technical monographs

Before discussing the detail of searching national patent collections, it is worth noting that there are a few publications available which perform a role similar to that of the scientific review literature. These may help to short-cut some types of portfolio assessment searches. Many patent offices provide a broad-brush overview of recent national patenting trends as a separate section in their annual reports. These documents are increasingly being made available via the office's website. In addition, both the *United Kingdom Patent Office* at **http://www.patent.gov.uk/** and the *EPO* offer an occasional monograph series. The EPO series is called Applied Technology and published commercially. These are paper-only publications at present, but up-to-date subject listings are available at the websites.

The IFI/Plenum Data Corporation has for many years published an annual Patent Intelligence & Technology Report, analysing granted US patents by assignee, subject matter and a variety of other criteria. This is a priced publication, but contact details can be obtained from the company website at **http://www.ifiplenum.com/**. Subsets of the data have been available on diskette in the past. Similarly, the CHI Research Corporation has created the Tech-line series of databases which attempt to analyse company strength and competitive position as a function of patent-related statistics. These files remain a commercial service, but examples of their work appear on their website at **http://www.chiresearch.com/**, as is the case for visual mapping software of Manning & Napier at **http://www.mnis.net/** and other statistical analysis tools. It must be said that the conclusions and inferences based upon these tools are somewhat controversial amongst patent information professionals, and it is not advised that they be used by anyone who is not familiar with at least the basics of patent procedure and some of the pitfalls of patent statistical method.

# Searching patent documents

The most appropriate Internet sites to use for actual searching of patent documents will vary according to the kind of search required. When patents are being used as sources of information in the context of financial or business intelligence, the most common searches will be:

- for evaluation of the IPR assets of a specific company or group (portfolio search)
- in pursuance of due diligence requirements preceding a merger or acquisition, in order to establish the assets and liabilities relating to

a company's IPR

- to establish an overview of the geographical markets of a particular company or sector.

Each of these search types presents a different challenge in the patents field. In some cases, the nature of the data available through the Internet sources is simply not appropriate for a particular search type, and the searcher is best advised to resort to alternative methods. Sometimes the data are available on the Internet, but the balance of time vs expense makes commercial sources more cost-effective. **Appendix 2** at the end of the chapter discusses some of the aspects of Internet first-level data sources and commercial value-added sources.

Most Internet patent sources, particularly those aimed at end-users, encourage searches based upon text (titles, abstracts) and there is a great deal of pressure from some quarters to add to the free full-text files currently on offer. However, a large proportion of the information content of patents is not in textual form at all, but embodied in graphical representations such as chemical structures, diagrams or images. Consequently, there will always be limitations to the effectiveness of a text-based search system, no matter how well devised the strategy. In order to improve the recall and precision of patent searches, various classification systems have been devised, such as the International Patent Classification (IPC). The schedules of these systems are available on the Internet: the *IPC* is found at **http://classifications.wipo.int/** and the US national classification at the USPTO site.

A portfolio search, particularly if it relates to a small company with a limited market reach, can sometimes be conveniently conducted in the patent files of a single country. A number of national patent offices have started to make available some searchable bibliographic files over the Internet. Most are exclusively in the languages of the country concerned, and cover a small to medium range of years – up to ten is fairly typical. There are established Internet search sites available via the following web pages (mostly national patent offices) for publications from:

- Australia at **http://www.ipaustralia.gov.au/services/S_home.htm**
- Canada at **http://patents1.ic.gc.ca/intro-e.html**
- France at **http://www.inpi.fr/inpi/brevet/html/rechbrev.htm**
- Germany at **http://www.patent-und-markenamt.de/depanet/index.htm**
- Hungary at **http://www.hpo.hu**
- Italy at **http://web.tin.it/fildata/indexen.htm**
- Japan at **http://www.ipdl.jpo-miti.go.jp/homepg_e.ipdl**
- Mexico at **http://www.impi.gob.mx/impi/welcome.pl**
- New Zealand at **http://www.iponz.govt.nz/search/cad/dbssiten.main**
- UK at **http://www.patent.gov.uk/dbservices/index.html**
- USA at **http://www.uspto.gov/patft/index.html**
- WIPO at **http://pctgazette.wipo.int/**.

These are all free sites, and in some cases offer full-text document delivery for any retrieved records. Most only offer so-called gazette data (bibliographic references). A few, such as the US site, offer searchable full texts.

Early Internet sites which loaded more than one patent file were generally handicapped by their inability to perform cluster searches across all files simultaneously. The former *IBM* site, now known as *Delphion*, at **http://www.patents.ibm.com/** provides access to documents from the USA, the EPO, the WIPO's PCT documents and English abstracts of Japanese applications, with more countries being tested and loaded all the time. Recently, it has become possible to search more than one file simultaneously, but there is the deduplication facility. The *Derwent Innovations Index* site (details from http://www.derwent.com/) has merged some of the Patent Citation Index with ISI's *Web of Science* and the value-added fields from the World Patent Index database.

There are now a few websites which offer multifile searching. The *MicroPatent* website at **http://www.micropat.com/** offers a limited amount of free access to recent US material, but the bulk of its offering comprises a suite of four files containing texts of US, EP and PCT documents (coded WO) and English-language abstracts of Japanese documents. These are available on a subscription basis, at a daily or annual rate. The commercial host Questel has a companion Internet product, *QPAT* at **http://www.qpat.com/**, which provides subscription access to full-text US and EP documents, and addition of the WO documents is imminent.

Finally, the largest single source of multiple-country patent document files is *Espacenet*, a cooperative project of the EPO and its 19 member states. *Espacenet* is accessible via the central EPO website (URL) or one of the national servers, each using an interface in the national language(s) of the state concerned. The URL for each national server is in the form **http://xx.espacenet.com/**, in which the 'xx' represents the two-letter country code for the member state concerned; in the case of the UK and Irish servers, these codes are GB and IE respectively.

*Espacenet* is a modular system, offering bibliographic access to the most recent two-year's-worth of EP-A and WO documents (two files), a set of corresponding single country files of national patent documents (for example, in the case of the GB server, two-year's-worth of GB-A documents), a full set of English-language abstracts of Japanese unexamined applications since 1976, and a much larger merged bibliographic file, the so-called world-wide module. A substantial proportion of these documents is available in the form of scanned images, as PDF files. The world-wide module offers genuine multi-country search facilities, in that it contains an English abstract for at least one member of each patent family represented in the database. Fuller details of the country and year coverage can be found at the EPO site.

In addition to the national patent offices and the established database producers, some other private-sector organizations have extended their activities into Internet patent searching. A typical example is the German publishing firm WILA Verlag, which offers its commercial current awareness service *PROFILDienst* at **http://www.wila-verlag.de/** in direct competition to the German Patent Office products. The Dutch company *Univentio* at **http://www.univentio.com/** offers an extensive range of documents for searching, but it is unclear from their website which countries, documents or year ranges are actually covered, which makes it difficult to evaluate this site as a source for commercially significant searches.

A few universities have sought to introduce their students to patents by loading files onto the websites, and have subsequently made them more widely available. The *Technical University of Ilmenau* in Germany at **http://www.patent-inf.tu-ilmenau.de/welcome-eng.html** offers an alternative access to the Patent Abstracts of Japan file, and unique Internet access to Russian patent abstracts in English.

The WIPO is engaged in an extensive project to create WIPONet, which amongst other things will create a network of Internet-based intellectual property digital libraries (IPDLs). The *PCT Gazette* at **http://pctgazette.wipo.int/** is one of the first fruits of this project, and other test files are being worked on at the time of writing.

As noted near the beginning of this chapter, many of the existing portals provide an overview of the legal resources for patents on the Internet, but are less useful in tracking down patent information sources and databases as such. There are partial listings on the FPLC site, the Patent Portal and IPMENU. However, there is a long-established Internet discussion group created by the membership of the *Patent Information Users Group* (PIUG Inc) at **http://www.piug.org/**.

The PIUG, together with the UK-based *PATMG* at
**http://www.luna.co.uk/~patmg/** represent a forum of experienced
patent information users, and their websites are growing in importance
as a reference point for selection of patent information tools. This is an
associated list-server for person-to-person advice.

# Interpreting the results

In addition to providing a new medium for distributing patent
databases, the Internet is also being used to disseminate the support
documentation for many existing commercial sources. Each of the
major online sources for these files has its own website with a
collection of database summary sheets, fact sheets, example searches
and training materials. The three most important are *STN* at
**http://info.cas.org/stn.html**, or **http://www.fiz-karlsruhe.de/** for
European-based users, *Questel-Orbit* at **http://www.questel.orbit.com/**
and DIALOG at **http://www.dialog.com/**. In addition, the websites of
Derwent Information and the EPO provide access to manuals and
support materials for the World Patent Index and INPADOC files
respectively. The latter is perhaps the most useful for users of the
*Espacenet* service, as it provides some level of explanation for many of
the document types which a user will locate via the world-wide
module. The EPO site also contains entry points for several dedicated
e-mail help desks, including one for *Espacenet*.

Beyond these help materials, it is recommended that anyone
searching patent information should familiarize themselves with the
peculiarities of patent-granting procedure of at least the major
industrialized countries. Without this background, it is easy to be
misled into drawing inferences from poorly understood data. The FAQ
sites mentioned previously will be some help. In addition, it is possible
to enlist the aid of professional searchers by posting of specific

questions on specialist list-servers, such as that run by the PIUG/PATMG. Other professional sites include the *Society of Competitive Intelligence Professionals* (SCIP) at **http://www.scip.org/**, some of whose members utilize patent data for company analyses, and the *US Pharmaceutical Education & Research Institute* at **http://www.peri.org/** and the *Association of Information Officers in the Pharmaceutical Industry* (AIOPI) at **http://www.aiopi.org.uk/**, whose members concentrate on aspects of information work in the pharmaceutical sector, including patent analysis.

# Document delivery and translations

The transmission speeds available over the Internet have made it possible to deliver large quantities of patent documents in electronic format. Owing to the variety of languages and scripts used for the originals, the earliest available common electronic formats were scanned image files, which are relatively large. However, more and more documents are becoming available in SGML format, which occupies less space for the same document than a scanned TIFF. The widespread availability of TIFF viewers, and of the Adobe Acrobat PDF viewer software for PDF files, makes it relatively easy to integrate viewing of the full texts with the browser-based searching step.

All of the major patent offices noted in the previous section (UK Patent Office, USPTO, JPO, EPO and the Canadian Intellectual Property Office CIPO) offer electronic delivery of complete documents corresponding to the bibliographic details retrieved by searching on their systems. Charges vary – some are free and the remainder are extremely competitive (rarely more than a few pounds per document, irrespective of length). The IBM site also sells complete texts, as do MicroPatent, Patent Explorer and Univentio.

Established patent supply services who have transformed their operations to include electronic delivery include the Dutch firm IPRO, trading in the UK as *Direct Patent* at **http://www.direct-patent.nl/**, the *British Library's Patent Express service* at **http://www.bl.uk/**, *Services menu, Leeds City Library* at **http://www.leeds.gov.uk/library/services/patents.html** and the USA firms *Optipat* at **http://www.optipat.com/** and *Patentec* at **http://www.patentec.com/**. There are a total of 13 members in the United Kingdom's PIN library network, all of whom are capable of providing at least a paper copy service (on the *BL* site at **http://www.bl.uk/**, search for 'PIN'). The corresponding network in the USA is the *PTDL (Patent and Trademark Depository Library)* system at **http://www.uspto.gov/go/ptdl/**. Some other European countries such as Germany (*PIZNet* at **http://www.patentinformation.de/)** and France (**http://www.inpi.fr/inpi/html/quelqmots/effect/indexbis.htm**) also have established national networks for the dissemination of patent documents.

In many cases, the existence of a patent family may reduce – or eliminate – the need for specially commissioned translations of patents. It is often sufficient to locate an equivalent member of the patent family in English, or at least in a less complex language. However, as was noted above, a large proportion of the patent literature is comprised of Japanese-language applications, and there are frequently no equivalents to these. Therefore, translation of Japanese texts is a critical problem in disseminating patent information. The British Library and Derwent Information both offer a custom translation service, as does the specialist translation bureau *Japanese Language Services* (JLS) at **http://www.jls.co.uk/trans/**. Increasingly, machine translation is being used to derive a rough draft at reduced cost, in order to assess the importance of obtaining a full professional version. *ISTA Inc* in the USA at **http://www.intlscience.com/** are specialists in provision of machine and professional translations from Japanese.

For other languages in Roman scripts, the Internet service from

*AltaVista* known as *Babelfish* at
**http://babelfish.altavista.com/translate.dyn** provides a rapid machine
translation of short texts, such as abstracts of European patents in
French or German. Software packages for PC translation are falling in
price, and can be useful as a first draft to establish relevance.

# After grant – licensing opportunities and legal aspects

The location of a patent bibliographic record, or even the full text of
the corresponding document, may only be part of the process of
establishing patent rights. By analogy with other types of tangible
property, intellectual property assets such as patents can by bought, sold
or leased to other parties. The process of leasing a patent is referred to
as licensing. Some patent holders may wish to have the benefit of an
income from the exploitation of the patent rights, but have insufficient
or inappropriate resources to do it themselves. By publicizing the
patent as being 'available for licence', they hope to conclude an
agreement with a suitable third party, who becomes entitled to use the
patent rights in return for a royalty payment.

Part of the commercial operation of the IBM patent website is the
introduction of their so-called pink dot scheme. This allows a patent
holder to authorize the tagging of the bibliographic record of their
patent(s) with a pink dot whenever these patents are being offered for
licence. The pink dot is a hyperlink to the contact details for the patent
owner.

The process of licensing involves commercially sensitive
information, and it is difficult to locate definitive information about
whether a patent has been licensed at all, much less details of the actual
royalty rates. For this reason, it can be an extremely difficult exercise to
derive commercial data on 'patent worth', such as the revenue stream
which can be attributed to a specific patent or group of patents. For

more details on this aspect of patent information, the website of the *Licensing Executives Society* (LES) at **http://www.les-europe.org/** is a useful starting point. If the parties to the agreement are known, it is possible that their individual company websites, or established news and business information sources like the *Financial Times* at **http://www.ft.com/** and *CNNfn* at **http://www.cnnfn.com/**, may contain texts of press releases pertaining to these agreements.

If a patent has been the subject of litigation, certain aspects can be located from established online sources like the European Patent Register. This service is not currently on the Internet, but is expected to be loaded by the end of the year 2000 on the EPO website as part of the *Espacenet* service. In the UK, the courts service has placed extensive material on its website at **http://www.courtservice.gov.uk/**, and some details of hearings and cases relating to patents in Britain can also be found on the UK Patent Office site.

# URLs mentioned in this chapter

*Association of Information Officers in the Pharmaceutical Industry*
   **http://www.aiopi.org.uk/**
*Association of South-East Asian Nations* **http://www.asean.or.id/**
*Australian Patent Office*
   **http://www.ipaustralia.gov.au/services/S_home.htm**
*Babelfish* **http://babelfish.altavista.com/translate.dyn**
*British Library* **http://www.bl.uk/**
*British Library's Patent Express* **http://www.bl.uk/**
*Canadian Patent Office* **http://patents1.ic.gc.ca/intro-e.html**
*Chartered Institute of Patent Agents* **http://www.cipa.org.uk/**
*CHI Research Corporation* **http://www.chiresearch.com/**
*CNNfn* **http://www.cnnfn.com/**
*Commonwealth of Independent States* **http://www.infcis.com/**

*Cornell Law School* http://www4.law.cornell.edu/uscode/35/
*CourtService* http://www.courtservice.gov.uk/cs_home.htm
*Derwent Information* http://www.derwent.com/
*DIALOG* http://www.dialog.com/
*Direct Patent* http://www.direct-patent.nl/
*EPO* http://www.european-patent-office.org/reps/search.html
*European Commission's Directorate-General for Enterprise*
    http://wwweuropa.eu.int/comm/dgs/enterprise/index_en.htm
*European Patent Institute* http://www.epipatent.com/
*European Patent Office* http://www.european-patent-office.org/
*Financial Times* http://www.ft.com/
*Franklin Pearce Law Center* http://www.ipmall.fplc.edu/
*French Patent Office* http://www.inpi.fr/inpi/brevet/html/rechbrev.htm
*German Patent Office* http://www.patent-und-
    markenamt.de/depanet/index.htm
*Hungarian Patent Office* http://www.hpo.hu/
*IBM* http://www.patents.ibm.com/
*IFI/Plenum Data Corporation* http://www.ifiplenum.com/
*Innovation Unit* http://www.innovation.gov.uk/home.htm
*Institute of Patentees and Inventors* http://www.invent.org.uk/
*Intellectual Property Magazine* http://www.ipmag.com/
*Intellectual Property Today* http://www.lawworks-iptoday.com/
*Inventors' World* http://www.inventorworld.com/
*IPC* http://classifications.wipo.int/
*IPMenu* http://www.ipmenu.com/
*IPR Helpdesk* http://www./ipr-helpdesk/en/home.html
*ISTA Inc* http://www.intlscience.com/
*Italian Patent Office* http://web.tin.it/fildata/indexen.htm
*J W Piper & Co* http://www.piperpat.co.nz/index.html
*Japanese Language Services* http://www.jls.co.uk/trans/
*Japanese Patent Office* http://www.ipdl.jpo-miti.go.jp/homepg_e.ipdl
*Japanese Patent Office* http://www.jpo-miti.go.jp/

*Journal of Information Law & Technology* http://
    bubl.ac.uk/journals/lis/com/jilt/
*Journal of Information Law & Technology* http://elj.warwick.ac.uk/jilt/
*Leeds City Library*
    http://www.leeds.gov.uk/library/services/patents.html
*Licensing Executives Society* http://www.les-europe.org/
*Manchester Business School* http://info.sm.umist.ac.uk/ipc
*Manning & Napier* http://www.mnis.net/
*Manual of Patent Examining Procedure*
    http://patents.ame.nd.edu/mpep/mpep.html
*Mayall's IPLinks* http://www.mayallj.freeserve.co.uk/index.htm
*Mercosur* http://www.mac.doc.gov/ola/mercosur/index.htm
*Mercosur* http://www.mercosur-news.com.uy/
*Mexican Patent Office* http://www.impi.gob.mx/impi/welcome.pl
*MicroPatent* http://www.micropat.com/
*National Endowment for Science, Technology and the Arts*
    http://www.nesta.org.uk/
*New Zealand Patent Office*
    http://www.iponz.govt.nz/search/cad/dbssiten.main
*Oppendahl & Larsen* http://www.patents.com/
*Optipat* http://www.optipat.com/
*Patent and Trademark Depository Library* http://www.uspto.gov/go/ptdl/
*Patent Information Users Group* http://www.piug.org/
*Patentec* http://www.patentec.com/
*PATMG* http://www.luna.co.uk/~patmg/
*PCT Gazette* http://pctgazette.wipo.int/
*PIZNet* http://www.inpi.fr/inpi/html/quelqmots/effect/indexbis.htm
*PIZNet* http://www.patentinformation.de/
*PROFILDienst* http://www.wila-verlag.de
*QPAT* http://www.qpat.com/
*Questel-Orbit* http://www.questel.orbit.com/
*Society of Competitive Intelligence* http://www.scip.org/

*Spinoza* http://www.unimaas.nl/~spinoza/iplib.htm

*Spoor & Fisher* http://www.spoor.co.za/

*STN* http://info.cas.org/stn.html

*STN* http://www.fiz-karlsruhe.de/ (European users)

*Technical University of Ilmenau* http://www.patent-inf.tu-
    ilmenau.de/welcome-eng.html

*United Kingdom Patent Office* http://www.patent.gov.uk/

*United Kingdom Patent Office*
    http://www.patent.gov.uk/dbservices/index.html

*United States Patent and Trademark Office* http://www.uspto.gov/

*United States Patent and Trademark Office*
    http://www.uspto.gov/patft/index.html

*US Pharmaceutical Education & Research Institute* http://www.peri.org/

*US Trade Representative* http://www.ustr.gov/

*Univentio* http://www.univentio.com/

*VRN* http://www.vagn.dk/patent

*WIPO* http://clea.wipo.int/

*WIPO* http://pctgazette.wipo.int/

*WIPO* http://www.wipo.int/

*World Intellectual Property Organization* http://www.wipo.org/

*World Trade Organization* http://www.wto.org/

# Appendix 1  The patent granting process

The vast majority of industrialized countries operate a patent-granting procedure called *deferred examination*. Under this system, the process of obtaining a patent falls into two distinct steps, each associated with a published document, or *specification*.

During the first stage, the application is filed at a patent office for a small – sometimes zero – fee. Provided that the contents comply with certain formal requirements (such as identifying at least one inventor), the application is allotted a national application number. The patent office will then arrange for a search of the literature, in order to identify the most closely related known references. Approximately 18 months after first filing, the search report and the application are published.

At this point, applicants can decide to withdraw from any further processing. Typically, they may do so if the search report indicates that the subject matter is already well known and therefore their application is unlikely to be granted.

If, however, applicants wish to proceed, they pay a further fee to request *substantive examination*. The subject matter is then processed in detail by one or more patent examiners at the patent office, in order to determine absolutely whether the patent application fulfils the criteria for grant, namely that the invention is novel, contains an inventive step and is capable of industrial application. The substantive examination stage can take anything from two years upwards, and its length varies greatly depending upon the complexity of the case.

If, at the end of this process, the patent examiner is persuaded that the applicant is entitled to a patent, the applicant is informed that the application will be granted. The specification is published a second time, incorporating any amendments which may have been imposed during the examination procedure. In most countries, this second document is the granted patent, although a few countries still issue a third-stage grant, in the form of either a certificate or the complete specification.

There is no 'world patent' as such, so if the applicant wishes to obtain patent protection in more than one country, the above processes must be pursued in parallel with the national patent-granting authorities in each state. International patent agreements allow for all these individual national filings to be deemed simultaneous for the purposes of denoting the starting point for processing (the so-called *priority date*). Consequently, several countries may each independently and near-simultaneously publish an 18-month unexamined application relating to the same invention. This cluster of documents forms a *patent family*. The first to publish is the *basic* and all the corresponding documents from other patent offices are termed *equivalents*. As each state proceeds to examine the application, the family is gradually supplemented further by the corresponding granted documents. It is not unknown for companies to claim 'We have 20 patents on technology X' when strictly they are referring to a single invention for which they have applied for a patent in different countries, creating a family of 20 members.

From the information searcher's point of view, it is important to realize that first-stage published documents are *not* granted patents. They confer only very limited legal rights, and many 18-month publications never proceed to substantive examination. Many are withdrawn by the applicant. A further proportion of those cases which do proceed to the second stage are rejected by the patent office and never reach grant. Many of the Internet sources of patent information concentrate on making available the 18-month unexamined applications, for notification purposes. They provide a snapshot of the applicants' intentions and research efforts, but they do not provide any follow-up information on the ultimate fate of these patent applications. It is vital that this further 'legal status' data is collected if searchers – or their customers – are intending to make any commercial decisions based upon the search results.

# Appendix 2  To use the Internet or not?

The vast majority of patent information available on the Internet comprises what is sometimes referred to as *first-level data* – files based upon raw data tapes directly from the source producer. Individual patent offices have for many years been making this sort of machine-readable data available to commercial database producers, such as Derwent Information and IFI/Plenum. These organizations have added value to the first-level data by introducing standards for data formats, vocabulary control on field content, and additional indexing and/or classification. Internet databases which are based purely on first-level data lack these enhancements, making it much more difficult to conduct certain search types in these files.

As was noted in **Appendix 1**, most patent offices operate a deferred examination system, which generates two documents for each granted patent: an early-published unexamined application (typically 18 months after priority date) and a second examined version of the specification. Most Internet files contain *only* the unexamined applications for a specific patent-granting authority, such as the European Patent Office, the UK, Germany or Japan. Consequently, these files are unsuitable for any search which requires the actual (granted) status of the patent. Typically, these enquiries occur when transfer of rights in the intellectual property is being contemplated.

A second consideration relates to subject-matter searching. This field represents a major value-added aspect of the files offered by the commercial database producers. Patents by their very nature are territorial documents, and publish in the official language(s) of the state or authority conferring the rights. A large proportion of the patent literature is thus in a language other than English. In order to search first-level data sources such as Internet files, it frequently becomes necessary to use the appropriate official language. To take a single example, nearly 30% of the entire annual output of *Chemical Abstracts* relates to Japanese patent applications. Without the advantage of specially written English abstracts, first-level data files of this enormous amount of literature would remain effectively unsearchable for the non-Japanese-speaking population. Few Internet sources can offer the benefit of single-language searching across documents of many countries. In addition to this fundamental problem, it should be noted that the abstracts and titles which come with the first-level data files are almost always of a much poorer quality than those prepared by the commercial organizations.

A third aspect of first-level data sources is the lack of control over the contents of searchable data fields. For example, most patent records contain a field for the patent assignee – the organization or individual who owns the patent rights at the time of publication. Professional searchers will readily recognize the hazards of searching large numbers of such records spread over many publication years. Company names change through merger, acquisition, rebranding or simply as a result of spelling errors or natural variation. A first-level data file may record an assignee name as 'IBM' on one document but as 'International Business Machines Inc' on a second one. Obviously this has implications for anyone wishing to create a comprehensive report on IBM's patent portfolio. Value-added database producers make the searcher's job easier by standardizing or controlling such data variation. Commercial online hosts offer index-browsing facilities to examine the variation in term usage. Today's Internet systems generally provide neither facility.

Having noted these negative aspects, it is worth pointing out that Internet sources generally offer one distinct advantage over commercial sources – namely speed of updating. The process of adding value to create a commercial database inevitably takes time, which delays the loading of the data onto the server. Since Internet sources are based upon unmodified first-level data, no such delays are imposed and many producers are able to update their files with new records on the day of publication, or certainly within one or two days. This speed of availability can be more important than any other factor in consulting the patent literature.

# 12

# Information technology and telecommunications

*Ian Tilsed*

## Introduction

It should come as no surprise that the Internet contains extensive resources in the fields of information technology and telecommunications. Ever since the dawn of the world wide web, the IT industry in particular has seized the opportunities the new medium presented for delivering information and services. The telecommunications industry has not been far behind. With increasing levels of convergence between the two industry sectors, it is appropriate that this chapter should address both together. The aim is to present an overview of information technology and telecommunications resources currently available on the Internet. Inevitably, given the extensive growth of these areas, the resources highlighted below represent only a fraction of what is available at the time of writing. The websites and subject areas have been chosen either for their importance or as being representative of the resources in a given area. The metasites and portals listed at the close provide further signposts to the wide range of available resources.

# Internet service providers

Early 1999 witnessed a revolution in the world of internet service providers (ISPs). Freeserve, launched by Dixons in late 1998, threw down the gauntlet to the traditional ISP revenue model by offering 'free' Internet access, meaning no monthly subscription fee and local rate charges for dial-up. Traditionally ISPs had, until then, charged anything between £5 and £20 per month. It was inevitable, then, for other ISPs to feel the pinch and follow suit, and that is exactly what has happened. Some of the well-established ISPs were initially slow to react but British Telecom and LineOne, amongst others, eventually dropped subscription charges.

However, the advent of free Internet access has not been without problems and Oftel, the UK telecommunications watchdog, has issued a consultation document on interconnections and the pricing structures for Internet access – *Oftel – Consultation Paper on the Relationship between Retail Prices and Interconnection Charges for Number Translation Services* at **http://www.oftel.gov.uk/pricing/nts0399.htm**. Oftel has admitted that it has reservations about the current arrangements, partly because it fears that those who use phone lines purely for talking are subsidizing free access. Several pressure groups have also formed in both the UK and Europe to campaign for unmetered charging systems for local phone calls, as is commonplace in the USA, in order to facilitate greater Internet use. CUT, the *Campaign for Unmetered Telecommunications* at **http://www.unmetered.org.uk/**, is the primary UK pressure group, comprising both personal and business members. The CUT website contains extensive resources, including an up-to-date listing of news, responses to statements and government policy, and expositions of the issues. CUT also aligns itself with other European campaigns, further details of which may be found on the *telecom.eu.org.* site at **http://www.telecom.eu.org/uk/index.htm**. There is no doubt that the next few years will continue to witness dramatic changes in the UK and European ISP markets.

Keeping track of all the ISPs, both free and subscription-based, has been made easier through a number of websites. A 'top-level' site is the *Internet Access Providers Meta-List* at **http://www.herbison.com/herbison/iap_meta_list.html**, based in the USA. US-based ISPs are organized by state; the rest of the world by country. Alongside the Meta-List, there is advice on choosing a provider and even information on becoming one. Both *ISP-Planet* at **http://www.isp-planet.com/** and *The List – the Definitive ISP Buyer's Guide* at **http://thelist.internet.com/** are sites that offer comprehensive resources on the ISP community. *ISP-Planet*, describing itself as 'the intelligence center for the ISP community', includes news, features and regular columnists alongside the expected listings. *The List* has fewer of the added features but covers over 8300 providers.

There are several resources that provide invaluable information to those in the UK searching for a free ISP. The websites reflect the nature of this particular industry sector, with quite a few relocations over the last year. However, there are a couple of sites that have remained constant. *Net4Nowt* at **http://www.net4nowt.com/** is one of the more comprehensive resources, offering far more than a simple listing. What is notable, and invaluable in a time of rapid change, is the section on free calls information. Each major ISP or telephone company has an entry, giving up-to-date news on deals that can reduce the cost of Internet access. *Easy as 1-2-Free* at **http://www.12free.co.uk/**, despite its questionable colour scheme and design, has much to offer, with news and reviews. The *FISP List* – Free UK ISP Listing at **http://www.fisplist.co.uk/** is a less featured but nonetheless useful site that offers a listing of free ISPs, alongside the occasional rating provided by a reader. Given the fast pace of change in what is essentially a young industry sector, it is good practice to consult several of these sites, and to check directly with ISPs and telephone companies before committing to a deal.

# Mobile and wireless computing

An observer of IT and telecommunications in the last few years could not have failed to notice the increasing convergence of the two industries, particularly with reference to mobile telephony and the Internet. The proliferation of personal mobile phones, the ever expanding use of personal digital assistants (PDAs) and 'palmtops', and the development of the first protocols for delivery of web pages to mobile phones, all present new and exciting possibilities for the future. Inevitably, in a fast-changing industry sector, provision of up-to-date news is paramount, alongside access to press releases and informed commentary.

The mobile and wireless computing branch of the *WWW Virtual Library* at **http://mosquitonet.stanford.edu/mobile/** is perhaps the best starting point for resources. The section on projects is a particular strength, with an extensive listing, invaluable to any researcher. In the mobile computing arena there are several notable sites that bring together industry information and news on developments. *Mobile Start* at **http://www.mobilestart.com/** is aimed at professionals working with mobile terminals and content, although it also targets reports towards a broader Internet population interested in new mobile services and products. Describing itself as a 'newsportal', it makes reports available in nine categories, including WAP (Wireless Application Protocol), palm computing, phones, ethernet, operators and business information. Each section has both current news and previous stories going back to April 1999. *MobileInfo* at **http://www.mobileinfo.com/**, claiming to be a 'one-stop shop', has a wider remit. Whilst its news service is not as comprehensive as that of *Mobile Start*, there is extensive information on applications, vendors and technical briefings. *Thinkmobile* at **http://www.thinkmobile.com/**, a 'portal for the mobile community', is notable for its considerable *Yahoo!*-style resource index. In addition, news headlines are presented alongside a products and services index, and financial information. Registration is required for full access to all the site resources.

In the realm of wireless computing two sites are worth a mention. *The World of Wireless Communications* at **http://www.wow-com.com/**, produced by the Cellular Telecommunications Industry Association, covers news, law and public policy, technology, statistics and surveys, consumer resources and conferences. It is heavily USA-oriented but nonetheless an important resource. *UnWiredGuru* at **http://www.unwiredguru.com/** offers a different approach to the subject, being essentially a news portal, with the stories (under the banners wireless and WAP) linking directly to the original source online. There is also a discussion forum, for which registration is required.

Perhaps *the* acronym of the moment is WAP – Wireless Application Protocol. Essentially WAP is a simplified version of the Internet protocols for mobile phones, allowing condensed information to be displayed on small handset screens. Currently restricted by the relatively slow speed of data transfer over a mobile phone network, a wide range of services and hardware are increasingly being offered, although proposed improvements to the network will open up the market further. If there is one site that should be bookmarked for information on this fast-developing area, it should be that of the *WAP Forum* at **http://www.wapforum.org/**. To quote:

> the WAP Forum is the industry association comprising more than 200 members that has developed the de-facto world standard for wireless information and telephony services on digital mobile phones and other wireless terminals.

The Forum website includes news, technical specifications (most for immediate download), e-mail lists and event listings.

# Companies and support sites

Until the advent of the web, most people had to rely on manuals, specialist databases and other more traditional media to obtain information on the IT and telecommunications industries and their products or services. Technical support was provided via the telephone, often at a premium rate, via third-party companies and through specialist books. The web changed all that. Now, technical support is often provided via dedicated web pages, offering the latest in software drivers, product information, 'knowledgebases' or frequently asked question (FAQ) files, and discussion forums. Indeed, software is now increasingly sold online too, with secure credit card payment and the delivery of products via download.

Finding websites for IT and telecommunications companies can sometimes be fairly straightforward. Often the name is an integral part of the address – for example, the *Microsoft Corporation* at **http://www.microsoft.com/**. At other times it is less obvious. Two notable resources, however, take the guessing game out of locating manufacturers and service providers. An extensive list of companies in IT as well as telecommunications is provided by Analysys as part of the Telecommunications Virtual Library (*WWW Virtual Library – Manufacturers and Vendors* at **http://www.analysys.com/vlib/manufac.htm**). The *Computer and Communication – Companies* site at **http://www.cmpcmm.com/cc/companies.html** maintains an absolutely colossal list. According to the home page over 9500 links to companies are listed. Fortunately for the visitor, these are delivered in alphabetical sections and a search facility is provided. Also spread throughout the listings are entries for some of the more popular support sites, such as *WinFiles.com* at **http://www.winfiles.com/**, for Microsoft Windows information, and *MacWindows* at **http://www.macwindows.com/**, the site for Macintosh/Windows integration.

*Google*, the search engine at **http://www.google.com/**, has recently
released an Apple-specific search engine (*Google Apple/Macintosh
Search* at **http://www.google.com/mac.html**). This engine indexes
corporate information in addition to product news and, like the main
*Google*, rates the relevance of a page returned as a hit partly by the
number of sites linking to it.

When looking for technical information, begin with a visit to one of
the lists of companies and go direct to that site for the particular product
or service. It is highly likely that sufficient information will be provided
to answer the query. Failing that, turn to the portals that host forums,
where experts field questions and provide advice. Alternatively, e-mail
the company concerned – contact details for technical support are
commonplace now. If, for whatever reason, a search on the Internet is
needed, prepare carefully. Throughout both IT and telecommunications
there are differences between UK and US usage of terms, practice and
acronyms. Think ahead, consider the possibilities and consult glossaries.
Only then should a search be attempted, as a large proportion of the
Internet is about computers and communications!

# Policy, regulation and standards

Both the IT and telecommunications industries are heavily reliant on
technical standards and extensively regulated by government
departments and official bodies. The growth of the Internet has seen a
dramatic increase in standards activity, but it has also witnessed the
development of tensions between the 'open' nature of, for instance, web
development and the need for strict standards to enable interoperability.
Many bodies, both professional and governmental, contribute to the
development of policies and standards and it would be impossible to
include them all here. The standards section of the *Computer and
Communication* metasite at

http://www.cmpcmm.com/cc/standards.html is one of the best
attempts at providing a comprehensive listing and would be a good
starting point. The (long) page includes 134 entries, each with many
subcategories, and it is heavily cross-referenced.

Governmental bodies include *Oftel* at http://www.oftel.gov.uk/, the
'watchdog' for the UK telecommunications industry, a government
department that is independent of ministerial control. Despite the poor
presentation of the site, there is a wealth of information, covering Oftel
press releases and publications, industry guidelines, and numbering
information, aimed at both consumers and service providers. BABT
(the British Approvals Board for Telecommunications) acts as the
approvals authority for telecommunications terminal equipment in the
UK and provides many other technical and approval services both in
Europe and beyond. The *BABT* website at http://www.babt.co.uk/
includes details of services and news, but the information services
section is the most useful, allowing the download of technical
information sheets, regulations and much more.

In the USA several bodies contribute to the regulation of the
telecommunications industry. The Federal Communications
Commission, an independent government agency, is charged with
regulating interstate and international communications by radio,
television, wire, satellite and cable. The *FCC* website at
http://www.fcc.gov/ has extensive resources, again for both the public
and companies. The National Telecommunications and Information
Administration (NTIA at http://www.ntia.doc.gov/), an agency of the
US Department of Commerce, contributes to domestic and
international telecommunications and information technology issues.
The NTIA works to 'spur innovation, encourage competition, help
create jobs and provide consumers with more choices and better quality
telecommunications products and services at lower prices'.

Internationally, the International Organization for Standardization
(*ISO* at http://www.iso.ch/) is a world-wide federation of national

standards bodies from some 130 countries. Its work in developing cooperation leads to international agreements, which are published as international standards. Many of these apply to the IT and telecommunications industries. As would be expected from the ISO, its site is comprehensive and well presented.

The International Telecommunication Union, based in Geneva, is an international organization through which governments and the private sector coordinate global telecom networks and services. It is also a leading publisher of telecommunications technology, regulatory and standards information. Different ITU 'sectors' deal with radio communication, standardization and development. Each sector has its own section of the *ITU* website at **http://www.itu.int/** detailing publications, working groups, projects, databases and membership. Elsewhere on the site access is provided both to the publications catalogue and to the various ITU databases.

The International Institute for Communication and Development approaches the topic of telecommunications arena from a different starting point, namely 'for gathering information on issues with information and communication technology (ICT) and sustainable development relevance'. Originally established in 1997, its remit is to assist key players in developing countries to obtain access to ICTs, to become involved in decision-making processes, to consider the impact on traditional cultures, and to foster sustainable development. The well-presented website (**http://www.iicd.org/**) includes details of projects and provides an electronic journal and a 'meeting place' section with a contacts list and interactive noticeboard.

No mention of standards would be complete without a mention of the bodies responsible for overseeing the development of the Internet. Several bodies work together to coordinate the development of technical, policy and social aspects of the Internet. The *IETF – Internet Engineering Task Force* at **http://www.ietf.cnri.reston.va.us/** is a large, open international community concerned with the evolution and operation of the Internet. The IETF working groups contribute to technical development, which is overseen by the Internet Architecture Board (IAB). The IAB in turn publishes RFCs (requests for comments), the official document series, and Internet drafts, which are quite often, but not necessarily, precursors to RFCs. The websites of these bodies are typically functional in style, but contain vast amounts of information. Those wishing to look up RFCs, however, would do well to avoid the IETF search page (unless the RFC number is known) and head to the *RFC Editor* site at **http://www.rfc-editor.org/**, which allows searching by keywords, authors etc.

The Internet Society is a non-profit, non-governmental, international organization that focuses on standards, education and policy issues. The *Internet Society (ISOC)* website at **http://www.isoc.org/** includes details of projects and publications, as well as an excellent collection of links to sites on the history of the Internet. Perhaps one of the more well-known bodies, at least to the public, is the World Wide Web Consortium (W3C), whose extensive and comprehensive site (*W3C – World Wide Web Consortium* at **http://www.w3c.org/**) is the authoritative source for all information regarding the web and its development. As to be expected, recommendations, guidelines, details on projects, and research, together with its public mailing lists, are delivered in an accessible style.

# Professional organizations

Professional organizations, whether they be professional bodies, associations or special-interest groups, can be difficult to find on the Internet. Searchers must, for instance, remember the British and American spellings of organization, and also find a way through the jungle of acronyms (do you want to find the IEE or the IEEE?). Website names are not always obvious either – the Computer Society of the

IEEE (*IEEE Computer Society* at **http://www.computer.org/**) being an appropriate example. Rather than trying to list all known associations, it is best to commence a search by consulting one of the lists. Most of the metasites and portals (of which there will be more below) include sections on professional organizations, but they differ in quality, coverage and ease of use. Perhaps one of the most thorough listings is to be found on *Computer and Communication – Organizations* at **http://www.cmpcmm.com/cc/orgs.html**. Over 400 organizations are recorded in a long alphabetical listing, each entry including both a link and a short description. Whilst US resources feature heavily, there is excellent coverage of European and world-wide sites. Another, albeit less comprehensive, list is to be found on the *WWW Virtual Library – Associations* at **http://www.analysys.com/vlib/assoc.htm**. This has a more European view, but some entries lack descriptions.

The use of portals such as *Yahoo!*, *Excite* and *Galaxy* to find appropriate listings is a little more difficult. For example, *Yahoo!* lists telecommunications and IT in several different areas of its directory. To give an example, telecommunications listings are found under computers and the Internet at **http://dir.yahoo.com/Computers_and_Internet/Communications_ and_Networking/Organizations/Professional/**, electrical engineering at **http://dir.yahoo.com/Science/Engineering/Electrical_Engineering/ Telecommunications/Organizations/** and business and the economy at **http://dir.yahoo.com/Business_and_Economy/Companies/Computers/ Industry_Information/Professional_Organizations/**. A similar situation is true of computing at **http://dir.yahoo.com/Science/Computer_Science/Organizations/ Professional/**. This is not to say that consulting such directories is a waste of time – far from it. However, patience is needed to tease out the information. Start with the dedicated 'one location' listings and use the general portals to supplement these where necessary.

# Online publications

It was inevitable that publications such as learned journals and magazines would seize the opportunities that the web offered in terms of delivery and 'added value'. Not surprisingly, the computing press was one of the first to deliver content on associated websites, thereby enabling direct linking to resources, reviews and vendor sites. It would not be appropriate, or even possible, to list all the known 'online' computing and telecommunications publications, not least because of the speed at which sites appear and disappear! However, a good place to start exploring the web content of many well-known and more popular computing titles is the listing provided by Microsoft (*Microsoft – Computer Magazine WWW Homepages* at **http://library.microsoft.com/compmags.htm**). The document is plain and simple but effective – a straightforward list of titles beside which the associated website addresses are given. There is no comment, no evaluation – just a list. A similar approach, albeit with the addition of some basic sorting, is the list of journals and magazines at the Virtual Computer Library (*Virtual Computer Library – Journals/Magazines* at **http://www.utexas.edu/computer/vcl/journals.html**). Entries are divided into three categories – article abstracts only, full-text articles and indexes. Again there is no attempt to offer any evaluation or comment.

*ZDNet* at **http://www.zdnet.com/** is worth mentioning, as it is the top-level domain for the *Ziff Davis* site, known for its PC and Internet information, and a portal site for a wide range of computing information. Many of the entries in the two lists above will point to an area of *ZDNet*, as it publishes 14 titles, including *Computer Shopper, PC Magazine, Macworld* and *Yahoo! Internet Life*. It is worth noting that the content of some of the sites differs from what may be published in UK hardcopy editions.

*Data Communications* at **http://www.data.com/** is a publication of

CMP's TechWeb. As indicated by the title, it is aimed at a specific industry sector. The site offers news, test lab reports, reviews and contents of back issues. It also links through to the site of *Network Magazine*, which incorporates *Data Communications*. The multimedia potential of the web is put to good use by *HotWired* at **http://hotwired.lycos.com/**, described as the 'journal of record of the future'. The website offers contents listings of both the current and back issues, with most of the features and columns of back issues provided in full text.

# Dictionaries and glossaries

The information technology and telecommunications industries are well known for their seemingly impenetrable 'languages'. Both areas, with good reason, use extensive lists of acronyms to communicate technical terms, as well as having their own terminologies. Whilst this increases the efficacy of communication between the IT and telecommunications professionals, it does mean that those from other disciplines, and those new to the subject, find information inaccessible or just plain bewildering. Increased emphasis on communications skills in recruitment in the industries will help 'break down' the communications barriers, but help is also at hand on the Internet through the provision of dictionaries, glossaries and encyclopedias.

One of the original glossaries to be published on the Internet is known as *BABEL* – the glossary of computer-oriented abbreviations and acronyms. First published in the late eighties, *BABEL* at **http://www.geocities.com/ikind_babel/babel/babel.html** is presented as an extensive text listing by Irving and Richard Kind. Updated three times a year in January, May and September, it is available for download, subject to conditions. Staying with computer terminology, *FOLDOC – Free On-line Dictionary of Computing* at

**http://foldoc.doc.ic.ac.uk/foldoc/index.html**, edited by Denis Howe, is a commendable UK-based searchable dictionary, with several international mirrors. Started in 1985, it now contains around 13,000 definitions covering 'acronyms, jargon, programming languages, tools, architecture, operating systems, networking, theory, conventions, standards, mathematics, telecoms, electronics, institutions, companies, projects, products, history, in fact anything to do with computing'. It is extensively cross-referenced and contains the occasional bibliographic entry too. TechWeb's *TechEncyclopedia* at **http://www.techweb.com/encyclopedia/** offers a searchable database of over 13,000 computer terms and concepts. More commercial in design than *FOLDOC*, it offers cross-references and lists the entries before and after the query term in its alphabetical listing. A curious 'feature' also allows a user to call up a random definition! A smaller, but popular, site is *whatis.com* at **http://whatis.com/**, a knowledge exploration tool about information technology, particularly about the Internet and computers. It contains over 2000 individual encyclopedic definition/topics and a number of quick-reference pages.

Perhaps the best-known dictionary site is *Webopedia* at **http://www.webopedia.com/**, produced by internet.com. One of its strengths is the facility for searching subsections of the overall database, with categories including communications, companies, graphics, hardware, internet, mobile computing, multimedia, software and standards. In addition, entries include not only definitions, but also cross-references and links to other websites such as FAQ files. This latter component makes this resource stand out from the crowd. Another comprehensive site is the *Sun Global Glossary* at **http://www.sun.com/glossary/glossary.html**, which lists over 2000 English-language terms and definitions for Sun software, hardware and terminology.

In the telecommunications arena the *MCI WorldCom Communications Library* at **http://www.wcom.com/tools-**

resources/communications_library/ is perhaps the most extensive glossary, claiming to be 'the definitive source of information on terms and issues related to the technology and business of telecommunications'. What is notable about this site is the inclusion of some company information. Querying is possible by either a search box or a browse index. The USA telecommunications industry has its own Federal Standard (1037C) for telecommunications terms. A revision to the 1996 standard is currently being developed, but use of the 1037C standard by all Federal departments and agencies is mandatory, and the website (*Federal Standard 1037C – Glossary of Telecommunications Terms* at **http://www.its.bldrdoc.gov/fs-1037/fs-1037c.htm**) provides a comprehensive glossary for those outside the USA. Visitors to the site are advised to select the search engine link from the home page, for ease of use.

# Metasites and portals

A good place to start looking for online resources in any subject is a metasite or subject directory listing. Unlike search engine databases, these are compiled by humans, offering the added advantage of commentary and selection. However, the latter point also leads to a warning: entries are included in directories because they have come to the attention of a person compiling the site and have been judged to be appropriate for inclusion in terms of content and quality. The absence of a site in a listing may simply indicate that it has not met certain criteria or that it is not known to the compiler.

Perhaps the best-known and oldest subject directory is the WWW Virtual Library. First created by Tim Berners-Lee back in 1994, it is run by a loose confederation of volunteers, who compile pages of key links for particular areas in which they are expert. It is not necessarily the biggest index of the web and some subjects are better covered elsewhere, but the site is known for its quality. The telecommunications area of the Virtual Library is *WWW Virtual Library – Telecommunications* at **http://www.analysys.com/vlib/**, hosted and compiled by Analysys Ltd, and is one of the best metasites. It has about 30 main categories, ranging from associations to videoconferencing, and also includes links to related virtual libraries (such as electrical engineering and networking). Each entry carries both a hyperlink and a one-line description. There is no attempt to rank the sites – they are simply listed in alphabetical order. Highlights of the site (many of which have already been mentioned) include the lists of manufacturers, associations and regulators. Despite the telecommunications tag, this site has much to offer those interested in IT, not least because of the increasing convergence between the two areas. There is, for instance, a section on software services, and computer companies feature heavily in the manufacturers section.

The corresponding *WWW Virtual Library – Computing* at **http://src.doc.ic.ac.uk/bySubject/Computing/Overview.html** is not as impressive, whether in terms of content or presentation. Delivered as one continuous document, it is awkward to use. Nonetheless, it is worth consulting, especially for the section on university computer science departments (the only section to be given its own page). Those searching for more general IT information would be well advised to follow the computer science link on the *WWW Virtual Library* home page at **http://www.vlib.org/** – this leads to a more general subject area, including links to virtual libraries for networking information and mobile computing, as well as the *Virtual Computer Library* at **http://www.utexas.edu/computer/vcl/**, based at the University of Texas at Austin. This is one of the better metasites for computers. Whilst not as complete or well presented as the Analysys site, it contains a useful collection of resources in such areas as academic computing, conferences and user groups. The computer and communication site (*Computer and Communication* at **http://www.cmpcmm.com/**) is an excellent and seemingly comprehensive subject directory of resources in both IT and telecommunications. The presence of several of its sections elsewhere in this chapter is indicative of the extent and quality of this site. Described as a 'one-stop shop [for] information about the developing global information infrastructure – currently represented by the Internet', the site has been in existence since 1993 and is well maintained, with extensive cross-referencing. One of the strengths of this site is the coverage of both computers and communications in one resource. An alternative, but less well-designed, telecommunications site is that entitled *{Tele}Communications Information Sources* at **http://www.vtcif.telstra.com.au/info/communications.html**. With sections on companies, service providers, authorities and events, all the information is regrettably delivered in one extremely long document, making navigation problematic. It does, however, seem to be well maintained. *Yahoo!* is also an extensive resources, with information in many subject branches.

Alongside subject directories there are portals, which are websites designed to be places where people start their daily web explorations – sites that become browser 'home pages'. A portal is a site so designed that it offers everything to everyone, demands attention and, as one commentator has remarked, 'never lets you go'. Subject-specific portals, aimed at industry professionals and other interested parties, have followed those of the first generation aimed primarily at general audiences. In the IT and telecommunications world there are many to choose from. Many require prior registration and offer news feeds and newsletters, along with personalized 'entry pages'. An example is *The IT Portal* at **http://www.theitportal.com/** – a UK-based venture that describes itself as 'page ONE of the web for IT professionals'.' The site provides over 2000 documents, covering news, commentary, features, online polls, FAQ files, discussion groups, career links and many other resources. It is a fairly 'young' site, but one that promises much for the UK IT industry. *Computing Central* at http://www.computingcentral.com/, a service of MSN, is another portal with more emphasis on technical information. To quote the site:

> Computing Central is an information marketplace for people who use computers at work and home. Through a range of activities and resources, Computing Central serves people who want to stay current on computing news and products, solve technical problems, share or develop ideas and expertise, and meet other people.

The site utilizes interactive chats and newsgroups, multimedia, news, and shareware and shopping to provide visitors with everything and anything to do with computers. At the heart of the site are the forum managers – experts in the topics they cover online as well as expert community builders. The site is heavily USA-oriented, meaning that live chat forums may be inaccessible owing to time differences, but the rest of the site still has much to offer.

Two other portals typical of the genre are *CNET* and *ZDNet*. Both are similar in style and objective, providing a 'one-stop shop' for technology and computing information. News, resource directories, links to online publications, discussion forums, newsletters and software are all typical. *CNET* at http://www.cnet.com/ is best known for its software download site, while *ZDNet* at http://www.zdnet.com/ links to the online content of its 14 hardcopy titles. Mix and match your portals carefully and a wealth of information may be accessed.

# Conclusion

As is to be expected of the information technology and telecommunications industries, the Internet is a substantial and ever-growing information resource, available for consultation, searching and developing. In this chapter an attempt has been made to introduce some of that resource. Given the breadth and depth of both subject areas it has not been possible to give selections from all possible subcategories. Indeed, what has been covered is merely the tip of an iceberg. For instance, there has been no mention of the developing area of teleworking (see, for example, **http://www.homeworking.com/**), no coverage of legal and financial resources, and no mention of continuing professional development and jobs (see, for example, **http://www.jobserve.com/**). That is not to say that they have been forgotten. Each of the metasites introduced above has sections devoted to these (and many more) subject areas. Remember that both industries are fast developing, and converging, so explore the subject directories of the metasites at will – and keep revisiting.

# URLs mentioned in this chapter

*BABEL* **http://www.geocities.com/ikind_babel/babel/babel.html**
*BABT* **http://www.babt.co.uk/**
*Campaign for Unmetered Telecommunications*
   **http://www.unmetered.org.uk/**
*CNET* **http://www.cnet.com/**
*Computer and Communication – Companies*
   **http://www.cmpcmm.com/cc/companies.html**
*Computer and Communication – Organizations*
   **http://www.cmpcmm.com/cc/orgs.html**
*Computer and Communication* **http://www.cmpcmm.com/**
*Computer and Communication*
   **http://www.cmpcmm.com/cc/standards.html**
*Computing Central* **http://www.computingcentral.com/**
*Data Communications* **http://www.data.com/**
*Easy as 1-2-Free* **http://www.12free.co.uk/**
*FCC* **http://www.fcc.gov/**

*Federal Standard 1037C – Glossary of Telecommunications Terms*
   http://www.its.bldrdoc.gov/fs-1037/fs-1037c.htm
*FISP List* http://www.fisplist.co.uk/
*FOLDOC* http://foldoc.doc.ic.ac.uk/foldoc/index.html
*Google Apple/Macintosh Search* http://www.google.com/mac.html
*Google* http://www.google.com/
*HotWired* http://hotwired.lycos.com/
*IEEE Computer Society* http://www.computer.org/
*IETF – Internet Engineering Task Force*
   http://www.ietf.cnri.reston.va.us/
*International Institute for Communication and Development*
   http://www.iicd.org/
*International Organization for Standardization* http://www.iso.ch/
*International Telecommunications Union* http://www.itu.int/
*Internet Access Providers Meta-List*
   http://www.herbison.com/herbison/iap_meta_list.html
*Internet Society* http://www.isoc.org/
*ISP-Planet* http://www.isp-planet.com/
*The IT Portal* http://www.theitportal.com/
*The List – The Definitive ISP Buyer's Guide* http://thelist.internet.com/
*MacWindows* http://www.macwindows.com/
*MCI WorldCom Communications Library* http://www.wcom.com/tools-
   resources/communications_library/
*Microsoft Computer Magazine WWW Homepages*
   http://library.microsoft.com/compmags.htm
*Microsoft Corporation* http://www.microsoft.com/
*Mobile Start* http://www.mobilestart.com/
*MobileInfo* http://www.mobileinfo.com/
*National Telecommunications and Information Administration*
   http://www.ntia.doc.gov/
*Net4Nowt* http://www.net4nowt.com/
*Oftel* http://www.oftel.gov.uk/

*Oftel* http://www.oftel.gov.uk/pricing/nts0399.htm
*RFC Editor* http://www.rfc-editor.org/
*Sun Global Glossary* http://www.sun.com/glossary/glossary.html
*TechEncyclopedia* http://www.techweb.com/encyclopedia/
*{Tele}Communications Information Sources*
   http://www.vtcif.telstra.com.au/info/communications.html
*telecom.eu.org* http://www.telecom.eu.org/uk/index.htm
*Thinkmobile* http://www.thinkmobile.com/
*UnWiredGuru* http://www.unwiredguru.com/
*Virtual Computer Library* http://www.utexas.edu/computer/vcl/
*Virtual Computer Library*
   http://www.utexas.edu/computer/vcl/journals.html
*W3C – World Wide Web Consortium* http://www.w3c.org/
*WAP Forum* http://www.wapforum.org/
*Webopedia* http://www.webopedia.com/
*whatis.com* http://whatis.com/
*WinFiles.com* http://www.winfiles.com/
*The World of Wireless Communications* http://www.wow-com.com/
*WWW Virtual Library – Manufacturers and Vendors*
   http://www.analysys.com/vlib/manufac.htm
*WWW Virtual Library – Telecommunications*
   http://www.analysys.com/vlib/
*WWW Virtual Library* http://mosquitonet.stanford.edu/mobile/
*WWW Virtual Library* http://www.analysys.com/vlib/assoc.htm
*Yahoo!*
   http://dir.yahoo.com/Business_and_Economy/Companies/Comp
   uters/Industry_Information/Professional_Organizations/
*Yahoo!* http://dir.yahoo.com/computers/index.html
*Yahoo!*
   http://dir.yahoo.com/Computers_and_Internet/Communications
   _and_Networking/Organizations/Professional/

*Yahoo!*

http://dir.yahoo.com/Science/Computer_Science/Organizations/
Professional/

*Yahoo!*

http://dir.yahoo.com/Science/Engineering/Electrical_Engineering
/Telecommunications/

*Yahoo!*

http://dir.yahoo.com/Science/Engineering/Electrical_Engineering
/Telecommunications/Organizations/

*ZDNet* http://www.zdnet.com/

# 13

# The food industry

*Dr Iain Swadling*

## Introduction

The Internet provides an invaluable global source of information, as well as a state-of-the-art communications medium for academia, governments, and professionals working in the food industry. The number and variety of food-related websites is rapidly expanding as the potential of the world wide web is being more fully realized. However, one of the biggest drawbacks commonly cited about the web is that it is disorganized and difficult to navigate. The quality of the information available on the different sites varies tremendously and selecting useful ones often proves to be time-consuming and difficult, not to mention frustrating. This need not be the case, and often accessing useful, informative websites can prove to be very rewarding.

The Internet is mainly used for providing information (87%) and communication (67%). The leading countries in Europe for Internet usage are Scandinavian countries, the UK and Germany, with the UK's largest food retailer, Tesco, being ranked number two in the top corporate websites in Europe. Currently, one in three companies in Germany use the Internet, and according to a study by the Institute of the German Economy in Cologne, a further 3750 million DM will be spent on net access and website construction over the next year. It has generally been recognized that European businesses are too cautious in their approach to e-commerce, and as a result the corresponding food sector currently lags behind too. However, the question still remains at the present time as to the efficacy of the Internet as a standalone marketplace for information and communication for the food sector.

The purpose of this chapter is to provide an overview of food-related information on the Internet by analysing the different types of websites, newsgroups and mailing lists available about the food industry. Several different search engines and directories will be mentioned and some of the more informative websites described; these include research institutes/organizations, government, marketing, publishing and patents/legislation.

# General directories and search engines

Information on the web is becoming increasingly available in a structured format via the use of search engines or directory/indexing sites. These enable keyword or topic based searching of websites. The search results are displayed with hypertext links, allowing direct access to the sites described. *Yahoo!* at **http://www.yahoo.co.uk/** is one of the biggest and best-known directories. The websites are registered and organized into a hierarchy of categories, with the additional facility of being able to use search engines to select specific sites. The web pages in *Yahoo!* are added by recommendation, although this is usually from their author, and the number of sites included is only a small fraction of those available. A simple search on 'food' for example, produced 14,138 sites, which were listed in 4070 categories. The types of categories were health > food safety, science > genetically modified foods, and health > diseases and conditions > allergies. *Yahoo!* is particularly useful for searching company names and URL addresses. Narrowing the search to food companies in the business and economics category identified 42 sublistings, including food safety, trade magazines and brand names.

Search engines can also be used to select websites. These differ from directories in that the searches are not limited to registered sites but are made of all accessible websites. Unfortunately, as a result this type of search usually leads to repetition of site information and yields a high proportion of non-relevant sites. Some of the better-known search engines include: *AltaVista* at **http://www.altavista.co.uk/**, *Excite* at **http://www.excite.co.uk/**, *HotBot* at **http://hotbot.com/**, *InfoSeek* at **http://www.go.com/** and *Lycos* at **http://www.lycos.co.uk/**. A comparison of these five different search engines, using a hierarchical-type search on food > meat > poultry > vitamins, is shown in Table 13.1. At first glance, the number of successful hits made by the different search engines seems impressive. Unfortunately, a closer inspection of the results reveals a high proportion of irrelevant sites and repetitions. In summary, general web directories and search engines can be useful starting points but their use can also be time-consuming and often leads to inappropriate information sources.

**Table 13.1**  *Comparison of five different search engines showing the number of successful hits using a hierarchical-type search (September 2000)*

| Topic<br>Search Engine | Food | Meat | Poultry | Vitamins |
|---|---|---|---|---|
| AltaVista | 10,013,685 | 815,055 | 382,805 | 612,980 |
| Excite | 1,150,000 | 113,000 | 38,200 | 377,000 |
| HotBot | 13,388,800 | 1,613,600 | 460,220 | 818,000 |
| Infoseek | 2,234,982 | 325,408 | 83,552 | 282,841 |
| Lycos | 1,931,987 | 214,175 | 52,149 | 168,048 |

# Food-specific directories/umbrella sites

There are a number of directories on the Internet that focus specifically on food-related topics. These sites are more effective for finding food-related information than the general directories. A fully searchable database that provides summary descriptions, including hypertext links, of quality food and nutrition websites is the *Food and Nutrition Internet Index* (FNII). The index is produced by the *International Food Information Service* (IFIS) at **http://www.ifis.org/** and is accessible at **http://www.fnii.ifis.org/**. The main focus of FNII is on food science, food technology and human nutrition, although food business and company information are also covered. The website is designed by food professionals especially for the food industry, and provides a fast and effective means of finding quality information on the Internet. The website covers a diverse range of food information on businesses, professional and trade associations, conferences and exhibitions, regulatory and food safety information, research institutions etc.

The *Arbor Nutrition Guide* at **http://arborcom.com/** is another extensive food directory, particularly specializing in sites associated with food, nutrition and health. This award-winning site supplies a search engine and summary descriptions, and covers a wide range of other food topics as well. Subject categories included on the site are:

1  *searching* provides access to general and nutrition search engines, and lists.
2  *homepages* provides links to a variety of organizations, governments and universities.
3  *clinical nutrition* has information on nutritional diseases, high-risk groups, nutrition in medicine, special diets and sports nutrition.
4  *applied nutrition* contains links on public health, dietetics, nutrition education, alternative medicine and nutritional diseases.
5  *food science* includes access to a variety of sources on food composition, genetic engineering, functional foods, food safety and food law (world-wide).
6  *food* contains information on the food industry and food service, including eating and dining.

Other food-related directories have a more commercial bias and are much more specific regarding the information they contain on their sites. *The International Food Ingredients Directory* produced by Miller Freeman at **http://www.mfbv.com/directory/food/index.html** is a good example. This site contains searchable information on over 1000 ingredient companies, describing products, trade names and company profiles. The database can be searched using the company name, brand name, or by selecting a maximum of five items on a drop-down list of products. One of the largest food ingredient databases on the Internet, containing the details of over 7500 ingredient suppliers, is *IngrID* at **http://www.ingrid.co.uk/**. However, only the company names, country, fax and telephone numbers are provided free of charge, with the full company details provided on a subscription basis.

Umbrella sites are another form of directory that supplies lists of links to useful websites. This type of directory usually consists of an index of resources relating to a specific food topic. The coverage of these topics tends to be more expansive than the general directories, and as a result the lists of links are much more discriminating. *The International Food Science and Technology* (IFST) website's resource page at **http://www.ifst.org/resource.htm** provides a comprehensive list of useful links to international food-related web resources, including most of the UK Government sites and a number of different newsgroups and mailing lists. Slightly further afield is the *Food Science Australia* umbrella site at **http://www.dfst.csiro.au/fdnet20a.htm**, which is a joint venture between the Commonwealth Science and Industrial Research Organization (CSIRO) and the Australian Food Industrial Science Centre (AFISC). This umbrella site has a world-wide list of Internet resources in food science and technology, including a list of research institutions, universities and links to sites providing information on food safety, food law and consumer information.

The *Foogene Training and Consulting* website has a very specialist links page at **http://www.foogene.co.uk/pages/links.htm**, which contains an alphabetical list of food safety, and general health and safety websites around the world. *Foodlink* at **http://foodlink.org.uk/linksmain.htm**, produced by the Food and Drink Federation, and the links page maintained by the *Society of Food Hygiene and Technology* at **http://www.sofht.co.uk/linkhyg.htm**, are two other useful umbrella sites. Not only do all of these sites provide a list of useful links, but they also contain other valuable information concerning food safety issues.

# Company sites

Companies representing the food industry, including manufacturers, retailers and suppliers, are well represented on the web. The primary purpose of company sites is promotional, and is aimed at customers, suppliers and investors. The information generally includes a list of products, company structure, company news, press releases, annual reports, financial statements and franchise opportunities. Sometimes, in an attempt to make their sites more user-friendly, companies include their own search engines and have several 'fun-based' features, such as competitions, games, recipes, teaching materials and even online shopping facilities. However, the quality and quantity of information provided by the different company websites varies tremendously and selecting useful sites can prove to be very difficult.

There are several business directories/databases on the Internet that provide food company information, including their full contact details, whilst other companies are actively encouraged to register their details on the database free of charge. However, a few of the more comprehensive directories are only accessible via registration and/or subscription. The *Europages* multilingual website at **http://www.europages.com**, which is accessible in English, Dutch, French, German, Italian and Spanish, and lists over 500,000 companies selected from 30 European countries, although this website is not restricted to the food industry. An easy-to-use search engine, where the search strategy selects a product or service, company name and geographical area, minimizes the number of false leads.

There are also a number of websites that focus on particular sectors of the food industry. For example, the multilingual *Gelatin Food Info* site at **http://www.gelatin.com/**, accessible in English, French, Italian and German, represents the interests of gelatin manufacturers across Western Europe. A list of gelatin manufacturers and associated international organizations is included, with additional information on the product history, markets, current research and different applications for gelatin. Similarly, the *American Glutamate Association* site at **http://www.msgfacts.com/** focuses on information about glutamic acid and its salts, and in particular safety issues regarding monosodium glutamate. Relevant world-wide news concerning the industry, background information, and a user comments page, are also provided.

# Universities, research institutes and organizations

Many of the principal organizations and universities involved in food research have sites on the web. Some of the sites are limited to summarizing the structure of their institution, describing relevant food science courses, and providing a brief outline of their current research, usually including profiles and contact details of key personnel. However, many of the better sites also include full details of published research and information sheets, which can be downloaded in a variety of formats, extensive links to other sites and interactive discussion forums.

The multiple-award-winning website of the *Institute of Food Science and Technology* (IFST) at **http://www.ifst.org/** is a good example. The IFST is an independent, incorporated professional body for food scientists and technologists. The site not only contains information about the Institute and its activities, but also provides other useful information about the food industry, and a search engine plus an index are provided to improve navigation. For food industry professionals, there are details on different careers in food science and technology, including places to study in the UK and abroad. There is a hot topic section that contains informative articles on food safety issues, eg allergens, as well as controversial topics, eg genetically modified foods and bovine spongiform encephalopathy (BSE). The *IFST* site also provides a large list of useful hotlinks to external food-related web resources.

A much smaller website, which is grant-aided by the *Biotechnology and Biological Sciences Research Council* (BBSRC) at **http://www.bbsrc.ac.uk/**, is that of *the Institute of Food Research* (IFR) at **http://www.ifrn.bbsrc.ac.uk/**. The IFR carries out independent, basic and strategic research on food safety, food quality, nutrition and health. Apart from a comprehensive description of IFR, which includes job vacancies and research activities, there is also a useful section on food information, containing food science information sheets, designed especially for the public, students and teachers. There is also a short list of science news, which targets coverage of scientific events, contract successes and advances in scientific research. Another site worth mentioning, which focuses exclusively on research in the European Union (EU) is the *FLAIR-FLOW* Europe home page at **http://exp.ie/flair.html**. The purpose of this site is information dissemination, especially to small and medium-sized food companies, and includes summary results from EU-funded food research and development projects.

Academic institutions are well represented on the web, which is not surprising as the Internet was originally developed as an academic tool. The information provided by university sites varies, and is often restricted to promoting the university, their food science courses and research departments. However, there are a few notable exceptions, where individuals or departments maintain their own home page at the university address, improving both the quality and quantity of information available. An excellent example is *David Juke's Food Law* site at **http://www.fst.rdg.ac.uk/foodlaw/main.htm** at the University of Reading. The site was primarily designed to assist students taking courses in food law, and includes sections on quality assurance and food legislation. It is a comprehensive guide to European food laws, complete with full-text articles dating back to pre-1980, UK food inspection statistics, UK food regulations, and information about the proposed development and role of the Food Standards Agency. Recent food law news, both in the UK and the EU, together with information about international food law, including university courses, make this one of the premier sites covering food law information.

# Government sites

There are several government sites associated with food, although locating the correct source of information can prove difficult. Fortunately, a comprehensive, alphabetical listing of all the UK public sector bodies associated with food can be found at **http://www.open.gov.uk/index/t_food.htm**. The key subject headings include agriculture, consumer protection, environment, exports etc, and a search engine is provided with an organization index to assist with navigating the site.

An excellent source of government-related food information, including full-text documents and reports by different advisory committees, is *the Ministry of Agriculture, Fisheries and Food* (MAFF) website at **http://www.maff.gov.uk/**. MAFF is responsible for assisting UK industries in improving their performance in the expanding European and world markets, whilst at the same time protecting health and conserving the natural environment. Complete records dating back to 1997 can be accessed covering all of the news releases and proceedings of meetings of 13 different committees advising the government. These include the Advisory Committee on Novel Foods and Processes (ACNFP), the Expert Group on Vitamins and Minerals, the Food Advisory Committee (FAC), the Joint Food Safety and Standards Group, the Meat Hygiene Group and the Spongiform Encephalopathy Advisory Committee (SEAC). The Advisory Committee on the Microbiological Safety of Food (ACMSF) is located at the *Department of Health* website at **http://www.doh.gov.uk/acmsf.htm#memb**. The MAFF site also contains a section on food and drink, where the objective is to assist UK food and drink manufacturing and retailing industries by promoting greater competitiveness and removing obstacles to growth. Other sections on the MAFF site include food safety and standards, animal health and welfare, fisheries and farming, and the environment.

# Market information

Many commercial sources provide extensive information on food and drink markets, but usually on a fee-paying basis, with the option to download entire or sections of reports. Examples include *Profound* at **http://www.profound.com/**, produced by the DIALOG Corporation, and the *Marketsearch* directory at **http://www.marketsearch-dir.com/**, which contains over 20,000 published market research studies. *Marketsearch* does provide a brief outline of the report contents for free. However, there is also a large amount of free market information on the Internet – not always as extensive as the paid services, but usually more than adequate. The *Food and Agriculture Organization* (FAO) website at **http://www.fao.org/** is an excellent example of a site that provides free access to a number of databases providing market information, and includes details on how to use the system. The databases are accessible in English, French or Spanish and include nutrition, agriculture, food quality control and fisheries. Selecting different domains, such as food supply, commodity balance and food balance sheets, refines the search strategy even further. An easy-to-use search engine is also provided, which can be used to search any or all of the databases, using a combination of individual countries or continents, commodities, and the year (1961–1997). This versatile site not only allows the user to select the information and display it graphically, but can also perform different calculations on the data.

The *Sugar Information Service* at **http://www.sugarinfo.co.uk/** is a single-point access on the Internet to a wide variety of information concerning the sugar industry. In addition to the market data, there is a variety of other links provided to categories that include:

- commerce (finance, banking)
- markets, brokers and traders (futures, domestic and international)
- prices and charts (futures, physical prices, freight rates)
- statistics analysis and reports (production/consumption, prices, trends).

Trade associations representing the different sectors of the food industry will generally also contain useful market data. The Biscuit, Cake, Chocolate, and Confectionery Alliance (BCCCA) is one of the food industry's largest trade associations, which was formed in 1987. In fact, approximately 90% of all the biscuits, chocolate and sugar confectionery products made in the UK, worth an estimated £7.3 billion in 1998, are products of BCCCA members. Included on their website at **http://www.bccca.org.uk/home.htm** is information on industry facts – the economics, finances and markets, different training, conferences and courses – plus a section dedicated to cocoa research. Similarly, the *Federation of Bakers* (FoB) at

http://www.bakersfederation.org.uk/ and the *British Society of Baking*
(BSB) at http://www.bsb.org.uk/ represent the interests of the bakery
industry. Issues regarding government consultation on labelling
legislation and nutrition are addressed by the FoB, whilst the BSB
provides a forum for learning more about the technical and marketing
aspects of the industry, through organized events and conferences.

# Patents, standards and legislation

Free patent data on the Internet, with the exception of US patents, was
until recently non-existent. However, an online web service at
http://ep.espacenet.com/ was recently launched by the *European Patent
Office* (EPO) at http://www.european-patent-office.org/. This service
supplies full-text documents and illustrations of European, PCT, World
Intellectual Property Organization (WIPO) and Japanese patents. The
*IBM Intellectual Property Network* at http://www.patents.ibm.com/ is
another extensive source of patent information. The sites allows you to
search and retrieve over 4 million patents and patent applications,
including 2 million US patents (published since 1971), 1.4 million
PCT applications from the WIPO (published since 1997), and Espace-
EP-A (1979–) and ESPACE B (1980–) documents produced by the
EPO. However, it is important to realize that, in general, free patent
services on the Internet do not always provide comprehensive coverage
of patent material. In fact, the site at http://ep.espacenet.com/ is only
really effective for searching recently published patents, providing that
adequate information is used during the search. To ensure a more
comprehensive and accurate search of patent material is completed, a
comprehensive patent database such as the *World Patents Index*
produced by *Derwent* at http://www.derwent.co.uk/ should be
searched online.

Information on the different standards and legislation operating in

Europe can also be accessed on the Internet. The *British Standards Institution* (BSI) at **http://www.bsi.org.uk/** and the *International Organization for Standardization* (ISO) at **http://www.iso.ch/** provide useful information about their organizations, recent developments, and details about their different standards, which include the British Kitemark and the ISO 9000 standard. Legislative information is also available from several different sources on the Internet, although the information changes continually and facts obtained from unofficial sources should always be validated. General material on European legislation can be found at the multilingual *European Union* site at **http://europa.eu.int/index.html**. Information includes access to press releases, official documents, legal texts and publications from the EU. *David Juke's Food Law* site at the University of Reading at **http://www.fst.rdg.ec.uk/foodlaw/index.htm** contains details relating more specifically to European food legislation. This site is described in more detail in the universities, research institutes and organizations section.

# Publications

Many of the different food publications and trade journals are well represented on the Internet. However, it is not uncommon for certain sections of the website to be restricted to fee-paying subscribers, particularly for access to current and recent back issues of the publication. Many of these sites provide good basic information about particular sectors of the food industry, usually including a number of interesting articles and links to other useful sites. An excellent example is *Nutraceuticals World* at **http://www.nutraceuticalsworld.com/**, a bimonthly trade magazine that reports on the latest developments, products and trends in the nutraceuticals industry world-wide. In the issue published on their website at the time of writing, only two of the main features could be accessed, with additional articles available from an archive section. However, the most impressive feature of this site is the web guide, which has amassed one of the most comprehensive, fully searchable web guides on the Internet of nutraceutical companies involved in research, manufacturing and marketing. Over 250 companies are listed, with a further 100 professional resources, and a suppliers index of companies providing products and services to manufacturers and marketers in nutraceuticals. Similarly, for the bakery industry, *Sosland Publishing* at **http://www.sosland.com/** provides extensive information on the bakery industry, including a calendar of events, selected features and daily news articles. The details of several trade magazines representing the bakery industry, such as *World Grain* and *Baking Buyer*, are also provided, the archives of which are available online.

There are also a number of electronic publishing services appearing on the Internet. *Bioline Publications* at **http://bioline.bdt.org.br/** is a collaboration between the UK and Brazil which was designed for bioscientists, and which contains useful information on the controversial subject of genetic engineering. Abstracts of online-only journals and established journals are provided free of charge, along with the contents lists and summaries of reports, newsletters and books. There is an option to download the full-text articles for a small fee. An online forum allows issues relating to biopolicy and biosafety published on their website to be discussed, and a bulletin board announces any new material and system upgrades.

# Mailing lists and newsgroups

The number of newsgroups on the Internet has increased rapidly since its first conception in 1979. Newsgroups are organized into seven main categories, with the prefix **sci.** representing discussions relating to scientific topics. The official newsgroup representing food science and technology queries is **sci.bio.food-science**, which was accepted in 1996, but there is also a long list of unofficial categories. There are also a number of newsgroups dealing with food and drink from the perspective of kitchen recipes, cookery, such as **rec.food.cooking**, **rec.food.drink** and a general food newsgroup **alt.food**. Other useful newsgroups representing the food industry worth mentioning are: **sci.agriculture** (farming and agriculture) including **sci.agriculture.fruit** (fruit, berries and nuts), **sci.agriculture.poultry** (the poultry industry); **sci.engr.manufacturing** (manufacturing technology); **sci.med.nutrition** (physiological impacts of diet); and **aus.foodtech** (Australian food technology).

Web-based chat rooms, which are text-based noticeboards attached to websites, are also becoming more popular, particularly as web producers try to make their sites more user-friendly. It is not uncommon to find discussion forums on websites, encouraging registered users to participate in discussing various controversial issues – something the food industry never lacks.

Mailing lists are similar to newsgroups, but are closed e-mail lists, restricted to a fixed list of subscribers, and are usually better quality and more disciplined. This is achieved using a moderator, who reviews all the postings, ensuring that they are relevant to the topic being discussed. *Food-For-Thought* (**mailbase@mailbase.ac.uk**), which is a forum for discussion on all aspects of food and eating, contains a bulletin board for announcements of meetings, employment opportunities etc. *Foodsafe* (**majordomo@nal.usda.gov**) is an international, interactive electronic discussion group with the primary aim of linking professionals interested in food safety issues from around the world. The diet, nutrition and health project mailing list (*DNH-PILOT* at **dnh-pilot-request@mailbase.ac.uk**) was designed to link together academic researchers across the EU along with industrial partners, and possibly to help secure future sources of funding. This mailing list discusses a variety of topics, and includes issues about food science and technology, agricultural economics and sociology. Finally, a mailing list that is devoted to discussing bovine spongiform encephalopathy (BSE) and new-variant (nv) Creutzfeldt-Jakob disease (CJD) is **listserv@uni-karlsruhe.de/**.

Newsgroups, mailing lists, newsletters, and interactive websites on the Internet have changed the way in which professionals communicate across the food industry. *The Gopher Hole* produced by Roger Trobridge at **http://internet-gopher.com/** provides an excellent review of these different methods for communicating on the Internet. The site explains how to use newsgroups and mailing lists effectively, and lists a number of useful examples.

# Conclusion

The Internet not only provides the food industry with most of its information needs, but also provides the ideal medium for communication between fellow-professionals and clientele. Many companies are now starting to realize the potential of electronic information and, as a consequence, more and more websites are beginning to appear on the Internet. Not only can companies use the Internet as an information resource to monitor advances in technology, solve manufacturing problems, generate new ideas and keep up to date with the latest news, but they can also use it as a sales and marketing tool, communicating with their customers and liaising with suppliers.

Probably one of the biggest drawbacks with the Internet is the sheer amount of information available, and the difficulty in accessing the right source. This may be a problem resulting from lack of training, or poor information management or technical support, or a combination of all three. However, the increase in investment made by companies into this rapidly expanding technology needs to be supported by an improvement in the training of staff and in the dissemination of information, whether via workshops, conferences or seminars. This chapter provides an introduction to the type of food industry-related information that can be found on the Internet and which is available to the food industry. A number of different options have been given to try and answer those all-important food-related questions, perhaps even to find inspiration, locate potential customers, suppliers or secure funding. The prospects for using the Internet in the food industry are endless, and it should be exploited to its full potential.

# URLs mentioned in this chapter

*AltaVista* **http://www.altavista.co.uk/**
*American Glutamate Association* **http://www.msgfacts.com/**
*Arbor Nutrition Guide* **http://arborcom.com/**
*Bioline Publications* **http://bioline.bdt.org.br/**
*Biotechnology and Biological Sciences Research Council*
    **http://www.bbsrc.ac.uk/**
*Biscuit, Cake, Chocolate and Confectionery Alliance*
    **http://www.bccca.org.uk/home.htm**
*British Society of Baking* **http://www.bsb.org.uk/**
*British Standards Institution* **http://www.bsi.org.uk/**
*David Juke's Food Law* **http://www.fst.rdg.ac.uk/foodlaw/main.htm**
*David Juke's Food Law* **http://www.fst.rdg.ec.uk/foodlaw/index.htm**
*Department of Health* **http://www.doh.gov.uk/acmsf.htm#memb**
*Espace* **http://ep.espacenet.com/**
*Europages* **http://www.europages.com/**
*European Patent Office* **http://www.european-patent-office.org/**
*European Union* **http://europa.eu.int/index.html**
*Excite* **http://www.excite.co.uk/**

*Federation of Bakers* http://www.bakersfederation.org.uk/

*FLAIR-FLOW* http://exp.ie/flair.html

*Food and Agriculture Organization* http://www.fao.org/

*Food and Nutrition Internet Index* http://www.fnii.ifis.org/

*Food Science Australia* http://www.dfst.csiro.au/fdnet20a.htm

*Foodlink* http://foodlink.org.uk/linksmain.htm

*Foogene Training and Consulting*
     http://www.foogene.co.uk/pages/links.htm

*Gelatin Food Info* http://www.gelatin.com/

*Gopher Hole* http://internet-gopher.com/

*HotBot* http://hotbot.com/

*IBM Intellectual Property Network* http://www.patents.ibm.com/

*InfoSeek* http://infoseek.go.com/

*IngrID* http://www.ingrid.co.uk/

*Institute of Food Research* http://www.ifrn.bbsrc.ac.uk/

*International Food Information Service* http://www.ifis.org/

*International Food Ingredients Directory*
     http://www.mfbv.com/directory/food/index.html

*International Food Science and Technology* http://www.ifst.org/

*International Food Science and Technology*
     http://www.ifst.org/resource.htm

*International Organization for Standardization* http://www.iso.ch/

*Lycos* http://www.lycos.co.uk/

*Marketsearch* http://www.marketsearch-dir.com/

*Ministry of Agriculture, Fisheries and Food* http://www.maff.gov.uk/

*Nutraceuticals World* http://www.nutraceuticalsworld.com/

*Open.gov.uk* http://www.open.gov.uk/index/t_food.htm

*Profound* http://www.profound.com/

*Society of Food Hygiene and Technology*
     http://www.sofht.co.uk/linkhyg.htm

*Sosland Publishing* http://www.sosland.com/

*Sugar Information Service* http://www.sugarinfo.co.uk/

*World Patents Index* http://www.derwent.co.uk/
*Yahoo!* http://www.yahoo.co.uk/

# 14

# Engineering on the world wide web

*Julia Dagg*

## Introduction

This chapter looks at various types of information relevant to the needs of engineers in the professional community and in the academic world. Engineering is very well served by the world wide web. Many organizations and companies involved with engineering have a website, and there are other websites which contain useful information. There is a great deal of substantive information available free of charge, some of which previously had to be purchased at considerable expense. However, it is important to bear in mind that information is a valuable commodity, and that much still has to be paid for, although the web does make it easier to discover what is available and to obtain it.

The main concern with using world wide web resources is how to evaluate their authoritativeness, and the breadth and depth of their contents. With purchased resources, you pay for what you get and you get what you pay for. Though some erroneous information is published, there are tried-and-tested ways of discovering where to go for useful and valid information. One of these is the way in which the item has been published: for example, a book published by a reputable publisher will tend to carry more weight than one self-published by an individual. With the world wide web everything is in practice self-published, though most reputable institutions exercise some supervision of what is posted on their websites. You are getting what someone for some reason has chosen to spend their time and, to a certain extent, their or their institution's money to post up free of charge. Websites therefore need to be evaluated carefully before the information they contain is relied upon. The key issues to be considered when using a world wide website rather than purchased resources are:

- Who has created it and why?
- How comprehensive is it?
- Is it being maintained, ie is it being updated, and are any onward links checked for currency?

It is also the case that, when purchasing information, you can usually, though not always, find a source, and it is just a question of balancing needs against funds available. With the world wide web there may be a marvellous source that provides the solution for one information need but absolutely nothing for another.

No one source can provide a definitive guide to useful resources on the internet and any selection will be to a certain extent subjective. This chapter simply tries to list some of the main gateways along with illustrative examples of the range of individual resources available.

Please note that a number of websites require registration before allowing you access to them, but when this is free it is usually clearly indicated.

# World wide web gateways

There are many websites which try to bring together a comprehensive set of links to relevant resources which can be both browsed and searched. For example, the UK Government has funded projects via the *Joint Information Systems Committee* (at **http://www.jisc.ac.uk/**) of the Higher Education Funding Councils to try to provide a comprehensive *Resource Discovery Network* at **http://www.rdn.ac.uk/**, with different subject hubs being managed by different institutions. Websites included have been selected and evaluated and should include all aspects of the subject covered. There is also the *World Wide Web Virtual Library* project at **http://vlib.org/**, which provides links to individual subject gateways that together provide a comprehensive directory of the web. Some of the major search engines also have directory sections, which tend to be aimed more at the personal user, but also cover areas of interest to industry and academia. Many institutions and individuals are also producing their own sets of links, often just to a specialist area of interest to them. The major funded resources are well maintained (though there may be issues concerning the long-term funding), but 'one-off' websites may need to be used with caution, as they may not be checked and updated.

# National/International academic gateways

These are attempts to offer systematic coverage of the whole of engineering. They provide links to evaluated resources for the benefit of the academic community, and many receive funding, directly or indirectly, from governments.

➡ *Edinburgh Engineering Virtual Library* (EEVL) at **http://www.eevl.ac.uk/** is the main UK engineering gateway to resources world-wide, based at Heriot-Watt University and forming part of the Resources Discovery Network.

➡ *Electronic Engineering Library* (EELS) at **http://www.ub2.lu.se/eel/eelhome.html** is produced by the

Swedish Universities of Technology Libraries.

➡ *Australasian Virtual Engineering Library* (AVEL) at **http://avel.library.uq.edu.au/** is a database of quality Australian resources, partly funded by the Australian government.

➡ *Internet Connections for Engineering* (ICE) at **http://www.englib.cornell.edu/ice/** was originally funded by the Council for Library Resources and is now maintained by reference librarians at Cornell University Library.

➡ The engineering section of *BUBL* at **http://link.bubl.ac.uk/engineering/** is part of a pioneering electronic service funded by JISC and originally intended for use by librarians but now has a wider remit.

➡ NISS's *Directory of Networked Resources* has an applied science section at **http://www.niss.ac.uk/cgi-bin/GetUdc.pl?6**, which forms part of a wider service, partly funded by JISC and providing information for education.

➡ The engineering section of the *World Wide Web Virtual Library* at **http://vlib.org/Engineering.html** forms part of the international cooperative attempt to catalogue the web.

➡ The last three also have computing sections: BUBL at **http://link.bubl.ac.uk/computing/**; NISS at **http://www.niss.ac.uk/cgi-bin/GetUdc.pl?518**; and WWWVL at **http://vlib.org/Computing.html**.

# Other gateways

There are a great many people world-wide compiling lists of useful websites, and most of the organizations, companies and university departments which can be traced using other sections of this chapter will have their own selected links. There are also many in-depth gateways to specific subjects, but whereas the comprehensive gateways listed above should provide some coverage of all areas of engineering, there is no guarantee that there will be a specialist one in a specific area. A selection of such gateways is listed below which were traced using world wide web navigators, the general gateways and sheer serendipity.

➠ *Aerospace resources on the Internet* at **http://www.cranfield.ac.uk/cils/library/subjects/airmenu.htm** from Cranfield University.

➠ *Chemical and process engineering resources* at **http://www.neis.com/cpe_resources.html** from the National Environmental Information Service.

➠ *Ceramics and industrial minerals* at **http://www.ceramics.com/**.

➠ *Offshore technology* at **http://www.offshore-technology.com/** is a website for the offshore oil and gas industry.

➠ *Nisee* at **http://www.eerc.berkeley.edu/** is the National Information Service for Earthquake Engineering from the University of Berkeley.

➠ *Nano-link* at **http://sunsite.nus.edu.sg/MEMEX/nanolink.html** has links to key nanotechnology websites from a collaborative project between Memex Research and the University of Singapore.

➠ *Railway technology* at **http://www.railway-technology.com/index.html** is a website for the railway industry.

# Web navigator directories

Search engines from the main web navigators can be frustrating tools for searching the Internet, but the directory sections are often useful such as:

➠ *Argus clearing house* at **http://www.clearinghouse.net/eng.html**

➠ *Lycos* at
http://a2z.lycos.com/Science_and_Technology/Engineering/
➠ *Yahoo!* at **http://www.yahoo.com/Science/Engineering/**

# Organizations

These are both well represented and well organized on the web.
Virtually every major scholastic and professional organization has a website. In many cases the URL is easy to guess as it is based on the standard
abbreviation, and if not it can be readily traced via a variety of sources.

➠ *American Association of Engineering Societies* at
**http://www.aaes.org/** has links to a range of US societies.
➠ *The Engineering Council (UK)* at **http://www.engc.org.uk/** has a list
of UK engineering societies and links to their websites.
➠ *Engineering links* at
**http://www.fdgroup.co.uk/neo/fsi/englinks.htm** from Flow
Simulation has links to organizations and university departments.
➠ *European Science Foundation* at **http://www.esf.org/** aims to
promote high-quality science at a European level, and has links to
65 organizations in 22 European countries.
➠ *IO net* at **http://csf.colorado.edu/isa/sections/io/internet.html** has
links to international organizations.
➠ *Professional Engineering Associations (UK)* at
**http://www.pei.org.uk/** is an umbrella site for regional websites,
which include links to local organizations and to the local branches
of national organizations.
➠ *Scholarly Societies project* at
**http://www.lib.uwaterloo.ca/society/subjects_soc.html** has links to
societies world-wide in all disciplines.
➠ *The UK Research Councils* have a joint home page at

http://www.nerc.ac.uk/research-councils.

➟ *World Federation of Engineering Organizations* at http://www.unesco.org/fmoi/fmoi/html/home/default.htm has 80 national members and nine international members, representing the whole engineering profession.

# Universities

Many of the gateways listed above will include individual university departments, but there are more direct ways of finding university websites in general.

➟ *NISS* has links to UK HE websites at http://www.niss.ac.uk/sites/he-cis.html.

➟ *Yahoo!* has links to college and university websites worldwide at http://dir.yahoo.com/education/higher_education/colleges_ and_universities/index.html.

# Governments

➟ The *Department of Trade and Industry* site at http://www.dti.gov.uk/ offers a range of information for consumers, small businesses, employees, anyone with an interest in the world of work, and many others.

➟ *Open.gov.uk* at http://www.open.gov.uk/index/orgindex.htm is the main gateway to UK government bodies, which includes government departments, local councils, NHS trusts, commissions, the Scottish Parliament, the Welsh Assembly etc.

➟ The *HMSO* website at http://www.legislation.hmso.gov.uk/ provides the full text of UK legislation from 1996 for Acts and from 1997 for statutory instruments.

➠ *Europa* at **http://europa.eu.int/** is the European Union server with links to all of the Institutions.

➠ *FedWorld* at **http://www.fedworld.gov/**, produced by the National Technical Information Services, is an online locator service for a comprehensive inventory of information disseminated by the US Federal Government.

➠ *GovBot* at **http://ciir2.cs.umass.edu/Govbot/** is a database of US government websites produced by the Center for Intelligent Information Retrieval.

➠ *Yahoo!* has a directory at **http://dir.yahoo.com/Government/Countries/** of government websites world-wide and a list at **http://dir.yahoo.com/Government/Embassies_and_Consulates/** of embassies and consulates world-wide.

# Books

It is now very easy to discover what has been published, as most major libraries, commercial publishers and professional organizations have online catalogues. There are also several online of booksellers with searchable catalogues.

# Library catalogues

➠ *The British Library catalogue* at **http://opac97.bl.uk/** covers the holdings of the reference collections (which date back to the beginning of printing) and of the Document Supply Centre.

➠ *The Library of Congress catalogue* is available at **http://lcweb.loc.gov/**.

➠ *Gabriel* at **http://portico.bl.uk/gabriel/en/welcome.html** has links to national libraries in Europe.

➡ *NISS libraries gateway* at **http://www.niss.ac.uk/lis/obi/obi.html** has links to all types of libraries in the UK and Ireland.

➡ *Webcats* at **http://www.lights.com/webcats/** is a gateway to selected libraries world-wide, but with a North American bias.

# Publishers and booksellers

➡ *The University of Sheffield* has a fairly comprehensive set of links at **http://www.shef.ac.uk/~lib/useful/books.html** to gateways and individual websites for publishers and booksellers.

➡ *The Publishers' Catalogues Home Page* at **http://www.lights.com/publisher/** has links to publishers from most countries.

➡ *Scholarly Societies project* at **http://www.lib.uwaterloo.ca/society/subjects_soc.html** has links to societies world-wide, many of which have online catalogues of their publications.

# Books published on the web

The web provides an opportunity to publish information without the constraints imposed by the medium of print, but nevertheless electronic books are available. Many are parallel versions of existing print publications produced for sale by commercial publishers, but there are also some publications produced by a number of sources which replicate the book, possibly to provide information in a familiar format in an unfamiliar medium. Below is a selection of free reference books that have been located.

➡ *The Basics of Engineering Design* at **http://www.machinedesign.com/bde/** is a web version of an established reference work made available free of charge.

➡ *The Composite Materials Handbook* at **http://mil-17.udel.edu/**, produced jointly by the US Army Research Laboratory, the Materials Sciences Corporation and the University of Delaware Center for Composite Materials, provides information and guidance necessary to design and fabricate end items from composite materials.

➡ *The Data Analysis BriefBook* from CERN at **http://www.cern.ch/Physics/DataAnalysis/BriefBook/** is a condensed handbook, or an extended glossary, written in encyclopedic format, covering subjects in statistics, computing, analysis and related fields, with the purpose of being both introduction and reference for data analysts, scientists and engineers.

# Journals

The web provides an excellent medium for access to journals. Most publishers now offer online subscription services for print or electronic delivery, and many provide a range of services free of charge, including free viewing of abstracts and an e-mail alerting service of the tables of contents of new issues of journals. Some examples are:

➡ *Blackwell Science Synergy* at **http://www.blackwell-synergy.com/Journals/default.asp** provides access to a listing and a searchable database of the contents of Blackwell's online journals; you can view tables of contents and abstracts, receive e-mails of tables of contents free of charge and purchase access to individual articles online.

➡ *Cambridge University Online Journals* at **http://www.journals.cup.org/cup/html/home.htm** gives free access to tables of contents, abstracts, search facilities and alerting services.

➠ *Elsevier ScienceDirect* at **http://www.elsevier.nl/homepage/** provides access to contents pages and has a free e-mail alerting service.

➠ *Oxford Journals* at **http://www3.oup.co.uk/jnls/** provides access to tables of contents and abstracts and has a free e-mail alerting service.

➠ *The Publishers' Catalogues Home Page* at **http://www.lights.com/publisher/** is a listing of publisher websites world-wide.

➠ *The Scholarly Societies project* at **http://www.lib.uwaterloo.ca/society/subjects_soc.html** provides links to professional institutions, many of which are publishers.

# Free electronic journals

There have been some attempts to take advantage of the world wide web to publish academic journals free of charge over the web. There are also some projects which aim to provide a free electronic archive of articles published in the conventional way.

➠ *Engineering E-journal Search Engine* at **http://www.eevl.ac.uk/eese/** searches 150 engineering e-journals available free in full text.

➠ *InterJournal* at **http://www.interjournal.org/** distributes self-organizing refereed journals on selected topics in science and engineering.

➠ *Scholarly journals distributed via the World Wide Web* from the University of Houston at **http://info.lib.uh.edu/wj/webjour.html** lists journals that offer English-language articles without requiring user registration or fee; it covers all disciplines but doesn't have a subject index.

# Free bibliographic databases

Journal indexes are expensive to compile, which means the subscription ones will continue to be necessary, but there are some specialist indexes available. The following is a selection of these resources:

➡ *Earthquake Engineering Abstracts* at **http://www.eerc.berkeley.edu/** from the National Information Service for Earthquake Engineering at the University of Berkeley indexes world literature on earthquake engineering from 1971.

➡ *Recent Advances in Manufacturing (RAM)* at **http://www.eevl.ac.uk/ram/aboutram.html** is a database of bibliographic information for manufacturing and related areas covering over 500 journals from 1990, and is particularly useful in that it includes business and engineering journals and covers the full range from trade and practitioner to academic publications.

➡ *Uncover* is a commercial document delivery service at **http://uncweb.carl.org/** which allows free searching of its database of 18,000 journals across all subject areas back to 1989; individual articles can be ordered by credit card.

# Commercial database hosts

The journal indexes available free of charge on the web are useful, but they are not a realistic substitute for the existing subscription databases. Most of these are now available on the web via the publisher or via datahosts.

➡ *Cambridge Scientific Abstracts* at **http://www.csa1.co.uk/** offers a wide range of bibliographic databases such as Metadex and Biotechnology and Bioengineering abstracts.

➡ *DIALOG* at **http://custom.netscape.com/technology/** gives access to a range of bibliographic and other databases.

➠ *ISI* at **http://www.isinet.com/** provides the Web of Science citation indexes and other products.

➠ *NISS* has a list of commercial and academic datahosts at **http://www.niss.ac.uk/lis/datahosts.html**.

# Patents

The world wide web has made a major impact on the accessibility of patents as a source of technical information. Comprehensive indexes are now available and the full text of some is available free of charge . However, if you are searching to see what patents exist for commercial or research purposes, then it may be advisable to have a professional search done, rather than relying solely on the information available on the web.

# Patent indexes and texts

➠ *Esp@ceNet* at **http://ep.dips.org/** has indexes for patents worldwide, with some full-text availability; full details of coverage can be found at **http://dips-2.dips.org/dips/help/index.htm**.

➠ *US patent and trademark office* at **http://www.uspto.gov/** includes a database containing the full text of US patents from 1976 at **http://www.uspto.gov/patft/**.

# Patent offices

➠ *UK Patent Office* at **http://www.patent.gov.uk/**.

➠ *US Patent and Trademark Office* at **http://www.uspto.gov/**.

➠ *Other offices* are listed at **http://www.wipo.org/eng/general/pcipi/otherwww/ipo_web.htm**.

## Gateways to other patent websites

➠ *BUBL's* patents links at **http://link.bubl.ac.uk/patents/**.

➠ *Patents on the web* at **http://www.aber.ac.uk/~dgw/patent.htm** is a wide-ranging set of links from the University of Wales, Aberystwyth.

➠ *Yahoo!*'s patent links at **http://www.yahoo.com/Government/Law/Intellectual_Property/Patents/**.

## Intellectual property links

➠ *Intellectual Property Network* at **http://patent.womplex.ibm.com/ibm.html** from IBM provides access to patents indexes of a number of patents offices and to other IP websites.

➠ The *World Intellectual Property Organization* site at **http://www.wipo.org/** includes (via the Library link) the full text of IP treaties along with other useful information and further links.

## Standards

Most standards-issuing bodies now make their catalogues available via the web, with online ordering facilities.

➠ *International organization for standardization* at **http://www.iso.ch/**.
➠ *British Standards Institution* at **http://www.bsi.org.uk/**.
➠ *European Committee for Standardization* at **http://www.cenorm.be/**.
➠ *American National Standards Institution* at **http://www.ansi.org/**.
➠ *American Society for Testing and Materials* at **http://www.astm.org/**.
➠ *IEEE* at **http://www.ieee.org/**.
➠ *National Institute of Standards and Technology* at

http://www.nist.gov/.

➠ *List of standardization bodies worldwide* from the ISO at
http://www.iso.ch/VL/Standards.html.

➠ *World Wide Web Virtual Library* standards section at
http://arioch.gsfc.nasa.gov/wwwvl/engineering.html#standardsl.

# Technical databases

There are a great many technical databases on the world wide web, but
they can be a little difficult to find using the standard search engines.
The gateways listed elsewhere in this chapter will have links to many
useful resources, and in *EEVL* at **http://www.eevl.ac.uk**, for example,
you can search or browse just for websites which provide technical
databases. Many professional organizations and university
departments, which can be traced using other sections of this chapter,
provide links to such databases, and may of course maintain such a
database themselves. The following is a selection of databases to give
some idea of what information is available and who is providing it.

*ChemFinder* at **http://chemfinder.camsoft.com/** is a source of data
on chemical compounds with links to further information. Individual
access to ChemFinder.com is provided as a free-of-charge service to the
scientific community. Access from corporations, academic institutions
and government organizations is charged on an annual enterprise
subscription basis.

*The Copper Page* at **http://www.copper.org/**, produced by the Copper
Development Association Inc, gives access to a range of resources
including technical and environmental data.

*The European Masonry Data Bank* at **http://www.fagg.uni-
lj.si/emdb/** is a European Union-funded online collaborative database
for the support and cooperation of masonry-related research and testing
activities.

*FACT (Facility for the Analysis of Chemical Thermodynamics)* at **http://www.crct.polymtl.ca/fact/fact.htm** from the Centre for Research in Computational Thermochemistry at the École Polytechnique de Montréal provides free access to a pure substances database, chemical reactions, and Gibbs energy minimization calculations.

*The International Nuclear Safety Center* has a materials properties database at **http://www.insc.anl.gov/matprop/**, which is intended to meet the needs of analysts using computer codes and doing experiments for safety evaluation of the world's commercial nuclear reactors.

*Material properties for MEMS* at **http://mems.isi.edu/mems/materials/** from the University of Southern California's Information Sciences Institute covers mechanical properties, electrical properties, optical properties and other values of Systems.

*Materials Safety Data Sheets archive* at **http://siri.uvm.edu/msds/** from the University of Vermont has links to manufacturers' datasheets and other information.

*MatWeb* at **http://www.matweb.com/main.htm** has property data for over 18,000 materials.

*Metals Powders and Compounds* at **http://www.micronmetals.com/** from Atlantic Equipment Engineers has full data for each element plus data on its metal powder and compound products.

*PolyContent* at **http://www.polymers.com/dotcom/polycon/** provides links to websites with technical content pertaining to plastics and polymers.

*The semiconductor data bookshelf* at **http://www.crhc.uiuc.edu/~dburke/databookshelf.html** has links to manufacturers' datasheets.

# Reports

## Technical reports

There is a great deal of report literature on the web, but it is not very easy to trace.

The *Virtual Technical Reports Center at the University of Maryland* at **http://www.lib.umd.edu/UMCP/ENGIN/TechReports/Virtual-TechReports.html** has made a start in providing links to a range of organizations world-wide which provide either full-text reports or searchable extended abstracts of their technical reports on the world wide web.

Otherwise, as with technical databases, you can use the resources listed elsewhere in this chapter to trace individual universities, organizations and companies which might post their reports. The gateways can also help, especially searchable ones such as *EEVL*.

## Government reports

The *United Kingdom Parliament* site has a searchable index at **http://www.parliament.the-stationery-office.co.uk/cgi-bin/tso_fx?DB=tsoof** of parliamentary publications, including reports of committees and commissions.

The *Stationery Office*, which publishes all other official publications, has a searchable index at **http://www.tsonline.co.uk/index.htm**.

The *National Technical Information Service* (NTIS) at **http://www.ntis.gov/** provides an index of scientific, technical, engineering, and related business information produced by or for the US Government and complementary material from international sources. You can search free of charge for items published since 1990, but only by keyword on the title, and you are only given a brief description of the item. There is a fee-based full-search service for the whole database and the resulting records include product summaries.

# Company and product information

This is an area which is extremely well served by the web. Most companies have a web presence, with many making the detailed specification of their products freely available, and there are many directories of companies and of company websites available free of charge. A guide like this can only give a brief indication of what is available, but some key gateways and a few representative websites have been listed below. Some websites giving extensive technical data are listed in the technical databases section.

# Company directories and websites

*Business Information Sources on the Internet,* Sheila Webber's site at **http://www.dis.strath.ac.uk/business/**, is an excellent gateway to a range of websites including directories.

*Engineering Industries Association* at **http://www.eia.co.uk/home.html** aims to be at the centre of information, trade and support for the engineering industry, especially for small and medium-sized enterprises, and includes a buyer's guide which is a searchable and browsable database of member companies.

*Yahoo UK and Ireland* has links to over 3,000 engineering companies' websites at **http://www.yahoo.co.uk/Business_and_Economy/Companies/ Engineering**.

*Yahoo!* has links to nearly 3,000 engineering company websites in the USA at **http://dir.yahoo.com/Business_and_Economy/Companies/ Engineering/**.

*Yahoo!* also has links to company websites world wide from its regional section at **http://dir.yahoo.com/Regional/Countries/** via the business and economy link for each country.

*Thomas Directory of American Manufacturers* at

http://www.thomasregister.com/ is a directory of 155,000 companies in the USA.

*Thomas Directory of European Manufacturers* at http://www.tipcoeurope.be/ is a Pan-European buying guide that covers 155,000 industrial suppliers in 17 countries.

# Typical product directories

*Chip directory* at **http://www.xs4all.nl/~ganswijk/chipdir/chipdir.html** contains numerically and functionally ordered chip lists, chip pinouts and lists of chip manufacturers, manufacturers of controller embedding tools plus links to other resources.

*DIAL industry* at **http://www.dialindustry.co.uk/** has information about 21,000 companies and their products.

*Principal Metals Inc* at **http://www.principalmetals.com/** gives property data for its products along with other useful databases.

*RS industrial products catalogue* at **http://rswww.com/** contains over 110,000 products and 14,000 datasheets.

# News

There are a number of newspapers and news services which provide some information free of charge, with a more comprehensive service available to subscribers. There are also some services looking specifically at science and technology.

# General

*University of Sheffield Library* web service at http://www.shef.ac.uk/~lib/useful/newseng.html has a wide range of links to newspapers and news services and to news search engines.

# Engineering

*Engineering UK* at **http://www.engineering-uk.co.uk/** provides news, jobs, company and product information and has a search facility.

*EurekAlert* at **http://www.eurekalert.org/** is a searchable news service for research in science, medicine and technology produced by the American Association for the Advancement of Science with help from Stanford University.

*TechWeb* at **http://www.techweb.com/** is a US site provided by CMP media inc, a high-tech media company providing information and marketing services to the technology sector.

# Ethical and policy issues

This section has links to a range of governmental and organizational websites which deal with ethical and policy issues relating to science and technology. In addition, the web makes it easy for anyone with an opinion on anything to communicate it to the rest of the world, and many pressure groups and individuals have mounted websites on topics of interest. These can usually be found using search engines.

*Center of excellence for sustainable development* at **http://sustainabledev.nrel.gov/** from the US Department of Energy has links to US case studies and to related websites worldwide.

*Council for Science and Technology* at **http://www.cst.gov.uk/** was established to advise the Prime Minister about the United Kingdom's strategic policies and framework for supporting science and technology, and maximizing their key contribution to the nation's sustainable development.

The UK Department of Trade and Industry's *Science and Technology* site has a section at **http://www.dti.gov.uk/scienceind/index.htm** on science and science policy.

*The European Science Foundation* has a section at

http://www.esf.org/policy/policy.htm on science policy.

*IO net* has links at
http://csf.colorado.edu/isa/sections/io/internet.html#ngo to non-governmental organizations, many of which are concerned with technology issues, and at
http://csf.colorado.edu/isa/sections/io/internet.html#enviro to environmental and development organizations.

*Online ethics center for science and technology* at
http://onlineethics.org/, sponsored by the National Science Foundation (US), has links to US case studies and to related organizations world-wide.

*Science and Engineering Indicators* from the US government at
http://www.nsf.gov/sbe/srs/seind98/start.htm has sections on public attitudes and on the economic and social impact of IT.

*Science policy information news* at
http://wisdom.wellcome.ac.uk/wisdom/spinhome.html from the Wellcome Institute is a database containing summaries of articles relating to science policy from over 150 journals and newspapers.

# URLs mentioned in this chapter

*Aerospace resources on the Internet*
    http://www.cranfield.ac.uk/cils/library/subjects/airmenu.htm
*American Association of Engineering Societies* http://www.aaes.org/
*American National Standards Institution* http://www.ansi.org/
*American Society for Testing and Materials* http://www.astm.org/
*Argus clearing house* http://www.clearinghouse.net/eng.html
*Australasian Virtual Engineering Library* http://avel.library.uq.edu.au/
*Basics of Engineering Design* http://www.machinedesign.com/bde/
*Blackwell Science Synergy* http://www.blackwell-synergy.com/Journals/default.asp

*British Library Catalogue* http://opac97.bl.uk/
*British Standards Institution* http://www.bsi.org.uk/
*BUBL* http://link.bubl.ac.uk/computing/
*BUBL* http://link.bubl.ac.uk/engineering/
*BUBL* http://link.bubl.ac.uk/patents/
*Business Information Sources on the Internet*
    http://www.dis.strath.ac.uk/business/
*Cambridge Scientific Abstracts* http://www.csa1.co.uk/
*Cambridge University Online Journals*
    http://www.journals.cup.org/cup/html/home.htm
*Center of excellence for sustainable development (US Dept of Energy)*
    http://sustainabledev.nrel.gov/
*Ceramics and industrial minerals* http://www.ceramics.com/
*ChemFinder* http://chemfinder.camsoft.com/
*Chemical and processing engineering resources*
    http://www.neis.com/cpe_resources.html
*Chip directory* http://www.xs4all.nl/~ganswijk/chipdir/chipdir.html
*Composite Materials Handbook* http://mil-17.udel.edu/
*Copper Page* http://www.copper.org/
*Council for Science and Technology* http://www.cst.gov.uk/
*Data Analysis BriefBook*
    http://www.cern.ch/Physics/DataAnalysis/BriefBook/
*Department of Trade and Industry* http://www.dti.gov.uk/
*DIAL industry* http://www.dialindustry.co.uk/
*DIALOG* http://custom.netscape.com/technology
*Directory of Networked Resources* http://www.niss.ac.uk/cgi-
    bin/GetUdc.pl?6; http://www.niss.ac.uk/cgi-bin/GetUdc.pl?518
*Earthquake Engineering Abstracts* http://www.eerc.berkeley.edu/
*Edinburgh Engineering Virtual Library* http://www.eevl.ac.uk/
*EEVL* http://www.eevl.ac.uk/
*Electronic Engineering Library* http://www.ub2.lu.se/eel/eelhome.html
*Elsevier ScienceDirect* http://www.elsevier.nl/homepage/

*Engineering E-journal Search Engine* http://www.eevl.ac.uk/eese/

*Engineering Industries Association* http://www.eia.co.uk/home.html

*Engineering links* http://www.fdgroup.co.uk/neo/fsi/englinks.htm

*Engineering UK* http://www.engineering-uk.co.uk/

*The Engineering Council (UK)* http://www.engc.org.uk/

*Esp@ceNet* http://dips-2.dips.org/dips/help/index.htm;
   http://ep.dips.org/

*EurekAlert* http://www.eurekalert.org/

*Europa* http://europa.eu.int/

*European Committee for Standardization* http://www.cenorm.be/

*European Masonry Data Bank* http://www.fagg.uni-lj.si/emdb/

*European Science Foundation* http://www.esf.org/;
   http://www.esf.org/policy/policy.htm

*FACT (Facility for the Analysis of Chemical Thermodynamics)*
   http://www.crct.polymtl.ca/fact/fact.htm

*FedWorld* http://www.fedworld.gov/

*Gabriel* http://portico.bl.uk/gabriel/en/welcome.html

*GovBot* http://ciir2.cs.umass.edu/Govbot/

*HMSO* http://www.legislation.hmso.gov.uk/

*IEEE* http://www.ieee.org/

*Intellectual Property Network*
   http://patent.womplex.ibm.com/ibm.html

*InterJournal* http://www.interjournal.org/

*International Nuclear Safety Center* http://www.insc.anl.gov/matprop/

*International Organization for Standardization* http://www.iso.ch/

*Internet Connections for Engineering* http://www.englib.cornell.edu/ice/

*IO net* http://csf.colorado.edu/isa/sections/io/internet.html;
   http://csf.colorado.edu/isa/sections/io/internet.html#enviro;
   http://csf.colorado.edu/isa/sections/io/internet.html#ngo

*ISI* http://www.isinet.com/

*ISO* http://www.iso.ch/VL/Standards.html

*Joint Information Systems Committee* http://www.jisc.ac.uk/

*Library of Congress Catalog* http://lcweb.loc.gov/

*Lycos* http://a2z.lycos.com/Science_and_Technology/Engineering/

*Material properites for MEMS* http://mems.isi.edu/mems/materials/

*Materials Safety Data Sheets archive* http://siri.uvm.edu/msds/

*MatWeb* http://www.matweb.com/main.htm

*Metals Powders and Compounds* http://www.micronmetals.com/

*Nano-link* http://sunsite.nus.edu.sg/MEMEX/nanolink.html

*National Institute of Standards and Technology* http://www.nist.gov/

*National Technical Information Service* http://www.ntis.gov/

*Nisee* http://www.eerc.berkeley.edu/

*NISS* http://www.niss.ac.uk/lis/datahosts.html;
    http://www.niss.ac.uk/sites/he-cis.html

*NISS libraries gateway* http://www.niss.ac.uk/lis/obi/obi.html

*Offshore Technology* http://www.offshore-technology.com/

*Online ethics center for science and technology (National Science
    Foundation)* http://onlineethics.org/

*Open.gov.uk* http://www.open.gov.uk/index/orgindex.htm

*Other Patent Offices*
    http://www.wipo.org/eng/general/pcipi/otherwww/ipo_web.htm

*Oxford Journals* http://www3.oup.co.uk/jnls/

*Patents on the web* http://www.aber.ac.uk/~dgw/patent.htm

*PolyContent* http://www.polymers.com/dotcom/polycon/

*Principal Metals Inc* http://www.principalmetals.com/

*Professional Engineering Associations (UK)* http://www.pei.org.uk/

*Publishers' Catalogues Home Page* http://www.lights.com/publisher/

*Railway technology* http://www.railway-technology.com/index.html

*Recent Advances in Manufacturing*
    http://www.eevl.ac.uk/ram/aboutram.html

*Resource Discovery Network* http://www.rdn.ac.uk/

*RS industrial products catalogue* http://rswww.com/

*Scholarly journals distributed via the World Wide Web*
    http://info.lib.uh.edu/wj/webjour.html

*Scholarly Societies project*
http://www.lib.uwaterloo.ca/society/subjects_soc.html
*Science and Engineering Indicators*
http://www.nsf.gov/sbe/srs/seind98/start.htm
*Science policy information news (Wellcome Institute)*
http://wisdom.wellcome.ac.uk/wisdom/spinhome.html
*Semiconductor data bookshelf*
http://www.crhc.uiuc.edu/~dburke/databookshelf.html
*Stationery Office* http://www.tsonline.co.uk/index.htm
*TechWeb* http://www.techweb.com/
*Thomas Directory of American Manufacturers*
http://www.thomasregister.com/
*Thomas Directory of European Manufacturers*
http://www.tipcoeurope.be/
*UK Department of Trade and Industry*
http://www.dti.gov.uk/scienceind/index.htm
*UK Patent Office* http://www.patent.gov.uk/
*The UK Research Councils* http://www.nerc.ac.uk/research-councils
*UnCover* http://uncweb.carl.org/
*United Kingdom Parliament* http://www.parliament.the-stationery-
office.co.uk/cgi-bin/tso_fx?DB=tsoof
*University of Sheffield* http://www.shef.ac.uk/~lib/useful/books.html
*University of Sheffield Library*
http://www.shef.ac.uk/~lib/useful/newseng.html
*US Patent and Trademark Office* http://www.uspto.gov/;
http://www.uspto.gov/patft/
*Virtual Technical Reports Center at the University of Maryland*
http://www.lib.umd.edu/UMCP/ENGIN/TechReports/Virtual-
TechReports.html
*Webcats* http://www.lights.com/webcats/
*World Federation of Engineering Organizations*
http://www.unesco.org/fmoi/fmoi/html/home/default.htm

*World Intellectual Property Organization* http://www.wipo.org/

*World Wide Web Virtual Library* (computing)
   http://vlib.org/Computing.html

*World Wide Web Virtual Library* (engineering section)
   http://vlib.org/Engineering.html

*World Wide Web Virtual Library*
   http://arioch.gsfc.nasa.gov/wwwvl/engineering.html#standardsl

*World Wide Web Virtual Library* http://vlib.org/

*Yahoo!* http://dir.yahoo.com/Business_and_Economy/Companies/
   Engineering/

*Yahoo!*
   http://dir.yahoo.com/education/higher_education/colleges_and
   _universities/index.html

*Yahoo!* http://dir.yahoo.com/Government/Countries/

*Yahoo!*
   http://dir.yahoo.com/Government/Embassies_and_Consulates/

*Yahoo!* http://dir.yahoo.com/Regional/Countries/

*Yahoo!*
   http://www.yahoo.com/Government/Law/Intellectual_Property/
   Patents/

*Yahoo!* http://www.yahoo.com/Science/Engineering/

*Yahoo! UK and Ireland*
   http://www.yahoo.co.uk/Business_and_Economy/Companies/
   Engineering

# Index

*Note: the names of organizations are shown in italic to denote that their online sites are being referred to here.*